Secret War Heroes

Marcus Binney

Secret War Heroes

HODDER &
STOUGHTON

Copyright © 2005 by Marcus Binney

First published in Great Britain in 2005 by Hodder and Stoughton
A division of Hodder Headline

The right of Marcus Binney to be identified as the Author
of the Work has been asserted by him in accordance with the
Copyright, Designs and Patents Act 1988.

A Hodder and Stoughton Book

1 3 5 7 9 10 8 6 4 2

A CIP catalogue record for this title is available from the British Library

ISBN 0 340 82909 5

Typeset in Sabon by Palimpsest Book Production Limited,
Polmont, Stirlingshire

Printed and bound in Great Britain by
Clays Ltd, St Ives plc

Hodder Headline's policy is to use papers that are natural,
renewable and recyclable products and made from wood grown in
sustainable forests. The logging and manufacturing processes are expected
to conform to the environmental regulations of the country of origin.

Hodder and Stoughton Ltd
A division of Hodder Headline
338 Euston Road
London NW1 3BH

For my stepfather George Binney whose name I bear

.

CONTENTS

AUTHOR'S NOTE ON SOE

Churchill's Special Operations Executive was an entirely new departure in warfare. On 16 July 1940, Churchill gave Hugh Dalton, Minister of Economic Warfare, the task of shaping the new organization, exhorting him to 'set Europe ablaze'. In *The Fateful Years* Dalton explains SOE's purpose 'was to co-ordinate all action by way of subversion and sabotage against the enemy overseas'. SOE, initially known as SO2, was to absorb the D section set up within the Secret Intelligence Service in April 1938

but would be on a much greater scale, with wider scope and largely manned by new personnel. It would be a secret or underground organisation. There would be no public announcement of my new responsibility, and knowledge of the activities would be kept within a very restricted circle. As to its scope, 'sabotage' was a simple idea. It meant smashing things up. 'Subversion' was a more complex conception. It meant the weakening, by whatever 'covert' means, of the enemy's will and power to make war, and the strengthening of the will and power of his opponents, including in particular, guerrilla and resistance movements.

SOE started in offices in Caxton Street near Victoria Street but soon moved to Sherlock Holmes territory in Baker Street, taking over the offices of Marks and Spencers and steadily expanding to occupy six large buildings in the vicinity under the cover name of the Inter-Services Research Bureau. SOE set up an extensive system of training schools, many in requisitioned country houses, as well as a series of deer-stalking lodges in the Western Highlands used for paramilitary training. SOE established a series of country sections for most European countries – Maurice Buckmaster was appointed to the F (French) Section in 1941, this was distinct from De Gaulle's parallel RF Section. DF Section organised SOE's escape lines.

Brigadier Colin Gubbins took over as head of SOE from Sir Charles Hambro in 1943. As the war spread across the globe, overseas headquarters were set up in Cairo and then Algiers, in India, Ceylon and Australia with a large number of sub-missions in other countries, particularly neutral ones. At its peak some 10,000 men and 3,000 women were working in SOE offices and missions, helping an estimated two to three million active resisters in Europe alone. In 1942, an American counterpart to SOE, the OSS, or Office of Strategic Services, was set up under 'Wild Bill' Donovan, who had many friends in SOE's top echelons. After the war, OSS developed into the CIA while Baker Street was closed down, and a few of its functions were absorbed within the Secret Intelligence Service.

In France, SOE operated a series of networks known as Circuits, usually consisting of an organiser, radio operator and courier (and sometimes a weapons instructor or sabotage specialist). At the time of D-Day, special Jedburgh teams were dropped behind enemy lines in France, consisting of teams of three officers, usually one American, one British and one French, to help train resistance groups, organise arms drops and provide radio links with Allied command.

INTRODUCTION

For years the French Foreign Legion provided an unending supply of stories of unusual, remarkable men determined to prove themselves by enlisting for service in exotic, dangerous places. Now, with every year that passes, Britain's wartime Special Operations Executive is emerging as an equally rich source of thrilling exploits. Although it existed for only five years, SOE, like the Foreign Legion, was an international force, filled with heroic personalities, some flamboyant, others diffident and retiring. Yet virtually all were determined to find a means of making their own personal contribution to the war effort – rebelling against the tedium and regimentation of military life and longing for adventure.

My interest in SOE was prompted by my stepfather, George Binney (whose name I bear), who carried off one of SOE's great early coups by bringing out five unarmed merchantmen through the German blockade of the Skagerrak, laden with a whole year's supply of ball bearings urgently needed for aircraft and tank production. He would tell the story to a hushed audience over the dinner table, blowing impressive smoke rings from his cigar.

SOE was separate from the existing Secret Intelligence Service, which included MI5 and MI6, and charged not with intelligence-gathering but with sparking resistance and carrying out operations in enemy-occupied territory – ranging from sabotage to attacks on enemy installations and personnel. It also provided an alternative to blanket bombing raids and a means of putting key industrial targets out of action without heavy civilian casualties.

SOE has the added fascination of being one of the few secret services for which a substantial archive is available. Its agents are not figures in the shadows, but distinct personalities whose family background, education and peacetime occupations and pursuits are known. There are war diaries and mission reports, files of different country sections containing details of operations, policy documents and correspondence with ministers – all once top secret material. In addition, as SOE was wound up in 1945 many SOE agents decided to write their stories.

Now some ten thousand personal files of SOE agents have begun to be opened at the Public Record Office. Often these include the agents' training reports and character assessments, their mission instructions, details of their cover stories, telegrams to and from the field, and the agents' own end-of-mission reports and debriefing summary.

From this emerges an astonishing saga of individual heroism, initiative, cunning and resourcefulness. There are stories of survival and endurance, both against the elements and against betrayal, imprisonment and torture. Here too are escape dramas as astonishing as many of the long-famous break-outs from prisoner of war camps.

SOE was also a vital means of showing that Britain and its allies could hit back successfully at German (and later Japanese) military might, which had subjugated whole continents. Much has been made of SOE disasters, for example of the *Englandspiel* in Holland, by which the Germans arrested incoming agents as they landed and then used their radios to ask for arms drops. Equally the astonishing story of the attack on the heavy water plant in

Norway which destroyed German nuclear hopes has been told many times. But there are many other extraordinary operations, such as the virtually bloodless liberation of the island of Madagascar, made possible by the courage and initiative of a single SOE agent and his wife.

SOE was a school of talent in which people of all ages could flourish. The young and audacious could rise rapidly to positions of command over hundreds, occasionally thousands, of Maquis and partisans. Talented people, too old at forty to enlist for active military service, could pit themselves against the enemy, working in the most dangerous circumstances in occupied countries, liable to discovery and arrest at any time of day or night. SOE was an international band – with recruits ranging from career British officers sent to arm and guide the partisans in the Balkans to people with no previous military experience, and even former conscientious objectors.

SOE could be described as the first genuinely pan-European fighting force, encompassing French, Dutch and Belgians, Spanish Republicans and Italian partisans, Scandinavians and recruits from every country in the Balkans – even Germans and Austrians. It was the more cosmopolitan for the fact that the first requirement for many destinations was fluency in at least one language other than English. Many of those enlisted held dual or even foreign nationality. As SOE expanded to cover the globe, recruits came not only from all over Europe, the Empire and the Dominions but from virtually every country where SOE was involved in fighting the Axis, notably in the Far East.

The courage and resilience of SOE agents and operatives are reflected in the remarkable number of awards given for both gallantry and conspicuous service. This included several George Crosses, George Medals, knighthoods, and an impressive number of DSOs. Amedée Maingard received his at the age of twenty-six.

DSOs were given to personnel who had shown a high degree of leadership and capability in planning operations, and also to junior officers who had shown sustained courage in the field. An impressive number of agents were also awarded Military Crosses. Bravery was also rewarded by the OBE and MBE (Military) – equivalent to the Queen's Gallantry Medal and the Queen's Commendation for Brave Conduct today.

The gap between courage and foolhardiness can be very narrow. Gus March-Phillips, leader of a dashing series of commando raids across the Channel, was gunned down on a reconnaissance raid on a Normandy beach which led to the death or capture of all his comrades. Agents needed self-confidence to survive. To be effective they had to take risks. Inevitably they also made mistakes. The most successful agents had a lucky streak. Some also had a sixth sense which alerted them to a trap or imminent arrest.

Again and again the importance of SOE's well-planned training comes through, particularly in terms of priming agents on how to maintain a cover story under duress. Preparation for vicious beatings and torture was more difficult. Denis Rake endured using the simple technique of counting, which he had been taught at the Beaulieu finishing school.

SOE's training officers included some remarkable characters, two of the best known being Gavin Maxwell, the author of *Ring of Bright Water*, and the notorious Russian spy Kim Philby. The most remarkable – and influential – of all was Eric 'Bill' Sykes, expert in unarmed combat and silent killing and able to draw and fire a handgun in a third of a second.

Quite apart from the bravery of the agents, courage of an

equal order was required by the local people who helped them. While the agents worked under aliases and their families were usually (relatively) safe at home in Britain or other free countries, their local helpers often lived in their own homes with their families around them. If they were caught, wives, parents, sons and daughters were liable to arrest and beatings – even torture, deportation and imprisonment in concentration camps from which many never returned.

Some of SOE's greatest coups, such as Operation Postmaster, had the advantage of total surprise. Others, though mounted against well-guarded factories and plant, still took the enemy unawares. But sometimes the mission was considered so important that, even though the odds bordered on the suicidal, the operation went ahead. In Operation Performance, merchant ships loaded with vital cargoes of ball bearings were escorted out of Göteborg harbour by the Swedish navy to confront waiting German guns, with gathering fog as their only protection.

Chapter 1

BILL SYKES – EXPERT
IN SILENT KILLING

Two of the most famous figures in SOE were not agents but instructors – William Ewart Fairbairn and Eric Anthony Sykes, experts in fast shooting and silent killing and inventors of the double-edged razor-sharp Fairbairn-Sykes fighting knife. There is a vivid description of them at work in the western Highlands, where a large Protected Area had been established for training purposes. It is provided by Major Henry Hall of the Dorset Regiment. They were not quite the Captain Mainwarings they first appeared.

'Our first meeting with Fairbairn and Sykes was impressive. We gathered at the foot of a large staircase in a big house and two old gentlemen aged approximately fifty-eight and fifty-six dressed in battledress with the rank of captain and both wearing glasses appeared at the top of the stairs and proceeded to fall down the stairs together and landed in battle crouch position with a handgun in one hand and a Fairbairn-Sykes knife in the other.'

In SOE Sykes was known to his colleagues as Bill, as he was to his family. The agent Peter Kemp wrote of him that he 'has the manner and appearance of an elderly, amiable clergyman, combined with the speed and ferocity of a footpad; lulled by his soft tones and charmed by his benevolent smile, we would be startled to hear him conclude some demonstration with a snarled "Then you bring up your right knee into his testicles"'.

Another testimony comes from William Pilkington, an instructor who first encountered Fairbairn and Sykes in SOE's new Baker Street headquarters in autumn 1940. 'He looked like a man of the cloth. He was an expert pistol shot and very skilled in ju-jitsu. I once wrestled with him only to suffer a very swift defeat . . . his physical power was amazing.'

Fairbairn and Sykes operated as a team until Fairbairn went to Canada in March 1942 to take part in training at Camp X on the shore of Lake Ontario, moving on to help set up training camps for the OSS, the American counterpart of SOE. Today Fairbairn is a familiar name in America to anyone interested in commandos, commando training and unarmed combat.

Sykes remained in Britain. The tributes to him in both letters from his colleagues and memoirs written by agents are formidably impressive. Donald Hamilton-Hill, in *SOE Assignment*, wrote of Sykes's wrists of iron.

He taught unarmed combat and quick shooting reactions such as how to kill four people in a room whilst falling down on the ground near the door lintel to make oneself a difficult target. His methods of unarmed combat and silent killing were such that many were able in the years to come to save themselves entirely owing to his instructions. The Germans in 1942 published a pamphlet which portrayed his methods, and used it in neutral countries to enlist sympathy against the diabolical British. 'Our man' in Lisbon picked one or two up and sent them to me for comment with a request for a UK posting, and training with Bill Sykes.

In SOE Fairbairn and Sykes were dubbed the Heavenly Twins. Sykes was sometimes known as the Bishop, thanks to his avuncular appearance, silver hair and round-rimmed spectacles. The story of his life has been brilliantly pieced together by John Harding, a Metropolitan police officer and safety instructor and a judo black belt. It is a romantic picture of a gentle giant who during twenty-six years of his adult life spent little more than three months in England. Sykes was a man of unexpected talents and traits. He wrote in a beautiful, even copperplate hand. Though an exponent of maximum force in warfare, he had a gentle manner. He fostered intense loyalty and admiration among those he taught, and his origins are wholly unexpected.

According to his passport, the man we know as Sykes only took this name, by deed poll, on 10 March 1917. He was born in Lancashire, at Barton-on-Irwell, on 5 February 1883, the son of Lawrence and Octavia Henrietta Schwabe. The family came from Leipzig and had settled in Manchester in the 1820s. His father is described on Eric's birth certificate as a merchant/cotton manufacturer. His grandfather on his mother's side was Godfrey Anthony Ermen, a business partner of the famous Frederick Engels (friend of Karl Marx) in the firm of Ermen and Engels.

In 1890 the family, now including a second son, Randolf, moved south to Hemel Hempstead. Both brothers were day-boys at Heathbrow school and together produced the school magazine. Randolf was later to become an accomplished artist and Professor of Fine Art at the Slade School.

Randolf's evident abilities as a teacher, as well as his dedication to his work, help shed light on his brother. After a spell at the Académie Julien in Paris, Randolf progressively built up a reputation as a draughtsman, etcher and lithographer. During the 1914–18 war he became a prolific war artist.

After teaching in the Camberwell and Westminster schools of art he went on to teach drawing at the Royal College of Art.

A colleague wrote: 'Schwabe has a remarkable amount of information on nearly all subjects . . . acquired by very wide reading. His slight stammer never hindered his flow of entertaining conversation; he had a quick and subtle sense of humour.' Later Randolf was to provide the drawings for the Fairbairn-Sykes classic *Shooting to Live*.

In 1907 Eric sailed for Shanghai, where he was to remain until 1940. One wonders whether his German blood would have made it difficult to enlist in British forces, though this had not prevented Randolf from becoming a leading war artist. Perhaps Eric's change of name was based on the same patriotic grounds as those that prompted Britain's royal family to adopt the name of Windsor in place of Saxe-Coburg-Gotha.

Claims that Sykes acted as a sniper in the First World War appear unfounded as letters written to his family imply he was in China throughout the war. In his will deposited at the British consulate at Tensin dated 18 August 1920 comes the first mention of Catherine Agnes Powell, the great love of Sykes's life. A year later, on 5 May 1921, they were married in the 1st Baptist Church at Reno, Nevada, by the Reverend Brewster Adams. At this stage Catherine was still married to her first husband, but clearly there was no deceit involved and this was not bigamy in the usual sense but rather a case of two young people passionately determined to pledge themselves to each other. On 25 March 1924 a second marriage service took place at the consulate-general in Shanghai, after divorce proceedings were completed on 31 January, giving legality to the union.

Catherine was the daughter of the Reverend Claudius Buchanan Brigstocke. Half Italian by birth, she had been brought up in Germany, spoke several languages and was an accomplished pianist. She had enrolled at the Schumann Conservatoire in Frankfurt, first as a student and then as a teacher of music. Her first husband had been Sidney John Powell, by whom she had a son, Trevor, and a daughter, Helen. On their return from America Eric and Catherine moved into what Helen described as 'a very pretty house in the Old Chinese style' at 54 rue Ghisi in Shanghai's French concession. The hall was adorned with the heads of animals, evidence of Eric's passion for game shooting. Eric was working at Reiss & Co. merchants, while Catherine taught music at the Shanghai American School.

After six months Eric was sent to take charge of the company's office in the city of Hankow. Here they lived in a large apartment on the river front until early in 1923, when Reiss & Co. collapsed. Eric sent Catherine and his step-daughter to the small house he had built for shooting weekends in Pei-tai-ho while he returned to Shanghai and began working for the China & Japan Trading Co.

Sykes's legendary association with Fairbairn appears to have begun about five years earlier. In 1919 Fairbairn set up the ballistic section of the Shanghai Municipal Police (SMP) and introduced the practice of marking the base of each bullet purchased for police use with a distinctive symbol. As the base of a bullet rarely deforms, he was able to assess the exact number of bullets fired by the police in any incident from an examination of those recovered. Wishing to avoid a possible British embargo on ammunition supplied to Shanghai, Fairbairn decided to obtain his ammunition from Remington, the American firm, whose representative in Shanghai was Sykes. In 1926 Sykes joined the Shanghai Municipal Police as a reserve officer.

A dramatic account of their joint participation in an

operation is provided in an article in the *North China Herald* on 14 January, 1928. Headlined 'Shanghai's Miniature Sidney Street – Kidnapper's Desperate Defence', it tells the story of a gun siege after police had dramatically freed a kidnapped Chinese merchant. 'The kidnappers fled upstairs, getting onto the roof. There were three of them. Sub-Inspr. Eaton followed and grasped and held one, whilst Chief Inspr. Fairbairn shot and wounded another and then secured him . . . The third, who caused all the subsequent trouble, jumped some ten feet from one roof to another and got into an attic.'

The man shot at all who approached. Mills bombs were thrown into the attic, the third blowing out the window sashes and beams. When one bomb failed to explode the kidnapper coolly threw it back. Three more bombs were thrown through the window as well as eleven tear-gas shells but still the man appeared at the window and shot back. After 10.30 p.m. all fell silent. All kinds of ruses were used to trick the kidnapper into showing himself. A hat was placed on a stick and dangled in front of the window. He was hailed through a megaphone and told he had five minutes to surrender. Four snipers, 'including Mr Sykes, the well-known revolver shot', attempted without success to take the man out.

Fairbairn also had a narrow escape. 'Whilst he was near the window, the man inside shot and the bullet grazed the inspector's eyebrows. The men undoubtedly are members of a Shaohsing gang who are well known to be the most daring of all bandits.'

This incident demonstrates Shanghai's importance as a training ground for the toughest type of close combat fighting. An examination of the criminal's corpse showed no less than eighteen bullet wounds and a mass of facial wounds caused by splinters thrown up by the Mills bombs.

'The state of the room is almost indescribable; he lay in a corner in a pool of blood, the floor was an inch deep in plaster dust, the walls were penetrated by hundreds of bullets and the floor was in splinters. Not a square foot was intact.' The kidnapper, continues the article, 'seemed to have a method of meeting every attack. When the soldiers threw in bombs, he crouched below the window, and most of the flying pieces of metal passed over his body . . . the teargas bombs failed to subdue him . . . He used extreme caution in meeting the police, conserving his ammunition. He never fired unless he had a target, and then usually but once. He could not have had more than 15 rounds for his .32 calibre pistol and at 8 a.m. he still had his last round which he fired at the police at the door.' After more Mills grenades were hurled into the room he was found dead on the floor.

Fairbairn had lived in Shanghai since 1907. Some graphic details of his work are provided in his book *Scientific Self Defence*, published in 1931. The preface by the legendary film star Douglas Fairbanks began: 'I do not know of any more interesting book to study . . . the author has a most extensive and practical knowledge of this art. I was forced to come to this conclusion when I attempted to grapple with him. Twenty three years of association with the Shanghai Police Force has [sic] given him an experience which he could not get in any other city in the world.' Fairbanks commended his book 'particularly to those who have not the fortune to be born with great physical strength'.

Fairbairn explained that the book, first issued under the title *Defendu*, was written for the police forces of the Far East that were faced with 'street ruffians, burglars and armed robbers' who would use any means to made good their escape. To this end he taught 'how to protect certain vital parts of the body'. He had, he said, for years been the instructor in self-defence to the Shanghai Municipal Police and included 'among his pupils, royalty and several of the highest Ju-Jitsu experts of Japan'. He was, he claimed, the first foreigner living outside Japan to be awarded a black belt degree by Kodokan Jiu-Jitsu University. He had studied 'under Tsai Ching Tung (then aged eighty-three), who at one time was employed at the Imperial Palace as an instructor to the retainers of the late Dowager Empress'.

Shanghai gloried in the title of the Paris of the East, and wasn't shy of being 'the whore of Asia'. By 1920 it was estimated that about 100,000 hoodlums in Shanghai were living partly off the illegal trade in opium which had been banned in 1917. G.W. Woodhead concluded in a series of articles in the *Shanghai Evening Post and Mercury* in 1931 that it was 'the considered opinion of some of Shanghai's most experienced foreign police officials that if it were not for the illicit traffic in drugs, serious crime such as kidnapping and armed robbery would be reduced by half, if not almost completely eliminated. The drug traffic attracts thousands of the worst criminal elements to Shanghai and fosters the formation of criminal organisations which are a constant menace to the peace and security of the law-abiding public'.

In 1930–31 Shanghai's annual gambling turnover was almost four times that of Monte Carlo, then regarded as the gambling capital of the world. Kidnapping was often abetted by servants or bodyguards – the sole mitigating factor was that there was an unwritten code that no victim would be seized a second time. Prostitution also flourished under criminal control. The numbers of prostitutes in the international settlement, listed as 9,791 in 1915, had risen five years later to more than 70,000 in the foreign concessions, ranging from high-class *changsan* to street-walkers or 'pheasants', women working in opium dens and fast-sex 'nailing sheds'. From these figures it has been calculated that one in every three women in the French concession was a prostitute in 1920.

Fairbairn had begun to keep precise records of the almost nightly shootings, personally answering every call for assistance where shots had been fired or were likely to be fired. When the police lost nine men at the hands of armed criminals, Fairbairn gave his blunt verdict: 'there is nothing wrong with the men. It is the antiquated methods you insist they be instructed in. More attention is being paid to winning silver cups than shooting to live'.

Fairbairn was allowed to develop his concept of shooting to live. Men were trained to fire instinctively in bursts of two shots without ever bringing their pistols up to the line of sight. They practised in the dark, when all that could be seen of an opponent was a shadow, firing up and down a staircase at moving objects. He obtained permission to pin down all safety catches. Instead men were made to holster their guns with a full magazine but no round in the chamber.

Fairbairn created a pistol range in an old warehouse which sounds today pure James Bond. It was also the fore-runner of SOE's commando training schools. It was known as the 'Mystery House' and fitted out to look like the interior of a Chinese lodging house occupied by armed criminals.

According to Fairbairn's own description, a trainee would step on floorboards that gave away under him as he entered 'a dimly lit room occupied by apparently harmless people (dummies) who vary from mere lodgers to dope fiends or stool-pigeons. He has to take in the situation in a flash'. Firecrackers, confetti, sticks and other objects were thrown at him. Anything approaching a deliberate aim was a sheer impossibility.

In 1928 Sykes took on the Colt firearms agency, in addition to that for Remington. He was now planning with Catherine to go and live on Vancouver Island, which promised an abundance of the game shooting and fishing that were his great passions. Catherine went ahead of him, but hardly had she arrived than he received the news that she had fallen ill and been taken to a clinic in California. Sykes rushed to join her, but it transpired that she had cancer requiring expensive treatment and he had to return to China to earn the money to pay for it. Then, in April 1929, came the news that she had died. Sykes was devastated. He never remarried.

Soon after Catherine's death he joined S.J. David & Co., Merchants, Land and Estate Agents, bringing the Colt agency with him. The next news of him comes in two letters to his brother Randolf. 'I count myself very lucky to have a salaried job,' he wrote on 21 May 1931, adding, 'it doesn't help me in the least to get out of this blasted country which is my main object in life'. In another letter, of 20 July 1933, he states that he has spent 'only three months and six days in England in the last 26 years'.

By the late summer of 1937 Sykes was spending the mornings at his office at S.J. David and the rest of the day at Fairbairn's office, where he had become the officer in charge of the sniper unit of the SMP.

When the Chinese air force bombed the international settlement in Shanghai on the afternoon of 14 August Sykes was told to call out the snipers and machine gunners and patrol the Nanking Road to prevent looting of shops. There were fears that the Chinese might that very evening attempt an armed entry into the settlements with the aim of attacking the Japanese in the rear. Sykes set up twelve machine guns on the road for two nights running until the threat receded.

Sykes was now living with Fairbairn, who had sent his wife and daughter to Hong Kong for safety. A letter from Fairbairn written on Shanghai Municipal Council paper thanks Sykes for a fine fishing trip. In August 1939 Fairbairn approached Robert Stanley Heaney, vice-consul at Shanghai, asking to be considered for police work in Malaya and to take Sykes as his assistant. The reply was negative and the two men began thinking of a return to England.

On 27 October 1939 Sykes wrote to Colt: 'Please to regard, from now on, Fairbairn and Sykes as a team, partnership, or what-have-you.' He adds that he will be advising S.J. David to relinquish the Colt and Remington agencies when he leaves Shanghai as he is the only employee with any knowledge of the subject. He continues: 'Fairbairn is due to leave Shanghai, on retirement at the end of February. I leave at the end of March on the same count. We have offered ourselves, jointly, to the Government for services of a special nature. If the offer is accepted, you may expect to hear from us later on from somewhere in Asia.' A letter from the consul-general for the Straits Settlements, Herbert Phillips, however, advised that no postings were available, and the two men set off back to England.

The question naturally arises as to whether Fairbairn and Sykes had any connection with British Intelligence while in Shanghai, a belief widely held in the United States. A photograph of Sykes at a farewell dinner for Fairbairn at the Police Club in Shanghai on 23 February 1940 includes two guests known to work for the Japanese Secret Service – Akagi and Uyehawa – a fact certainly known to their hosts. Heaney is also likely to have had connections with SIS. He worked as a passport officer, a cover often used for SIS agents on overseas postings. The American editors of the

China Weekly Review repeatedly complained that the SMP was top heavy with foreigners, most of them British, alleging that many of the activities of the SMP were connected with espionage and propaganda. The Deputy Commissioner, W.G. Clarke, who was the head of the CID, was assumed by many knowledgeable Shanghai residents to be a leading SIS agent in China.

Sykes travelled via Japan and Canada, arriving in Liverpool on 9 May 1940. He went to live with his brother in Oxford while he was vetted by SIS. Barely two months later he arrived at the Special Training Centre (STC) at Lochailort in the western Highlands as an instructor with the rank of acting captain.

A memo dated 29 September 1940, shortly after their arrival at Lochailort (where he and Fairbairn famously tumbled down the stair at Inverailort House), states that the two men 'were originally enlisted through D Section but were taken over by MI(R)'.

D Section had been established in May 1938 within the Secret Intelligence Service under Major Lawrence Grand of the Royal Engineers. His brief was to look at means of sabotage in enemy territory. MI(R) was set up by the War Office to study forms of irregular warfare under Lieutenant Colonel J.F.C. Holland, also of the Royal Engineers. All this is the more interesting as D Section had no known presence in the Far East, though it was involved in setting up the first training schools and research stations which were absorbed into SOE in the summer of 1940.

The origins of the famous Fairbairn-Sykes commando knife are also intriguing. In 1942 Fairbairn describes it in *Get Tough* as 'The Fairbairn-Sykes Fighting Knife developed by the author and a colleague'. The first batch of these knifes was made on the two men's instructions in November 1940, after they had both visited the director of the Wilkinson Sword works, John Wilkinson-Latham. His grandson, Robert Wilkinson-Latham, recalls that the men were taken through a showroom decorated with famous swords and firearms made by the company in the past, up a narrow staircase, through bales of wartime khaki, air force blue and navy blue to the office at the rear.

The urgent business of the meeting was to produce a knife for the new commando force. Until then, there had never been an official knife for the British armed services, although many types of knife had been authorised for use in the past. Bowie-style knives were carried by some of the Imperial Yeomanry during the South African War of 1900–01, and in the First World War cut-down bayonets, privately purchased hunting knives or captured German-issue folding knives were extensively utilised.

The two men sat down and described the type of knife they had in mind and the purpose for which it was intended. As discussions continued, preliminary sketches were drawn up and modified time and time again. Robert Wilkinson-Latham recalls: 'In order to explain exactly their point, the two men rose to their feet and one, it was Fairbairn my grandfather mentioned, grabbed the wood ruler from his desk and the two men danced around the office in mock combat.'

The concept was a knife with a heavy grip so it would sit well back in the palm of the hand, yet light in weight so as to be easily manageable and controllable. The grip was to be roughened or chequered for maximum purchase in wet weather. A cross-guard would protect the hand from slipping on to the cutting edge of the blade, which would be double edged with a stiletto-sharp point.

At the end of several hours of animated discussion, it was agreed that the Wilkinson prototype would be ready in a few days. Later that evening, after the two men had left, John Wilkinson-Latham met Charles Rose, the manager of the experimental workshop, to get the project under way immediately. Shortly thereafter a contract was issued to Wilkinson Sword for the first 1,500 'Fairbairn-Sykes fighting knives'.

The first-pattern Fairbairn-Sykes fighting knives were drawn by hand and there are slight variations in length – the blade measuring 6¾–7 inches and the whole knife 11¾–12 inches. These knives have the distinctive S-guard. The second-pattern knife comes with both polished and blackened blades, and some are made by J. Clark & Sons of Sheffield. The sheath for the first-pattern knife is of dark brown leather with a nickel-plate brass chap (tip) to protect the point. The leather frog includes a leather retaining strap with snap fastener. There were also leather tabs on each side so the sheath could be sewn inside battledress.

Major Henry Hall, who described Fairbairn and Sykes tumbling down the stairs at Inverailort, had arrived there on a three-week course in February 1941, part of a group of fifteen officers and sergeants on a guerrilla training course. Fairbairn and Sykes, he says, lived in the big house with the other officers. The students were lodged in Nissen huts.

The paramilitary training in the western Highlands was initially based on the idea of semi-military bands operating in enemy-occupied territory but evolved into the training of agents working as saboteurs and leading a clandestine life in civilian guise. The syllabus included physical training, silent killing and weapons training, use of explosives and fieldcraft. According to the official SOE history of the training section, 'weapon training concentrated primarily on making a student a good shot with an automatic pistol (.32 or .45 calibre) and a Sten Carbine. A feature of this training was the method taught of instinctive shooting (ie without using the sights) introduced by the late Major Sykes and which was later adopted in part of the army'.

A vivid description of Inverailort is provided by Hall. 'We were given intense training in close-quarter combat, knife work, gun work and hand-to-hand fighting,' he says. He continues, 'their favourite weapon was a nine-millimetre Browning automatic. We were trained in instinctive firing from the navel, using one hand not two'. Fairbairn and Sykes kept the knife in the left trouser pocket and the gun in the right. 'The pocket was slit down at the side so you could slip your hand straight in – normally you lift your hand to reach into your pocket. The holster was sewn into the pocket and the pocket sewn on to the trouser leg so it would not move as you drew the gun. I modified my own trousers in this way and wore them throughout the war.'

Fairbairn and Sykes also gave Hall instruction in the use of catapults and sticks as well as methods of garrotting. 'Any stick would do, from a clipboard to a broom handle. We were taught to hold the stick with both hands and deliver blows to the solar plexus, the neck or over or under the nose. A clipboard would be used to whack an opponent on the bridge of the nose or the Adam's apple.'

They also experimented with a range of coshes. Hall continues, 'their preference was for spring-loaded coshes, a metal tube with a spring inside and a lump of lead at the end. As you swing the cosh, the spring shoots out the lead. This way it conforms to the shape of what you hit and does more damage than a solid piece of metal or wood'.

It was Sykes who trained the agents who were sent to assassinate Reinhard Heydrich, deputy chief of Himmler's SS, in Prague. Sykes, says Hall, helped to design the grenade that the agents used, 'full of nasty things and made in the workshops at Inverailort'. Hamilton-Hill, who saw the three Czech agents involved fly out of RAF Tempsford, recalled: 'Later, we received a radio message that the Czechs had landed safely . . . Their message ended: "Give Bill Sykes our best wishes – tell him we won't miss."'

A colleague who has a vivid memory of Sykes in Scotland is Angus Fyffe, the commandant at Inverlair, often known as 'The Cooler' and used to detain trainees who had failed to qualify but knew too much about SOE's work until they were no longer considered a risk. He explains:

Sykes was concerned that we were losing agents as a result of Sten guns that misfired and jammed after four or five shots. He argued instead that agents should use a .45 revolver which with training could be accurate at up to hundred yards and was an effective way of picking off a sentry or a guard. We spent several afternoons practising. At a hundred yards he could hit the head of a six-foot target four times out of five. We would take a gun from the armoury at random, just drawn off the rack, usually a Colt .45 or sometimes a Colt .38 on a .45 chassis. I was quite a good marksman myself and after practice could achieve three out of five but often he would hit five times out of five.

Sykes, he continues, 'used the army position, leaning against a tree and gripping the pistol with both hands, firing with a very gentle pull on the trigger, not a jab'. Though Fairbairn had the more authoritative manner, it was Sykes, says Fyffe, who was 'the better marksman and fastest on the draw'. Sykes's 'masterpiece', in Fyffe's phrase, was to draw and fire a gun in a third of a second. He would grab it, cock it, point to the target and fire. Fairbairn and Sykes taught the double tap system – always put two bullets in an opponent, to be doubly sure he was out of action and could not suddenly fire back.

Sykes asked Fyffe to make a prototype steel bow and arrow for silent killing in the forge at Inverlair. The forge had been set up by a brilliant Italian engineer, Eduardo Parisiol, who was one of the residents at Inverlair and who salvaged a large amount of metal from the British Aluminium workings near by. The bow was collapsible, so that one half could be slipped down each trouser leg. It was intended to be lethal at up to 80 yards. After tests they settled on hardwood arrows with very thin aluminium feathers, barely more than a millimetre thick. 'The prototype was sent to London but they decided it would take too long to train people to use it,' says Fyffe.

He continues, 'They were also masters in the art of knife fighting. They would never hold a knife high as you see in the films. That way you can grab an opponent's wrist, twist it fiercely and he will scream in agony.' When giving training in unarmed combat, the two men taught that there were twenty-two points on the human body where a lethal blow could be delivered. Special dummies were made for agents to practise on.

Ernest Van Maurik, another instructor in Scotland, recalls how 'Sykes demonstrated that even if an enemy had a gun pressed into your back, it was possible to spin round and disarm him'. This apparently impossible feat is based on the simple fact that action is faster than reaction, and that, moving fast, you can turn and move from the line of fire before your assailant can pull the trigger, giving you time to lock your arm around his and disarm him.

A warm letter of thanks from Major A. G. Brown dated 31 December 1941 offered appreciation of what Sykes had achieved: 'the STC has gone from strength to strength and your efforts have undoubtedly gone a very long way to putting Lochailort on the map – armed close combat is now on sane lines throughout the army, entirely due to your care and forethought – last but not least, your delightful personality, knowledge of human nature and unique method of putting over the instruction, will have a lasting effect'.

On 1 January 1942 Sykes was formally transferred to SOE, beginning work as a travelling instructor based principally at STS 17 Brickendonbury in Hertfordshire, where he supervised training in weapons and unarmed combat. Brickendonbury was SOE's 'demolition' school, where agents were given training on the use of explosives. Sue Ryder, who worked there, wrote: 'STS 17 specialised in industrial sabotage, and some 1,200 men had passed through its various courses by the time the war ended in 1945.' The commanding officer was Lieutenant Colonel George Rheam. Among the members of staff, Ryder recalled, were Sykes himself, 'an expert in pistol shooting and silent killing, but he looked like a retired bishop'; George Howard, a small-arms expert; Sergeant England, who gave instruction on demolition; and Hatcher, ex-bomb disposal unit, who also taught demolition.

Leslie Fernandez was one of a group of ten future instructors who took a three-week course with Sykes on unarmed combat. 'He was a likeable man, quiet yet dynamic too, suddenly bursting into action.' Sykes, he says, had been deeper into the subject than anyone one else they met. 'He knew all about pressure points, how to paralyse a man in an instant.' He also provided extensive instruction on illegal entry and escape. 'For example, he devised a system of scaling twelve-foot barbed-wire enclosures with overhangs. It was very difficult to get through barbed-wired fences without cutting the wire and setting off alarms. He invented a pair of stirrups, each with a hook on the back. You would put all your weight on one foot and then lift the other.'

The year 1942 also saw the publication of *Shooting to Live with the One Hand Gun*, written jointly by Fairbairn and Sykes. Sykes had originally mentioned the book in a letter written from Shanghai on 27 October 1939 to the Colt Company in Hertford, Connecticut: 'we are at work on a book on pistol shooting from the practical angle. The target side of shooting we are content to leave to the experts, regarding the practical side as our field, backed up by police records of actualities in the way of shooting affrays over a great number of years'. Later he added with decided modesty: 'Fairbairn's wide experience of the practical side is invaluable. As for me, I do believe I can clean a gun better than anyone I have ever met!'

The book is written with great directness and clarity:

'In the great majority of shooting affrays the distance at which firing takes place is not more than four yards. Very frequently it is considerably less. Often the only warning of what is about to happen is a suspicious movement of an opponent's hand. Again, your opponent is quite likely to be on the move. It may happen that you have been running in order to overtake him. If you have reason to believe that shooting is likely, you will be keyed-up to the highest pitch and will be grasping your pistol with almost convulsive force. If you have to fire, your instinct will be to do so as quickly as possible, and you will probably do it with a bent arm, possibly even from the level of the hip. The whole affair may take place in a bad light or none at all, and that is precisely the moment when the policeman, at any rate, is likely to meet trouble, since darkness favours the activities of the criminal.

Fairbairn and Sykes put forward three crucial points. First was extreme speed both in drawing and firing. Second came instinctive as opposed to deliberate aim. And third, practice under circumstances that approximated as nearly as possible to actual fighting conditions. They continued, 'the average shooting affray is a matter of split seconds. If you take much longer than a third of a second to fire your first shot, you will not be the one to tell the newspapers about it. It is literally a matter of the quick and the dead. Take your choice'.

Instinctive aiming, they said, was an entirely logical consequence of the extreme speed to which they attached so much importance.

There is no time to put your self into some special stance or to align the sights of the pistol, and any attempt to do so places you at the mercy of a quicker opponent. In any case the sights would be of little use if the light were bad, and none at all, if it were dark, as might easily happen.
We cannot claim that the system produces nail-driving marksmanship, but that is not what we look for. We want the ability to hit with extreme speed man-sized targets at very short ranges.

George Millar, a soldier who became an SOE agent after an amazing escape from Germany, relates how effective the gun training could be in his book *Maquis*. He was told by an agent, back from France on a refresher course, of a young French operator. He had been captured by the Gestapo, who 'searched him, but failed to find the small automatic hidden in a special holster. The pistol, following our rule, was ready cocked and at "safe"'. They handcuffed him and drove him off. The radio operator had never fired a pistol except at the training school. Despite the handcuffs he was able to reach his gun, and shoot the driver of the speeding car twice in the neck. The car overturned and he promptly shot the other two Germans in the car and escaped.

In 1942 cracks began to appear in the close relationship between the two men. Fairbairn went to Canada, then on to the United States to help train the OSS, SOE's American counterpart. Sykes remained in Britain, reportedly criticising

Fairbairn's *All-in Fighting* (published in the United States as *Get Tough*) as being too complex and police oriented. Later Rex Applegate, who was in charge of close combat and weapons training for OSS, said that in all the time he was with Fairbairn in the United States he never once heard him mention Sykes. William Pilkington quotes Sykes as saying 'We seem to be serving a one-man army, everything we invent or create he channels into his own record'.

In his preface to the book Fairbairn writes:

the method of hand-to-hand fighting described in this book is the approved standard instruction for all members of His Majesty's forces. The Commandos, and parachute troops, harrying the invasion coasts of Europe, have been thoroughly trained in its use. Britain's two-million Home Guard are being daily instructed in its simple but terrible effectiveness. The units of the United States Marine Corps who were stationed in China between 1927 and 1940 learned these methods at my own hands when I was Assistant Commissioner of the Shanghai Municipal Police.

He continues:

there will be some who will be shocked by the methods advocated here. To them I say 'In war you cannot afford the luxury of squeamishness. Either you kill or capture, or you will be captured or killed' . . . The methods described in this book I have carefully worked out and developed over a period of many years. They owe something to the famous Japanese Judo (jujutso), and something else to Chinese boxing. But largely, they were developed from my own experience and observation of how most effectively to deal with the ruffians, thugs, bandits and bullies of one of the toughest waterfront areas in the world.

His advice was for the student not to try to master them all, but to select about ten 'which for reasons of your height, weight, build, etc., seems [sic] most suitable, and specialise in mastering them thoroughly. Do not consider yourself an expert until you can carry out every movement *instinctively* and *automatically*. Until then spend at least ten minutes in daily practice with a friend. At first practice every movement slowly and smoothly. Then gradually increase your speed until every movement can be executed with lightning rapidity'. To this he added a word of warning – namely that almost every one of these methods, applied vigorously and without restraint, would result, if not in the death, then certainly in the maiming of an opponent. The manual goes on to describe and illustrate chin jabs, bronco kicks, wrist holds, bear hugs, sentry holds, hip and wrist throws, how to secure a prisoner, and disarming an opponent of his pistol.

According to Leslie Fernandez, agents would practise close combat with boxing punchbags, but for the women, who had less physical strength, Sykes introduced straw-filled dummies hung from cords. Students would be sent in for two-minute sessions.

Sykes continued to work intensively and was promoted to a temporary major on 8 September 1943. In 1944 he received an additional assignment – to assist with the training at Milton Hall near Peterborough of the Jedburgh teams who were to be dropped behind German lines on and after D-Day to help arm, train and organise the resistance.

Sykes is the author of an unpublished manual that largely forms the basis of the SOE syllabus on close combat. Here, in trenchant fashion, he gives his views.

There is nothing new or original in any of the methods that are going to be described here. All of them in fact are widely known. At this date I doubt indeed if anything new in unarmed combat remains to be discovered. That is not to say that there are a great many people who know the entire subject from A to Z. I certainly do not. There may be some who do but I have never met them. It is true that every so often a man will think out or discover by accident something hitherto unknown to himself and his immediate associates but the probability is that somewhere someone else knows about it already.

Sykes's manual deals with the whole gamut of close combat – blows with the side of the hand, kicking, chin jabs, the use of knees and elbows and finger jabs. The SOE syllabus explains that the course is 'designed to teach and kill without firearms. Since the course includes the use of the knife . . . silent killing is a more appropriate description . . . It is essential to confine the teaching to what is simple, easily learned and deadly'.

Instructors introduced the course as follows:

'this system of combat is designed for use when you have lost your firearms, which is something you should not do, or when the use of firearms is undesirable for fear of raising an alarm. At some time or other, most of you, probably, have been taught at least the rudiments of boxing under the Queensberry rules. That training was useful because it taught you to think and move quickly and how to hit hard. The Queensberry rules enumerate, under the heading of 'fouls', some good targets which the boxer is not trained to defend. This, however, is *WAR*, not sport. Your aim is to kill your opponent as quickly as possible . . . That may sound cruel but it is still more cruel to take longer than necessary to kill your opponent . . . There have been many famous boxers and wrestlers who time after time have won their contests with their favourite blows or holds. The reason is that they had so perfected those particular blows and holds that few could withstand them. The same applies to you. If you will take the trouble to perfect one method of attack, you will be far more formidable than if you only become fairly good at all the methods which you will be shown.

Sykes's rapid influence on training of British forces is evident in a letter of 12 January 1942 from HMS *Excellent* in Portsmouth, sent to him at Inverailort. It reads: 'Dear Captain Sykes, I am sure you will be interested to hear that the Board of Admiralty have approved that your method of instruction in pistol shooting should be adopted forthwith in the Navy . . . Though this decision will not, by itself, win the war, I am quite sure it will help us to shoot more Germans, and we have a lot to thank you for.'

Sykes also had a role in advising on the development of specialist weapons by SOE. One example is the Welrod, a small 9mm or .32-inch-calibre handgun with a very effective built-in silencer. The stock-cum-magazine could be easily detached from the barrel, making it easy to conceal. During November 1942 some examples of a four-shot version were made to the requirements set down by Sykes and the Chief of Combined Operations. In December 500 were ordered for Station XII at Aston House in Hertfordshire which housed the research and development section responsible for placing orders with outside manufacturers. The Welrod was designed as an assassination weapon, and in February 1944 about a dozen Gestapo staff were assassinated in France by the Gaullist 'Armada' circuit in a campaign suitably named Ratweek. Even after SOE's disbandment the Welrod was used in operations in Korea, Malaya, Vietnam and Northern Ireland.

Sykes was also involved in the assessments of the Sten gun used by so many agents and resistance forces. This was a simple, cheap sub-machine gun that took its name from its designers, R. V. Shepherd and H. J. Turpin, who worked at Enfield. The Sten could keep firing even when coated in sand, mud or water, but it jammed easily and had an alarming tendency to fire off a whole magazine if dropped or jarred accidentally. Various attempts were made to improve it, for example by fitting a bayonet and by replacing the stock with a pistol grip. Sykes reported that the pistol grip seriously reduced accuracy but the bayonet showed some promise.

A Special Confidential Report in Sykes's personal file, covering the thirteen months ending December 1943, gives his age as fifty (actually it was sixty) and his health as A1. It states that he had been employed supervising weapon training and unarmed combat and describes him as 'a most conscientious, hard-working and energetic officer who is an acknowledged expert in his subjects. Universally respected and popular'.

Sykes paid ready tribute to his mentors in unarmed combat. One was Lieutenant Colonel W. A. Ord of the South Staffordshire Regiment, 'whose knowledge of the subject must be unrivalled'. Ord, born in 1910 in Montreal, joined the 5th Staffordshire TA in 1938. At this time he was a trainee consulting engineer with the LMS Railway and his hobbies were listed as 'Wrestling (Amateur International), Swimming (County Champion), Rugby (County), canoeing and sailing'. In September 1940 he joined No. 6 Commando as an acting captain at Lochailort, serving as an instructor in fieldcraft and close combat. In June 1941 SOE was interested in using him for service overseas, apparently 'because of his expertise in railways and knowledge of paramilitary skills including demolitions. Worked as a trainer in all subjects including silent killing . . . teaching field craft and close combat'.

In his manual Sykes continues: 'Any weapon is better than

none – half a brick, a bottle, or something that will serve as a club . . . ethically, it makes no difference whether you kill the enemy with blockbusters, bottles or your bare hands.' He was determined that his students, faced with the actuality of war, should forget all gentlemanly rules and conventions. 'We start with one advantage and that is the freedom to attack . . . Your watchword is attack and kill. Attack first and keep on attacking until you kill. That is the basis of this course of instruction.' He continued, 'do not go to ground ever if you can help it. If you have to, get up as quickly as possible. Don't go into a clinch'.

He also recommended *The Art of Wrestling as taught in the British Army* by G. de Relwyskow, published in London by Gate and Polder in 1919.

On 8 August 1944 Sykes was taken to Hertford Central Hospital suffering from heart problems. Though he was discharged on 9 September and returned to duty, he evidently feared for the future. A letter to him from a Colonel J. T. Young of 27 October 1944 tells him, 'it will ultimately be necessary for you to attend a medical board, as the particulars of your illness and admission to hospital have been passed to the War Office'. He is informed he will not have to leave STS 17 until the middle of December, at the earliest. When he came before the medical board, however, he was downgraded from A to E. Suddenly SOE had no role for him.

Sykes's value to SOE was warmly put in a letter he received from Lieutenant Colonel J.S. Wilson on 20 January 1945 expressing dismay at his retirement. 'It is a great blow to me, and to my Norwegians and Danes, to feel that we shall not have the benefit of your advice and example in the future. The work you have done for us has been of inestimable value and I am perfectly certain in my own mind that several of our Norwegian boys owe their lives solely to

the instruction in self-defence that you have given them in
the past.'

Another tribute, written on the headed paper of the Inter-
Service Research Bureau (the cover name for SOE) by F.T.
Davies, is equally vivid:

I remember so well the first time that you and Farbairn went to
Lochailort and it appears so long ago that I almost feel it was my
early youth . . . I remember also what a tremendous impression
you made on that first Commando School. In fact, I really believe
it might have slumped badly if you two had not been there to
introduce the unarmed and self-preservation tactics into Army
training. I think the gospel you preached has spread right
through the Army and even into the Home Guard, and it always
amuses me when somebody talks in an admiring tone of some
P.T. sergeant who has taught them unarmed combat . . .
Countless men in this Organisation and throughout the army are
carrying out your instructions . . . I only wish I had contributed
as much to the war as you have.

Within three months of leaving SOE Sykes was dead at
the age of sixty-two – in a boarding house at 69 Egerton
Road, Bexhill. A doctor certified the cause of death as
coronary thrombosis and arteriosclerosis (hardening of the
arteries). Sykes was accorded only the briefest of obituary
notices in *The Times*. With him he had no more than two
suitcases of possessions. But he had the solace of a close
friend, Gwynneth Lipsum Ward. She wrote a strong, well-
measured plea to his commanding officer. 'I feel he should
not be allowed to sink into oblivion with no word of recognition for all the good work he did. He died for his country
as much as any member of the forces, for the doctor tells me
the heart trouble was caused by overwork, anxiety and
standing about in snow, rain and mud. With his fine
physique he should have lived many more years.'

She continued, 'Two years ago I asked him to give up but his sense of duty was so strong that he couldn't do it.' Sykes's quiet dedication and unstinting commitment had been his own death warrant.

Chapter 2

GEORGES BÉGUÉ – THE FIRST AGENT TO BE DROPPED IN FRANCE

In 1941 Georges Bégué was the first SOE agent to be parachuted into France. As a radio operator he laid the foundations for the communications that were to be used by SOE with such devastating effect behind enemy lines on D-Day. So great a mark did Bégué make that for a long time all SOE radio operators were known as Georges. He was George I; the rest were given other numerals to distinguish them, such as Georges IX or Georges 65. (One story has it that this was inspired by Pratt's Club in St James's where the menservants were habitually known as George 1, 2, 3 because elderly members had difficulty in remembering their names.)

Georges Bégué was the son of a French engineer who ran the tramway system in the Egyptian city of Alexandria. The young Bégué also trained as an engineer, and was then sent to the University College of Hull to learn English. He did National Service in the French army as a signaller and was called up in 1939. Thanks to his English he was given a job as a liaison officer to the British Expeditionary Force, escaping to England via Dunkirk. As France surrendered, Bégué immediately volunteered to join the British army and was enlisted as a sergeant in the Royal Signals.

In 1940, SOE's newly formed French section was looking for recruits to send to France. The man in charge of

34

recruitment was Thomas Cadett, seconded by *The Times* to be F Section's deputy head. Later he was to describe Bégué as 'the pick of the bunch'.

Bégué's personal file (PF) contains a brief summary of his career with SOE. To SOE he was known as George Noble. On 10 February 1941 he was 'put through the cards' (PTC) by MI5, 'with a view to employment as an organiser'. On 27 February STS 5 (the Special Training School at Wanborough Manor near Guildford) advised that he 'has dash and initiative, a natural leader, reserved and efficient. Has shown great interest'. Two months later, on 29 April, STS 31 at Beaulieu commented, 'A very alert and capable brain. A reserved but very pleasant personality. Thorough, painstaking and discreet. An excellent man.'

Alarms bells had rung briefly when it was found that Bégué had sent a telegram on 29 January 'to one Bégué in Alexandria, the text of which is ambiguous'. This was the more disturbing as a Bégué in Alexandria was already suspect. A letter of 26 February to Colonel Hinchley-Cooke states: 'Noble is at present under effective supervision and his correspondence is censored. His behaviour up to date has been good and he makes a good impression. He is quite young. On the other hand we do not wish to give him special training if there are any doubts about his good faith. He has shown himself, up to the present, to be outstandingly proficient.'

All was explained a few days later in a memo from FB.

I had a talk with Noble on Saturday afternoon and, in the course of general conversation, asked him whether he ever heard from his family. He said 'Yes' and that he had found a convenient means of letting his father know he was all right by sending a monthly telegram to Alexandria. Without pressing, he volunteered the information also that his father had recently, in a letter, asked him a number of personal questions about his occupation in this country. Noble said he realised he would be unable to give any detailed answers and that he had sent a telegram in which the final words had in effect been 'Silence golden' to indicate to his father that he could not answer his letter properly. This rather looks as if Noble's telegram, produced by MI5, is not too dangerous. If it were so, then it would mean that Noble is a very slick individual indeed, but I do not really think this is so.

Noble's cover story, dated 28 March, is on file – interesting as it is one of the very first. He was to be Georges Robert Mercier, born in Angers on 1 November 1911 (his real birth date was 22 November that year). His father, a mechanic, had conveniently died of blood poisoning in 1933, his mother of pneumonia six years earlier, so neither could be traced. His only surviving close relative, an aunt, had also been missing since the German offensive. Educated at the Angers Lycée, Mercier had done military service at Nancy as a wireless mechanic and then taken a job selling wireless sets and spare parts in Paris. Hearing 'that there was a possibility of Frenchmen being forced into factories for German war production [he] decided to scram ... finally crossing the demarcation line by bridge at Vierzon with a man whose identity he does not know, who got him across with a pass which he handed back afterwards'. One wonders whether the police would have become suspicious of so many dead ends had they ever begun to check, but it was not this which was to be Bégué's undoing.

Bégué's PF also contains his own brief account of his training. 'In January 1941 I found myself at Scarborough at the Royal Signals Holding Station waiting to be called for the special mission that my comrades and I had been hoping would be confided in us since August 1940. At the end of January I was summoned to London where it was explained to me in a few brief words what was being asked of me. Directed to a Special Training Camp I was sent back eight days later for W/T training. Having already mastered transmission, no real effort was required on my part.' This was followed by seven days' parachute training at Ringway and just five days at Beaulieu, which consisted of 'testing of my set and about seven hours of tuition on special subjects'.

Personal details in the PF are sparse, but Bégué had met his wife Rosemary while studying at Hull and listed his interests, rather grandly by English standards, as 'Sciences, Arts and Sports. Social and International Activities. Psychology and study of individuals ie other people's business. Objectively: Politics and New Ideas – The New World'.

An impressive briskness, even impatience, runs through his reports. On the day of his departure, 5 May 1941, he was driven by car to the aerodrome at Stradishall and then flown south to Tangmere near Chichester in Sussex. 'Excellent meal, though late,' he noted. 'Impossible to take a nap in advance. Uneventful flight to the area around Vatan. Red light a quarter of an hour before the jump. Twisted parachute cords caused a spiralling descent. Dropping point not accurate. A walk of 25 kilometres not 18. Hard to mask my fatigue. Meat and bread coupons were missing from my ration card. Impossible to find Frédéric, away on the day.'

Frédéric was Max Hymans, a socialist deputy for the Indre. Immediately after de Gaulle's famous broadcast calling for the French to fight on, Hymans had succeeded in sending a letter to a friend in London, saying he would do anything to help the Allies. This had reached Tom Cadett, who decided to take a chance and send Bégué to him. Hymans had not been warned of Bégué's arrival and it took five hours of questioning for him to accept that Bégué was an agent sent by the British and not a German agent provocateur.

Finally persuaded of Bégué's good faith, Hymans introduced him to some of his fellow socialists. One was the chemist M. Renan of 54 rue des Marins, who became SOE's first live letter box through whom incoming agents could make contact with Bégué. (Later it was to be M. Fleuret, a garage keeper at 68 rue de la Couture.)

Bégué continues: 'That evening I found myself a room, badly situated but suitable for a first W/T contact. The next day first contact with London established easily. ['Others should try and emulate this speed,' Buckmaster wrote in the margin.] Sent a telegram. Two days later further contacts. Sent and received several telegrams. Interrupted by a "jamming station".'

He goes on: 'at my departure I had been given some 15,000 francs, a sum clearly inadequate to cover my expenses over 6 or 7 months. I told London this and received with the arrival of Bernard a week later 20,000 francs'. Bernard was Lieutenant Louis Lefrou de la Cologne, who parachuted in on the night of 10/11 May with one of SOE's most important early agents, Baron Pierre de Vomécourt, code name Lucas. The speed of delivery was impressive, but the day after his arrival Bernard announced that he was '*brûlé*' and that he had been interrogated by the Sûreté and the Deuxième Bureau and felt it best to retire for a while.

Bégué himself was faced almost immediately with the threat of discovery by the Germans. Pinpointing a lone agent transmitting from rural France sounds like the proverbial search for a needle in a haystack, but the Germans very quickly picked up his signals. He was aware of this and at once turned his astute mind to ways of shortening transmissions.

The danger of exposure was increased by the use of postcards as a means of communication between agents in France (though these were often used by ordinary French people in preference to letters which might be opened and read). 'I received a first card from Albert [Major Cottin] in Brittany giving me an address and requesting money then a second giving another address at Landereau and then a third from Paris, in code which asked for seven hours work deciphering and money as soon as possible.' Bégué replied, demanding that the *cartes postales* should not be used and providing Pierre de Vomécourt with 2,500 francs to give to Albert in Paris.

Bégué described his usual daily routine: '7h–12h QSO; 1h–4h deciphering; 4h–6h letter drops, shopping, rendez-vous; 8h–12h and later coding etc . . . The current was often cut in the morning about 10 o'clock when I was transmitting. To avoid these setbacks – dangerous for my security – I requested earlier transmitting times, first eight, then seven in the morning.' He also complained that Lucas's first messages were not condensed and abbreviated as they needed to be. He described his problems in receiving parachute drops, though these sound minor compared to what reception committees were later to endure. Pierre's brother, Philippe de Vomécourt (Lionel), had had to spend two nights waiting – the first wasted. On the second night the aeroplane had flown six times over the target zone and dropped the containers in the trees. This was SOE's first arms drop, organized by Bégué, and took place on the night of 12/13 June. The containers were landed on Philippe de Vomécourt's estate near Limoges and were hidden in the shrubbery near the chateau.

Bégué was now using 'rush' signals or messages (he calls them telegrams). These consisted of fifty groups at the maximum, requiring less time to decipher. At the beginning of August two more agents arrived, an event that was to have fateful implications for Bégué – Captain G. C. G. Turck (Chris) and Captain Jacques Vaillant de Guélis (Jacques). De Guélis had dropped on rough ground, but although severely cut and bruised was not gravely injured. Turck was a French architect who had been the French Deuxième Bureau's liaison officer with Section D. He could not be found. Only later did they discover that he had been concussed on landing and had not recovered consciousness until the morning, when he found himself surrounded by peasants pointing guns at him while awaiting the arrival of the gendarmes. Turck provoked strong views. Philippe de Vomécourt distrusted him on sight. A woman near Marseilles 'had no confidence whatsoever in him.'

Faced with a flood of signals that all needed encoding and deciphering, Bégué now proposed a system of abbreviated texts. For example F W O W T P T would indicate Freddy Whitley Operation Will Take Place Tonight. Freddy was the name of the agent – Whitley the type of aircraft, indicating a parachute drop. J L O W T P T indicated Jacques Lysander Operation Will Take Place Tonight. The introduction of an N, as in J L O W N T P T, indicated the operation was postponed, while OK indicated confirmation. These were broadcast between 9 and 11 a.m., and in the afternoon between 2.30 and 3.30 and 5.25 and 5.40.

On the day of a drop planned at Loches, Bégué had to send a courier on the 6.10 p.m. train to Loches to tell Philippe de Vomécourt the latest news about the drop. The tight schedule was almost confounded when, at 4.15 p.m., just fifteen minutes after Bégué had deciphered a telegram and camouflaged his transmitter, a policeman arrived demanding to search his room. No sooner was this over than Bégué was due to go back on air to receive a further signal confirming or postponing that night's operations.

'Happily I received a telegram just in time to get to the station and prime my courier to tell Lionel to lie in wait another night. For Lionel it was to be the second night of waiting without result.'

The next night a combined drop of six 'bods' did take place, attended by Hymans and Bégué. 'Operation entirely successful despite the difficulties – first day of the hunting season, aeroplane waking up Châteauroux and failure of pilot to acknowledge my signals,' Bégué told SOE.

As more agents arrived, the risks grew. 'As I feared, surveillance around Châteauroux was becoming more intense: listening points at key places . . . frequent searches of suspects and premises in the town.' Meanwhile Lieutenant Bruce Cadogan (François) arrived – he had been landed at Barcerès from HMS *Fidelity*.

As fast communications between agents on the ground had become impossible, the resourceful Bégué asked for messages to be broadcast by the BBC with confirmation of planned drops. The three first messages were '*Lisette va bien*', '*Gabriel va bien*' and '*Claude va bien*'. These were the origin of the famous BBC *messages personnels* broadcast to France on an increasingly regular basis. The Germans, baffled at their meaning, thought there was a code to be broken, but in fact they were simple messages to individual groups announcing or postponing parachute drops of agents and arms, or ordering attacks on previously agreed targets.

Another close call took place on the night of 4 September 1941, when a Lysander was used for the first time to deliver and bring back returning agents. The little plane brought out Major Gerard Henri Morel (Gerry) and took back Captain de Guélis. De Guélis had installed himself at a hotel near the landing ground when on the night of his departure the police arrived and began a thorough check of the papers of everyone in the hotel. De Guélis remained calm as his departure time drew closer. As the police left he leapt on his bicycle and arrived at the ground just as the aircraft's engines could be heard. He rapidly laid out the lights and was soon on his way to London to make an extremely valuable report. But in his rush he had made a mistake, and as the aircraft took off it fouled some telephone wires, several yards of which were found trailing from the plane when it arrived back in England.

On Saturday, 4 October Marcel Fleuret, who was now acting as Bégué's letter box in Châteauroux, was arrested and imprisoned. By 8 p.m. Bégué had been warned through Hymans and he left the next morning. With Pierre de Vomécourt he went to the Château de Breuil to enable him to continue transmitting and to endeavour to get Pierre to London. Next he set off for Limoges with the hope of establishing himself there in greater safety. Meanwhile Cadogan and Pierre de Vomécourt took on the task of handling agents, either by personal visits or by posting anodyne messages in convenient places. This procedure had been proposed by London.

Arriving at Limoges, Bégué found the population 'had grown to 22,000 during the exodus. It was impossible to find a suitable place to work, even for a short period'. Instead he now went on to Périgueux to meet Pierre Bloch, a former socialist deputy recruited by de Guélis. In Périgueux a further shock awaited – the sight of two fellow agents being led out of the station in handcuffs. They were 200 metres ahead of him. Hoping to be able to signal to them, Bégué hurried to catch them in the main street. But suddenly they were masked from view and were gone.

With Cadogan he set off for Carcassonne, hoping to find Hymans, and then for Marseilles. On his arrival he rang Turck, who answered the telephone and told him to come at once as all was normal. At the Villa des Bois, where Turck was staying, he found the gate shut. He knocked and Turck came out of the villa and across the garden. But several metres from the door he stopped and asked, 'Who is there . . . is it Georges?' Suddenly Bégué and Cadogan found themselves surrounded by six policemen.

They were taken to the Villa Fantaisie, occupied by the ST (Surveillance du Territoire) of Marseilles. This villa was situated on the Corniche, opposite a little restaurant called Les Ombrelles, where Turck had taken him to dine a month before. This sowed further suspicions in Bégué's mind, but at this point his view was 'Until proved to the contrary, Christophe did not betray me, but cowardly allowed the ST of Marseilles to seize me. With François I was the last of our group to be arrested. Others before me had been seized, very probably the fault of Christophe'. To Bégué the fact that Turck said nothing while the inspectors of the Surveillance du Territoire were following him closely, yet allowing him to remain free, tipped the balance against him.

Bégué was now interrogated for four days at the Villa Fantaisie. He heard that the ST had lain in wait for several days and several nights at the Villa des Bois both before and after his arrest. He took heart from the fact that the police, at least those in Châteauroux, made a great mistake by first arresting Fleuret – putting Bégué on his guard.

The police had initially and rightly believed that Bégué was the 'radio de Châteauroux' but had found no papers or other evidence to incriminate him. The only papers that worried him were the texts of messages that he was bringing to Turck. They were in a suitcase he had deposited at the *consigne*, or left luggage office, on arrival at Marseilles. Having found a ticket while searching Cadogan, the police had gone to look for the luggage the next morning. Opening Bégué's case in his presence to examine the contents they had quickly discovered the remains of his money and a notebook with several pages carrying the texts of deciphered signals. So occupied were they with counting the money, however, he had been able to secrete the notes and later destroy them without anyone noticing.

I then composed a story telling them that I was only the assistant of the 'real Georges' who, alerted by the arrest of Fleuret had departed on holiday, leaving me the task of warning others. Therefore, I was not able to give them details of our transmissions nor to indicate to them where I transmitted from. They were far from satisfied, but on the last day their aggressiveness declined. The main point for them was to place before the judges a case which stood up and they demanded me to make a deposition which they typed out. This was, as far as I could make it, a mass of hollow phrases, which tallied more or less with depositions made previously by others to the police and which inevitably revealed part of the truth. (Fleuret had told them almost all he knew. I had foreseen this and avoided letting him know my name and addres . . .) They roasted me on the subject of Frédéric. They had his real name from Fleuret . . . They also wanted to know everything that had happened there . . . They had verified my identity (Georges Mercier). They must have found a Mercier at Angers but the date of birth did not tally (I heard them receive the reply by telephone.) I had to give them my true identity, explaining that I had departed from there, instructed by Captain May, sent from the other side to help Georges, and to be instructed by him in the use of the radio. In sum I did not have very much which could satisfy their curiosity.

Only after the war was the truth about the arrests to come out. It stemmed from the disaster that followed the drop of the Corsican mission which arrived by parachute on the night of 10/11 October to a reception committee arranged by Pierre Bloch (Gabriel), the former socialist deputy recruited by de Guélis. The agents were J.B. Hayes, Clement Jumeau, Jean Philippe Le Harivel and Daniel Turberville. They were all trained saboteurs but all four were arrested within ten days. Turberville had dropped wide of the others but with all the containers. He was arrested the next morning by the gendarmerie with the address of the Villa des Bois on him.

The police then set a trap at the Villa des Bois manned by someone who resembled Turck in voice and bearing. This explains why the man stopped 5 or 6 metres short of the gate when Bégué arrived at the villa. In this way two more agents, Robert Lyon and Pierre Bloch, had been arrested. On one of them Marcel Fleuret's name was found and he was arrested too. Gabriel was caught at his garage, Michael Trotobas was taken at Châteauroux.

Turck, when he returned from captivity in Germany, was able to tell his story. He had heard from a Vichy army friend in Lyons that the police were after him. He disappeared immediately, leaving no address. He went into hiding at his fiancée's flat in Paris but by bad luck was caught by the Gestapo at St Germain-des-Prés in July 1942. He said nothing under torture in Paris, and when he tried to protect a Senegalese soldier from a beating in the Compiègne transit camp he was beaten again and kept naked and starving in an empty cattle truck, ending up in Buchenwald and Dora for fifteen months. For his heroism he received an MC.

At the end of October Bégué was in the prison of Béleyme near Périgueux in the Salle des Détenus Militaries with Gabriel, Philippe, Jumeau, Hayes and Pierre. Several other agents, were in different cells on the first floor. The prison was later graphically described by Jumeau as 'degrading and humiliating to the last degree. We were all thrown in amongst deserters, thieves, murderers and traitors . . . hygiene and sanitation . . . were non-existent. Food was unspeakably bad. In addition we were plagued with vermin and disease'.

Bégué said of Béleyme: 'All having the idea of escaping, we needed an external contact if possible. Of all of us, I was evidently the one who could most easily renew contact but I was always concerned not to compromise anyone outside in making the contact. Repeatedly I found myself at odds with those of my comrades who were seeking in a dangerous fashion to renew contacts themselves with members of our organisation who were still free.'

Jumeau, in a report in his PF, said Madame Bloch:

provided food for more than a dozen persons during more than six months . . . I think she succeeded where a hundred magicians would have failed. She lived fifty kilometres away and had to travel three times every week throughout the winter in order to carry the numerous parcels of food which she was able to find. She had three young children to look after as well. The food she brought us had to be obtained on the black market. She was denounced to the police on several occasions. Her house was searched. Once or twice she was searched while carrying parcels of food to the prison. Yet she never gave up . . . I believe Madame Bloch to be capable of unlimited devotion to any cause she believes in. I say so because I believe every word of it to be true. On many occasions she carried letters and messages which male friends of ours had refused to carry because they thought it too risky.

On 15 May they were taken to the prison at Mauzac on the Dordogne, about 15 miles upstream from Bergerac. A vivid description is provided by another SOE agent in the camp, George Langelaan, in his book *Knights of the*

Floating Silk (an allusion to their arrival by parachute). He wrote:

After the prison of Béleyme, Mauzac seemed like Paradise. The open air, the large barracks full of sunshine, the wash-basins, everything seemed so marvellous after the dark, sordid and damp stone refectory of Béleyme, its stinking corridors and cells, its recreation yards where the walls were so high that the sun could only splash a very small space of ground at best. True, there was the barbed-wire enclosure, but we could look through it at fields and trees, and a road with real live people on it, and, in the distance, at roof-tops with smoke moving lazily up from the chimneys. It was like discovering poetry all over again. The civilian guards were much the same as the Béleyme jailers; some were churlish and unpleasant, others more amiable, and a few, a very few, quite friendly.

Bégué and his comrades were placed together in the same hut as prisoners from other organisations similar to their own. Some of these had already made plans to escape. 'The problem was not to prejudice each other's efforts . . . It seemed at first difficult to find a means of us all escaping together. I recommended digging a tunnel but met strong opposition from those who said I was not competent . . . Bit by bit Jumeau and I who were developing the escape plans found ourselves opposed by a dissident group putting difficulties in our way.' Bucheron, who had been in hospital, recovered and was deemed strong enough to join them.

Two others, Breuillac and Pigeonneau, then handed on a contact they had made with one of the guards as their plans were less advanced and they had some hope of being released. Bégué then conceived a brilliantly original and subtle escape technique. He made each agent observe the key to the door of their hut in minute detail. From these descriptions he succeeded in crafting a duplicate. At the same time, through Madame Bloch, he made contact with Virginia Hall, the brilliant American agent working for SOE in Lyons, and Philippe de Vomécourt to organise their escape route once outside the camp.

Langelaan takes up the story: 'Every night, after a final roll call and inspection, we were locked in our barrack. Night after night, we held interminable sing-songs in order to cover the noise Georges Bégué was making, filing away at a piece of iron.' Langelaan describes how the local priest, a First World War veteran who had lost his legs and used to arrive in a wheelchair, insisted one day on being lifted up into their hut to see their 'interior decorations'.

'I have a little present for you,' he said, 'but first post a sentry or two at the doors and windows, just to make sure no one is roaming near the barrack. Right. Now all you others gather round me . . . That is the idea! Now, one of you look under my cassock . . . where my legs should be if I still had any. There is a present for you.'

'Great Scott! It's a piano!' whispered Georges as soon as he saw the little suitcase which he knew contained a radio.

The priest replied, 'Yes. I was given to understand that you can get plenty of music out of it. It has been nicely tuned.' Working at night, says Langelaan, Georges was able to set up a hidden aerial under the edge of the roof and within a week was in communication with London, and through them with their contacts outside the prison, planning every detail of the escape.

Always cautious, Bégué, was nonetheless very sparing in his use of the transmitter. 'Unfortunately there was one of our number who had the annoying habit of writing a diary each day with all kinds of details which he hoped to secrete out of the camp by a very dubious means,' with the risk that it might be seized and read by the authorities who would then order a thorough search of the hut and find the transmitter.

They worked out that with careful planning they could slip through the barbed-wire enclosures between the rounds of the guards. The point of escape had to be, as far as possible, out of sight of the miradors, or lookout posts, and in the shadows cast by the barrack blocks when the arc lights came on. Teams of pétanque players were sent out every afternoon to find the best route and to choose hard ground where they would not leave tracks, measuring distances so times could be calculated precisely.

One big concern was that the guards might spot the open door as the agents slipped out one by one. They did not want to risk the sound of telltale creaks as it opened and closed while each prisoner left at carefully pre-planned intervals. Finally they hit on the ruse of a false door painted on sackcloth which could be pinned up in seconds once the real door had been unlocked and opened. From one of the windows they could watch the guard in the mirador and when he was not looking another man could slip out and dash into the shadow of the opposite wall.

According to Langelaan the Alsatian guard who had agreed to help them was due to be on duty in the mirador nearest their block from midnight to four on the night chosen for the escape. He was to give the all-clear by lighting his pipe. Tantalisingly they had to wait until nearly three o'clock for the signal. As Bégué's key opened the lock, the first man out pinned up the false door and the second, Michael Trotobas, came out carrying a strip of carpet under his arm to be placed across the barbed wire. He also unrolled a ball of string as he went to act as a signal line. One tug was to indicate all clear, three short tugs was a danger warning. They had allowed a sixty-second interval between each man to avoid bunching. Langelaan dived on to the carpet and wriggled across. He was almost through when a guard from another mirador appeared. Trotobas was ready to spring on him from the shadows, ready to put his silent-killing training into action, when the guard said 'Is it the English?' in a whisper.

'Yes,' replied Trotobas.

'Well, don't make so much noise,' said the guard, turning to walk away. Later they heard that almost everyone in the camp was watching. This particular guard was beaten and imprisoned for his supposed failure to spot what was happening.

The Corsican Albert Rigoulet was waiting for them with a lorry. He drove them 32 kilometres to a forest hideout where they camped for a week. Jumeau paid him a handsome tribute. 'He too towers far above the average . . . While we remained in hiding he and his wife provided us with the necessaries of life and acted as liaison between us and the outside world.'

Madame Bloch was of course promptly arrested after their escape but, says Langelaan, released within a matter of hours, 'for she had not one, but half a dozen cast-iron alibis.' At the time of the escape she had been on her way back from Vichy where she had been received by a series of officials, pleading with them for her husband.

After several days at Rigoulet's hideout they went in twos and threes to Lyons. Bégué and others escaped into Spain via Perpignan. Walking at night, it took three days to cross the mountains. On the other side they were told to take a train to Barcelona. This proved to be full of police and armed civil guards and they were arrested and imprisoned in Gerona. Bégué then spent six weeks in the notorious camp at Miranda before reaching London in October 1942. By this time the personnel in the French section had changed and Cadett had departed. Though he was appointed Signals Officer for F Section, Bégué felt his talents were not being put to best use. Buckmaster recognised his qualities but perhaps felt that Bégué was too well known to risk his return to the field. His assessment reads: 'Georges is a household word in London HQ. Extremely able technically and conscientious, he was persistent to a degree in everything he did. A great patriot, he is a worrier and frequently takes an unnecessarily pessimistic view, but his rare enthusiasm and transparent honesty, as well as his immense courage and charm, have endeared him to us all. A great man.'

Bégué received a well-earned MC, but soon after the war was over he emigrated to the United States with his wife Rosemary. Here he became an electronics engineer and took American citizenship. He lived to the age of eighty-two, and is survived by his wife and two daughters. He died in Falls Church, Virginia, and deserves to be remembered by Tom Cadett's handsome accolade, 'a Prince among French Patriots'.

Chapter 3

GEORGE BINNEY AND THE BALL BEARING RUN

In January 1941 my stepfather, George Binney, carried off one of SOE's first major coups, Operation Rubble, bringing five unarmed merchants ships through the German blockade of the Skagerrak laden with a whole year's worth of vital steel supplies needed for tank and aircraft production. Both he and the head of SOE, Sir Charles Hambro, received knighthoods in the June Birthday Honours 'for special services in the supply of valuable war material', though my stepfather was dubbed 'the secret knight' by the press, as no announcement was made as to why he, a forty-year-old businessman, had received this honour and was included in the select list of Prime Minister's Honours set above all the others.

At the outbreak of war George Binney had been running the export department of the United Steel Companies. He had been speedily appointed by Sir Andrew Duncan, the Steel Controller, to represent British iron and steel interests in Scandinavia. Before his departure he made contact with the Ministry of Economic Warfare, and was in touch with Hambro and Harry Sporborg, who both moved to SOE when it was set up in summer 1940. When the German occupation of Norway cut normal communications between Sweden and England, messages had to be sent by cipher from the British legation in Stockholm. On the advice of the commercial counsellor, Jack Mitcheson (who became one of his greatest allies), Binney was appointed an assistant commercial attaché with an office in the legation. Here Binney had the good fortune to recruit Bill Waring, a chartered accountant who had fled Norway with his wife Anne and their small son. Waring spoke both Norwegian and Swedish and played a major role in helping organise the shipments.

After the success of Operation Rubble, attention quickly turned to a repeat operation, and a new series of ten Norwegian ships trapped in Swedish ports was chartered, taking advantage of the last action of the Royal Norwegian Government before it went into exile, which had been to commandeer Norway's extensive merchant navy fleet.

The five Rubble ships had broken out of Swedish waters at the end of January, taking advantage of long Scandinavian winter nights and benefiting from a heavy night snowfall which greatly delayed German planes based at Norwegian airfields from attacking the next day.

Performance, the second operation, was planned for November 1941, intended again to use the cover of the long winter night as naval and air cover could be provided only when the ships were halfway across the North Sea.

The Rubble ships had been able to anchor in a remote fjord close to the Norwegian border and the mouth of the Skagerrak, providing the shortest route across to Kirkwall Roads in the Orkneys, the huge naval base that provided the first safe haven for shipping crossing the North Sea. The Performance ships, at the insistence of the Swedish government, had to be anchored deep in Göteborg harbour, a full 10 miles from the open sea.

Fascinating new detail about Performance and the extraordinary battles with the Swedes have now emerged from the Foreign Office's own files on the operation, withheld for over sixty years because of understandable political and diplomatic sensitivities. I examined them in the bowels of the old Admiralty building, where I found a trolley piled high with large cardboard boxes containing buff folders packed with carefully filed copies of telegrams to and from Sweden and official correspondence, including impressively printed versions of key letters to and from Anthony Eden, the Foreign Secretary.

Naturally the Germans had been irate at the escape of the Rubble ships, but Sweden was a neutral country and ships under British flags had as much right to free entry and exit from Swedish ports as the large quantity of German shipping trading with Sweden – much of it carrying iron ore essential to the Nazi war effort. A 'Most Secret' Foreign Office report on Performance states: 'The Swedish Government has viewed the success of the first operation with considerable sympathy, as they were anxious that some measure of trade should be maintained between Sweden and the United Kingdom. They had, however, been severely taken to task by the Germans for an alleged complicity in the operation and had been warned that connivance in any further operation would be regarded by Germany as an unfriendly act. This warning was frequently repeated.' Norway and Denmark had been invaded for less.

In April 1941 Binney notified Swedish government officials that he intended to try to run the blockade a second time and applied for licences for the goods he proposed to ship. These were granted. They covered substantial tonnages of 'semi-finished war materials, machine tools, machinery and equipment of great importance to Allied War production'. The only means of transporting these valuable cargoes to Britain was in these Norwegian ships. Sending merchant ships from Britain was also ruled out as it would have doubled the risks to ships and crews, both in short supply.

The Rubble ships had been managed by the Norwegian consulate at Göteborg. This time it was decided the ships should be directed controlled by His Majesty's Government. It was anticipated that the Germans would attempt to immobilise the ships in Göteborg by starting proceedings in the Swedish courts, claiming that the decree of the Norwegian government-in-exile was invalid. To forestall this the Norwegian government in London had chartered the ships to the British government, protecting them through the immunity of the British government from proceedings in Swedish courts. To prevent any claim that this was a mere device, British captains were to be appointed to manage the ships. Five British merchant officers with the necessary master's certificates were available in Sweden and five more were to be sent out from Britain.

For reasons of *amour-propre*, the Norwegian authorities in London were anxious that the ships should sail under Norwegian captains. It was agreed therefore that as soon as the ships passed out of Swedish territorial waters, then a 5-kilometre limit, the Norwegian masters would take charge. Meanwhile the Norwegian masters stayed aboard as representatives of Nortraship (the Norwegian Trading and Shipping Mission in London) and suffered no loss of income.

The five ships involved in Rubble had delivered not only their precious cargo but a substantial number of British and Norwegian merchant seamen trapped in Sweden. The British crews were the residue of ships lost in the fighting at Narvik. The Norwegians were chosen from hundreds who had escaped from Norway and were prepared to take any risk to reach England rather than vegetate in a refugee camp in Sweden. This time the Norwegian authorities agreed that two of the ships, MS *Dicto* and SS *Charente*, should be manned by British crews with British captains in sole charge for the voyage. As *Dicto* was a motor vessel and no British motor engineers were available, the Norwegians were to provide the engineering staff. In return the engineering staff for SS *Gudvang* and the chief engineer and one or two of the engineering staff for SS *Skytteren* were supplied by the British.

The strength of the Luftwaffe based in Norway meant that, as with Rubble, there was no prospect that the Royal Navy could sail out across the North Sea to provide the ships with an armed escort. It was also believed that, following Rubble, the Germans had laid a minefield across the North Sea between the Orkneys and the Norwegian coast. One possible route was to sail along the Norwegian coast and around the minefield, but there was a chain of aerodromes along the Norwegian coast from which the ships could be attacked at close range. And though an air escort had been promised by Coastal Command at dawn on the second day following the break-out from Göteborg, the chances of protecting ships using this route from continuous air onslaught were slim.

As an alternative the Admiralty had proposed a direct course from the mouth of the Skagerrak to the Scottish coast using a channel that was thought to run between both British and German minefields. This was at the ships' risk as there was no certainty that it existed. Binney was firmly of the belief that out to sea minefields were more a deterrent than a real threat. In addition six of the ships were tankers and unlikely to sink even if they struck mines as their holds were compartmentalised. With a shorter route Coastal Command could also provide more concentrated air protection.

The major drawback of the short course was that it demanded accurate navigation. In the bad weather they were hoping to use to escape detection, there would be no means of navigating by sun or stars. Only one ship, *Skytteren*, had a gyroscopic compass which made it possible to plot an accurate course in all weathers. The Admiralty therefore agreed to lay on direction-finding signals, though it was pointed out that at such long range the deviation could be substantial. A meteorologist, K. A. Clark, was sent out from England to help predict the most favourable sailing conditions and a special wireless service was established which provided in cipher fleet weather reports bearing on the North Sea and the Skagerrak.

To maximise the speed and engine efficiency of the ships a Swedish engineering expert was engaged to supervise repairs and maintenance and advise on means of boosting cruising speeds. Given the likelihood of German air attack, precautionary defensive measures had to be taken, and by degrees Lewis guns and ammunition were distributed surreptitiously to the ships. To protect the ships' bridges from machine-gun attack, circular steel 'pillboxes' were erected, each capable of holding three men. A special gearing device enabled the ship to be steered from within the pillbox.

Every member of the crew was also issued with a Swedish life suit – a loose fitting rubber overall completely protecting the body from exposure or immersion.

On 22 July 1941 Binney wrote to his colleague Mike Wheeler at the Ministry of Supply saying that one of the services the operation could offer was 'to transport a large number of British, Norwegian and Polish subjects eligible for service in their respective armed forces' – these including British volunteers from the 1939 Finnish

campaign, Polish aviators and at least 500 young
Norwegians. *Skytteren* had accommodation for 250
whalers, and if fifteen passengers were taken on each of
the other ships that would bring out 400 men in addition
to the 280 crew.

In July 1941 Marcus Wallenberg, Swedish representative
on the Anglo-Swedish War Trade Commission, told the
British legation in Stockholm that 'the Swedish authorities
did not intend to place any difficulties in Binney's way and
that, on the contrary, they secretly hoped he might again
succeed'. Nonetheless he warned that 'the German Navy
was absolutely determined to prevent another successful
Rubble Operation', adding that 'Admiral Raeder had reason
to believe that he would lose his job if he again failed to
prevent Binney carrying out his plans'.

The British minister in Stockholm, Victor Mallet (at that
time ministers and legations were the norm rather than
embassies and ambassadors), was very alive to Swedish con-
cerns that any blockade-busting operation might provoke
savage German retaliation against Sweden.

A 'Most Secret' briefing paper on Operation
Performance was sent by Hugh Dalton, the minister in
charge of SOE, on 3 October 1941 to Anthony Eden, the
Foreign Secretary, explaining that the break-out was now
planned for the middle of November. 'The most important items are ball bearings and the machinery for their
production since, both in this country and the United
States, there is a serious deficiency in equipment for the
production of ball bearings specifically for the War effort.
Tanks and aircraft require in large quantities sizes of ball
bearings not normally used in commercial industry.' To
meet this special demand a shadow factory was being
erected in Scotland, but Swedish supplies of the finished
bearings were needed meanwhile, and the new factory

was also dependent on 'machinery which can only be obtained from Sweden and has never yet been successfully manufactured in this country or the United States'. Without the cargoes, Dalton's paper continued, 'production of tanks and aircraft both in this country and in the United States will be affected, and tank programmes may be directly delayed for several months'. Other items to be shipped were illuminating devices for aerodromes, marine buoys, springs for Bofors guns and ground thread taps needed for the aircraft industry.

The briefing paper also asked Eden to take a strong line with the Swedish minister in London over the refusal of visas to six British master mariners being sent out to captain the ships. 'This is a serious blow to our preparations and represents extremely un-neutral conduct on the part of the Swedes, since they constantly grant visas for Norwegians and others to be sent to Sweden by the Oslo Shipping Companies ... Indeed, a Norwegian quisling captain and a party of men were granted visas by the Swedes only a fortnight ago, in an attempt to gain possession of one of the very ships which we intend to use for this Operation.'

The plan was now to attempt the break-out about the middle of November with eight ships, four of which would be in water ballast with the other four carrying 14,000 tons of cargo – the maximum that would then be ready to ship. Orders had been placed for 18,000 tons of cargo in all and up to twelve ships had now been identified for charter.

Serious consideration was now given as to whether Operation Performance might trigger a German invasion of Sweden. A paper of 2 October graphically sets out the difficulties the Germans would encounter if they attempted to invade Sweden in winter. These were continuous snowstorms and blizzards and freezing of the coastline, making landings difficult without ice breakers. Roads and railways would be blocked by snow. Long nights and short days would further hamper invading forces, as experience showed that the Germans were reluctant to operate at night. Though weather conditions in January were more favourable for snow warfare, they were also ideal for sabotage and guerrilla attacks.

Victor Mallet reported a visit by Marcus Wallenberg on 1 October. The Swede archly said he did not think the *immediate* reaction of the German government to the departure of the ships would be more than the stoppage of the Göteborg shipping traffic and possibly the sinking of any Swedish ships that happened to be on that route at the time. Karl Schnurre, the Nazi's special negotiator in Sweden, had also threatened Jacob Wallenberg that the German navy would go into Göteborg harbour, but Wallenberg had laughed at him and said that German ships would be sunk in that case. Marcus Wallenberg was careful to say that he was not suggesting any weakening of the line on the ships but added that Britain failed to appreciate how important the Göteborg traffic was to Swedish morale as it provided contact with the outside world and reduced the feeling of dependence on Germany. If the traffic halted, the whole of Sweden's economic system would then become dependent on Germany and the Swedish government would find themselves more and more forced to give credits and to sell to Germany steel and other manufactured goods. Why not, he suggested, keep the ships in readiness indefinitely and so hold down German naval ships? In which case the Swedish government might offer other quid pro quos, for example a secret advance of payments in connection with revictualling post-war Europe.

The Ministry of Economic Warfare's assessment was set

out in a letter from its headquarters in Berkeley Square to Chris Warner at the Foreign Office on October 8. It reads:

I do not believe Germany will attack Sweden unless she is quite sure she can conquer the country quickly without the destruction of Swedish industry and especially of the mining industry . . . The Swedes have a good deal of national pride, they have seen the Finns fight the Russians and the Norwegians fight the Germans and they have heard the criticism which was levelled at the Danes for refusing to resist. They look upon themselves as the leading Scandinavian race and I do not believe even their Government could face up to seeing the Germans treat Sweden as they treated Denmark.

Nonetheless, Swedish concern at possible German repercussions continued to grow, and on 30 October shortly before the intended departure, the Riksdag, the Swedish parliament, in secret session, passed a bill through all its stages in one day prompting the 'arrest' of all ten ships.

That day Binney cabled SOE that the over-executor of the Göteborg court was so distressed by this political interference 'that we could probably count on his good will' in allowing ships to remain free for a few days. 'I am therefore planning to get out the *Dicto* subject to favourable weather in next 2 or 3 days. She will not leave coast unless weather conditions are favourable.' He added that he was also preparing three other ships for departure.

The very next day, 1 November 1941, he cabled with grim news: 'All ships now arrested. Gothenburg [Göteborg] authorities clearly acting on instructions from Stockholm obstructed [the] obtaining of clearance papers for *Dicto* which we attempted to obtain last night and again this morning.'

A day earlier he had cabled SOE: 'I am convinced that Swedish Government regard Performance as a major political issue and it may even be that they have given specific assurances to the German Government that ships will not sail.' Another strongly worded memo proposes rallying public opinion in Göteborg. 'German ships every night anchor in Swedish territorial waters while we are forbidden to lay up anywhere except in the port of Gothenburg ... We have at the moment the very best opportunity of driving a wedge between the Swedish Government and the people [who are] very largely in sympathy with our cause ... The press and the people ... are completely unaware that their legal system is being tampered with in order to meet German demands.' The matter should be brought up in Parliament in London, and a press conference held at the legation in Stockholm. 'There is nothing which frightens the Swedish Government so much as the possibility of strained or broken relations with Great Britain.'

On 4 November 1941 Binney sent another anguished cable to SOE in London. 'The susceptibility of the Swedish Law Courts to political pressure indicates they are capable of indefinitely prolonging present lawsuits ... We should hit hard at small clique of Swedish ship owners, industrialists, and financiers, who consistently expect best both worlds. These men control policy of the Swedish Cabinet ... and they must be brought to realize we mean business as opposed to ineffectual wrath.' He suggested immediate retaliation – holding up two Swedish inbound vessels due to arrive at the Faeroe Islands on 7 November with cargoes vitally needed in Sweden. Simultaneously he urged lodging a claim for unwarranted detention of £200,000 per week.

A Most Secret memo of 14 November 1941 sets out a major incentive offered to 'certain Swedes'. If they could arrange for the most urgent export of 6,000 tons of the most urgent material needed for Performance, Sweden would be permitted to import enough aviation spirit to make up her war reserve to a total of 40,000 tons and two full tankers of crude oil. An attachment adds: 'Mr Wallenberg to return to Sweden quickly with this agreement in his pocket and to impress upon his Government the importance of immediately making to H.M.G. a statement that they will permit the litigation over the Norwegian ships to take its proper course with the least possible delay, that administrative delays and difficulties will be stopped and that, provided that H.M.G. are successful in the litigation, the ships will be permitted to sail in conditions giving them a fair chance to succeed.'

As the long winter set in, sabotage – ironically one of SOE's own specialities – became a problem. On *Skytteren*, sand was discovered in the main bearings of the engines, one auxiliary engine was tampered with and a small fire was started. On *Lionel* the lubricating system of the auxiliary engines was interfered with, while on *Buccaneer* there was trouble with the engines. Continuous watches were kept to prevent unauthorised persons boarding the ships, and the sentries at the gangway had instructions to admit no one without an officially stamped card from the British consulate. Naval ratings from HMS *Hunter*, lost at Narvik, were employed as special watchmen on the ships throughout the winter. Later on, double watches were kept, while Swedish soldiers guarded the approaches to the vessels on both the quayside and on the ice in the harbour. Pamphlets were distributed to the crews, repeated warnings were given to the captains, while the chief engineers sealed up vulnerable points on the engines and steering gear.

An intelligence report of November 1941 'from a secret and reliable Norwegian source in Göteborg' lists a number of crew members who had come under suspicion because of contacts with Nazi sympathisers. On *Lionel* a bosun appeared to have stolen a barrel of kerosene which had been hidden in one of the fore-holds. A motorman on *Lionel* went regularly to a Swedish family where the daughter was a German spy. A stoker on *Skytteren* who always had plenty of money met a woman journalist and teacher from Arjang every week. She came from 'a well-known Nazi family here in Sweden, who also have relatives in Oslo'.

Meanwhile the Swedes were seriously slowing the loading of the ships. Their tactics, cabled by Binney on 4 November 1941, included arranging a shortage of railway wagons, slow-timing port facilities, delaying the arrival of Norwegian seamen enlisted to crew the ships, and stalling on the supply of 400 tons of diesel fuel, promised in return for a guarantee that the ships would not sail in September.

A further point was that all the materials had been paid for – a commitment of a million pounds, a massive sum which made it all the more unacceptable for the Swedes to delay shipping of the goods. When legal proceedings had begun against Performance, Binney reported, 'we were assured by two eminent and independent Swedish maritime lawyers that our case for immunity was sound in accordance with existing Swedish law … this view has subsequently been confirmed by Sundberg, professor of international law at Uppsala University, who also confirmed view of other advisors that appeal court judgement could only have been dictated by political considerations'. Binney had also received a report on Muhl, the Swedish lawyer engaged by the Germans to conduct their case. Muhl was then in a Göteborg hospital and had talked to a British-born subject, Dinsdale, who was also a patient there and knew Muhl quite well, having employed him professionally. Muhl had admitted that the case was bad in Swedish law, but was nevertheless hoping to prolong the litigation for the duration of the war, adding that there were grounds for hope that even if he lost his case in the courts, the government would requisition the ships.

On 5 November Binney cabled SOE urging continued coverage of the ships on the BBC. 'It surprised HM Minister. It awakened the Swedish.' He suggested a report on the passing of special law by the Riksdag in secret session and the tampering with Swedish law 'which hitherto has enjoyed an international reputation for its integrity'. To this should be added a report on the number of Swedish vessels currently crossing the Atlantic on their way to Göteborg.

On 6 November a small victory was gained when the Göteborg town bailiff restored parts removed from *Dicto*'s engine to prevent her sailing. Better still was the news that the over-executor in Göteborg had 'liberated all ships from arrest this afternoon and according to our lawyers gave highly satisfactory reasoned judgement for his action. Presumably application for re-arrest will be made tomorrow. Meanwhile *Dicto* is to be cleared and all being well will leave Gothenberg [*sic*] harbour tomorrow morning . . . Reasons for clearing her are . . . to test bona fides of Swedish authorities in permitting her to depart [and] to test German reaction and if possible ascertain German dispositions off Swedish coast'. Binney continued: 'Suggest you endeavour to arrange for Coastal Command to send patrol to spot German ship movement . . . patrol should be operated between midday and dusk tomorrow.'

The very next day Binney cabled with more bad news. *Dicto* and all other ships 'were re-arrested at instance of appeal court'. On 8 November 1941 he cabled with more detail to SOE, citing filibuster techniques. 'Application for pass was made by telephone at 1515 but naval officer concerned was absent and his substitute stated only commanding officer could issue pass. Commanding officer returned at 1600 ... stated only authorities Stockholm could give final permission.' As to the rearrest, he added angrily, 'so far there has been no protest,' and Victor Mallet, the British minister in Stockholm, had simply said 'that on the next occasion he saw Eric Boheman [the Secretary-General of the Swedish Foreign Office] he would probably grumble but that we must be careful not to annoy the Swedes at this stage'. Binney continued, 'In my opinion we shall never get the ships out if in our diplomatic representation we continue to adopt a spineless attitude of deference.'

On 8 November the Foreign Office weighed in, cabling to Stockholm that 'it looked as though Swedish Government had decided to adopt a policy of appeasement towards Germany at expense of Great Britain', adding that this followed permission for a German division to cross Swedish territory (a grave breach of neutrality).

On 11 November 1941 Binney cabled SOE that this was the psychological moment to warn Jernkontoret (the Swedish counterpart of the British Iron and Steel Federation) that 'post war relationship between our industries would be very seriously affected by any attempt to hinder export of steel to United Kingdom purchased in good faith' on granting of an export permit.

The next day Victor Mallet swiftly set out his view that the Swedish government was 'conducting a rearguard action with some skill though at the cost of certain disadvantages to ourselves' and suggested using 'these months in fattening up Sweden for a possible fight against Germany' rather than 'starving her into a state of apathy'. He concluded pointedly. 'My three service Attachés have been consulted when drafting these telegrams and concur.' The next day he added, 'my Soviet colleague who is a shrewd judge only recently told me again that she thought Swedish Government were standing up pretty well'.

In London, the Foreign Office sharply disagreed. Christopher Warner, head of Northern Section, wrote on 14 November: 'we do not agree with Victor and I expect we shall be sending him a major political telegram to get him on the right lines'. The draft reply on the files tells Mallet to disabuse the Swedes of the idea 'that we were prepared to make almost any sacrifice of our own interests whenever Swedish Govt. think there is slightest risk of clash with Germans . . . we consider our interests to be more seriously injured than you have perhaps hitherto realised . . . it is surely only elementary psychology in dealing with frightened people to take rather a stiff line with them while trying to show them where their fears are exaggerated'. Mallet is asked to exert himself in combating the policy of appeasement to which the Swedes were tending and 'to impress on the Swedes that H.M. Government are justifiably incensed over the various devices to which the Swedish Govt. have resorted to prevent operation "Performance"'.

On 17 November 1941 Binney cabled:

neither Waring nor I were present when he [Mallet] discussed Performance issues with service attaché. I entirely disagree with defeatist attitude . . . I suggest therefore that PM should be asked to prepare a speech calculated to set Sweden by the ears on Sweden's present position vis-à-vis democracies, and that Prytz be given an advance copy of it. There will then be desperate efforts by the Swedish Cabinet to avert the denouement. So much so that imminence of an immediate crisis will over-shadow their forebodings as to possible German aggression next spring.

Renewed consideration was now given as to whether Germany might invade Sweden if Performance went ahead. The Foreign Office view was that the Germans were now heavily engaged in their attack on Russia and would need up to a million men to be sure of success and certain of overcoming Swedish resistance.

This assessment was based in part on a report of a dinner attended by leading Swedish civil servants, professors and writers – some fifteen to twenty leading figures, all men. The dinner had been given by Bertil Ohlin and the report came from an unnamed Danish friend of his who had attended the dinner. 'A certain exalted Handelsråd' had recently returned from Germany and told the other guests that 'the German army had lost up to the beginning of December more than 25% of its fighting strength'. The Dane reported that there was:

among them a real determination that Sweden could resist if necessary against any German attack ... Sweden would have enough oil for her navy and army for seven months of war, and stocks were being carefully husbanded. All present agreed that Germany would need an extremely strong force to subjugate Sweden. They were not impressed by Germany's poor showing in the Finnish woods and all seemed convinced that Germany would meet with no greater success in the Swedish woods.

On 7 January 1942 Hambro had written a secret memo seeking to obtain permission for a few of the ships, laden with the most important cargo, to make a break even though they were under arrest. 'Such an attempt is considered operationally possible by our experts on the spot. The vessels in question are fully loaded and supplied ... They could be warped out into the stream and could sail without the help of tugs and in spite of the fact that they are moored with their bows towards land.'

The 18,000 tons of cargo, he added, had a sterling value of £1.25 million. 'Perhaps the most important part of the material is the ball-bearings and the machinery for ball-bearing manufacture. In the immediate future production of a number of weapons (for example tanks) will be directly regulated by the availability of ball-bearings. The United States Government, from which considerable supplies were expected, have now stated that they consider their own supply position to be at least as bad as that of the U.K., if not worse.' Production could not expand before the end of 1942 and even this was dependent on the safe receipt of machines included in the cargo.

The next day, 8 January, Mark Wallenberg asked for a secret meeting with Binney with a view to finding a solution to the Performance deadlock. 'He told me that as a result of his conversations with the Swedish Cabinet during the last few days he was satisfied that no adverse influence whatever would be brought to bear on the Supreme Court.' But he also indicated that even if the judgement was favourable, problems lay ahead. 'The naval authorities would not grant facilities for the ships to lie up along the coast,' thereby depriving them of their best chance of avoiding detection. He also said it was very unlikely that the Swedish government would consent to eleven ships sailing and offered two as a compromise, the remainder to lie up until the next winter. Binney expressed shock, as earlier the Swedish government had given categoric assurances that it would abide by the Supreme Court decision.

A meeting at the Foreign Office on 12 January again considered the question of a break-out now that it looked as if the litigation would drag on beyond the period of long

nights. Hambro confirmed that production of key armaments would be delayed for several months. It was also likely
that the Swedes would seize any remaining ships and possibly agree to further German troop transits across Swedish
territory. The conclusion was that the importance of the
cargoes justified the risk. The legal advisers present also
thought they could put up quite a good defence for defiance
of the Supreme Court on the basis that 'the Swedish courts
and the Swedish Government had refused to consider
seriously the argument that the ships, being chartered to His
Majesty's Government, were entitled to immunity'.

Binney set out his views. 'Will the Swedish navy, who have
not fired a shot in anger for 140 years, take the responsibility of shooting (at point blank range) at a number of
unarmed merchantmen flying the white ensign and manned,
as they well know, by Norwegian and British sailors?' He
continued, 'the white ensign will upset their calculations
and . . . ensure their seeking further instructions from headquarters. If we win this first trick, we shall win the game.
No one in Stockholm in my opinion will take the individual
responsibility of ordering the navy to fire on us. It would
have to be a collective Cabinet decision, which would take
time . . . in the meantime the ships would be well on their
way down the river'.

On 22 January Binney received a cable stating: 'you now
have authority, to be exercised at your own discretion, to
sail all or any of the ships at any time from now onwards,
whether they are under arrest by the Swedish authorities or
not'. The Foreign Office was notifying Mallet accordingly,
though adding that Binney's unfettered discretion did not
preclude Mallet from raising important political considerations he felt should be taken into account. There was,
however, every advantage of 'Mallet "not being informed of
zero hour"'.

The same day the Foreign Office cabled to Mallet: 'Most valuable part of cargo is of so great importance to war effort that possible serious repercussions . . . must be faced . . . Decision of the Supreme Court at any reasonable date is out of the question . . . I fully realise you will be placed in extremely awkward position . . . It would be out of question to send ships to fetch cargoes. Hazards would be doubled.'

The best, indeed the only, chance of making an illicit break-out was for the ships to start towards dusk, preferably at a weekend when the garrisons of the harbour forts and the harbour police would be lightly manned. But Göteborg harbour was 10 miles long and the channel out through the Rivo and Vinga fjords was intricate and well guarded. To hinder any such attempt the ships had been made to anchor with their bows to the shore. In the narrow harbour it would have been exceedingly difficult to manoeuvre them without tugs into the stream. There was a severe danger of the ships running aground, most probably the larger and more valuable ones.

The position of any ships that failed to make their way out to open sea would be critical. Faced with the defiance of the Swedish courts, the Swedish government might seek to arrest or even to requisition all Norwegian shipping remaining in Swedish waters, and even possibly to hand over to the Germans tonnage equivalent to that which had left Swedish waters. The British legation in Stockholm would also be in a severe predicament as in their first note complaining of the ships' arrest they had expressed their intention of awaiting the decision of the Swedish courts.

On 20 January Mallet had cabled the Foreign Office to say he had been told confidentially by Erik Boheman, secretary-general or head of the Swedish Foreign Office, that the Supreme Court had given no indication of when judgement would be forthcoming but had agreed to give the government four days' warning to allow 'certain dispositions' including 'mobilisation' of the air force to prevent a possible German air coup against the ships in Göteborg harbour. The navy would also be warned to stand by. The garrison of the Göteborg forts was already being discreetly strengthened.

Next came the worst news of all. The Supreme Court had decided by four votes to three that, before they could reach a final decision on the question of immunity, more documents had to be served on the shipowners in Norway. This was a clear piece of filibuster and brought an understandably furious response from the Foreign Office. A telegram to Mallet on 25 January pointed out that although 'all the necessary documents were submitted to the Supreme court on the 29th of December, it was not until the 20th January that a decision was given upon this preliminary matter of procedure. These facts alone show that the Swedish Courts have no conception of the importance attached by His Majesty's Government to a speedy decision on the question of immunity'. At every stage delays over 'procedural matters' had 'promoted the interests of the German Government' and constituted 'a denial of justice' which was all the more inequitable as the Norwegian shipowners 'are acting under German duress and in some instances are actually in prisons under German control'.

On 29 January the Foreign Office cabled Mallet telling him of a series of cases in which sovereign governments had secured release of their vessels – in United States, Belgian, Argentine and even German courts – adding: 'During present war plea has been successful wherever it has been raised.'

The telegram continued by priming Mallet to inform Boheman: 'this country is in midst of life and death struggle and cargoes are of vital importance to our war effort.

Operation could only be undertaken during the depth of winter . . . We are convinced that it is Sweden's interest that the United Kingdom should win the war. Germany has already occupied two Scandinavian States and if she won, Sweden would be vassal State'.

Mallet's reply of 31 January 1942 is equally vivid in describing his meeting with the secretary-general the day before.

'I have never seen him so angry . . . The aspersion upon the Supreme Court was a thing the Swedish Government could not admit. He would lay the note before the Cabinet but he felt certain that its effect would be merely greatly to augment the existing irritation against His Majesty's Government. The Swedish Government were furious at the way in which the Ministry of Economic Warfare had gone back on their agreement with Wallenberg and were now refusing navicerts for essential supplies already purchased in South America. His Majesty's Government seemed to have no consideration whatever for Sweden's appalling difficulties. They expected her to take grave risks on their behalf without even helping her to get the wherewithal to maintain herself if attacked by Germany . . . The departure of these ships would expose Sweden to mortal dangers. If the war then came to Sweden no help could be expected from His Majesty's Government which had invariably been unable to save any small nation from German aggression.'

He added that 'The German Government were furious at the case having been left to the Law Courts to decide', as they believed this was a ruse to eventually set them free. 'I contested his arguments one by one and answered back with much violence, but our arguments got us nowhere,' added the vexed Mallet.

To increase pressure on the Swedes the British government had now indicated that they could hold up supplies of oil and rubber which the Swedes desperately needed. Boheman's reply, as reported by Mallet, was that the war trade agreement with Britain would go by the board and Sweden would be forced to sell to Germany 'up to 150,000 motor cars with tyres now lying idle in Sweden, 50,000 of which the German Government had asked for many times already. Swedish industries would have to follow Swiss example and harness themselves increasingly to the German war effort'.

A memo from Harry Sporborg of 17 February suggests that Boheman had a point. After the shipments of rubber, hides and wool to Sweden had been agreed in December, the Ministry of Supply had stepped in and stated that even when the Swedes had actually purchased goods within the agreed quotas they might not be allowed to ship them. This new policy had arisen out of the enormous demand for raw materials created by the American armaments programme. Fortunately Sporborg was able to quickly secure the agreement of Lord Beaverbrook for the shipments on the basis that the Swedes would probably make Performance impossible without it. Five days later Binney cabled to report 'excellent effect of rubber concessions' but also the grim news that 'Ice conditions in Gothenburg harbour are unprecedented and our ships are so firmly locked that it will take many hours with tugs and possibly an icebreaker to release them.' Agonisingly there was no question of a clandestine departure for some weeks.

The Lloyds agents Lindahl and Collin, '100% pro-British', were prepared to exert their substantial influence with the Göteborg Tug Company but this could not be tested in advance and there remained a possibility of political interference. A second telegram followed saying that after discussions with two of the captains who had long experience of the Skagerrak, Binney had decided on a short southerly route which offered 'better chance of evasion as Germans are likely to be looking for us on Norwegian south westerly coast'. In addition this 'practically halved our fuel requirements of which we are growing desperately short'. Also, 'by following shallow water route we are more likely to secure continuous fog belt'.

The next day Mallet reported that Boheman still now anticipated the Supreme Court judgement by 15 March, 'and that it would be in our favour'. Binney continued: 'In present position we shall not secure ice breaker or tugs and are therefore impotent. It is not anticipated Gothenburg will be ice free until 1st or 2nd week in March.'

He had also learnt that 'from outset Swedish Navy has had instructions to use all measures to stop us and we must therefore anticipate serious casualties,' with the possibility of the clandestine departure being aborted by blockage of the harbour channel.

On 8 March Binney had asked to be informed what aircraft would be sent out to support Performance so there would be no possibility of the ships' gunners mistaking them for enemy planes. Two days later he heard that they were likely to be Beaufighters and Blenheims.

Finally, on 17 March, the Supreme Court ruled that the ships were free to sail, but huge packs of ice remained, continuing to make departure impossible. The very next day came news that German patrols had been observed at Kristiansand south and Hantsholm – two or three vessels in each place evidently aimed at stopping the ships. This was followed on 20 March by an aircraft report of long lines of ice remaining in the Skagerrak with bands of brash ice as well. Much of the ice was in heavy packs as much as 350 yards wide.

On 20 March Mallet and his American opposite number were summoned to the Foreign Ministry, where the secretary-general told them that the German minister had arrived the evening before to remind the Swedes of Ribbentrop's declaration in September 'that if any single ship left Gothenburg and arrived in a British harbour or in British hands this would be considered an unfriendly act of the Swedish Government'. Mallet noted astutely that Ribbentrop's original term had been 'hostile' and 'unfriendly' had been substituted. The Germans now asserted that if the Swedish government refused protection for (the quisling) Norwegian shipowners, and if they actively supported the departure of the ships by issuing clearance papers, 'this would be a one-sided act of collaboration in favour of Great Britain'. The secretary-general added that he considered these claims unfounded but laboured the point that if the Germans closed the Göteborg traffic Sweden's capacity for defence would be seriously affected. In six months an oil shortage could cripple the Swedish fleet and air force.

With the nights becoming shorter, Binney reported on 23 March that he had gone out on the harbour ice breaker to the Vinga lighthouse to examine the ice. Here he had found one narrow channel kept open. The ice in the fjord was at least 2 feet thick. Beyond, ice flows were a major hazard – greatly reducing speed though hampering German patrol vessels too. Two days later came the dismal news that weather prospects had again deteriorated, meaning a further delay of at least three days.

When the ice began to melt Binney wrote to the ChaHarMiks, as he called Charles Hambro and Harry Sporborg at SOE and Mike Wheeler at the Ministry of Supply on 28 March 1942: 'All our ships are now lying at the mouth of the harbour in as advantageous position as Gothenburg can offer, but of course they are easily seen by any watchers on shore. Admiral Akemak, who I saw yesterday in

Gothenburg, and Boheman, with whom I lunched at the Minister's today, admit that the Germans will inevitably get the news as soon as we begin to move, but nothing will induce them to offer any alternative anchorage in Swedish waters.'

The fuel position was also dire. 'The Swedish authorities have curtailed our fuel supplies, firstly by refusing to allow us to take up 100 tons of Norwegian Government oil,' available on a lighter, and 'by refusing to allow us to bunker some English coal belonging to a British controlled company . . . Throughout the winter the authorities raised no objection to this. Now they frankly state they do not want to give the Germans the slightest excuse to infer that we have received any assistance . . . this was apparently a Cabinet decision and unalterable. The Swedes completely close their eyes to the fact that our shortage of oil and coal is solely due to their wrongful detention of the ships'.

Binney fumed that in spite of the good efforts of Swedish friends 'the Swedish Government has played and continues to play as dirty a game as they can hope to get away with'.

The new berths were at and around the oil quays towards the outer limits of the harbour, less directly under observation – except from the Swedish navy, whose wharves lay opposite. There was in any case little prospect of leaving by stealth as the Admiral in Command at Göteborg, acting under orders from Stockholm, had given orders that the ships must notify the Swedish naval authorities of the precise hour of their departure. The Swedish navy would then put to sea four hours ahead of the ships, and this would naturally alert the Germans to an imminent possible sailing. In addition, the Göteborg customs authorities refused to allow the deposit of the ships' clearance papers to be delayed until ten days after departure as they had done with the Rubble ships. These measures pointed more and more to a single end result – that the Performance ships would be driven straight out of Swedish waters on to German guns.

On 29 March came news that the Swedes were proposing to place four or five naval ratings on board each ship immediately prior to departure. They would remain for the first half-hour of the voyage. A protest had been made but the secretary-general had told Mallet that similar measures were to be taken with German ships in the harbour to ensure that they did not break wireless silence or seek to create an incident. Mallet continued: '[The Swedish] naval authorities have learned that one or two German ships propose to follow our ships out of the harbour in order to give away to the German patrol our whereabouts or alternatively to attack our ships.'

The Germans, besides maintaining air and surface patrols, had sent into Göteborg a number of armed merchantmen with instructions to follow the ships out of port. The one redeeming factor was that William Kjellberg, the shipping agent, had persuaded the Swedish naval authorities to let the Performance ships leave at sundown, and had established that the armed German merchantmen would not be allowed to follow them.

The Swedish Admiralty had also refused the ships the safety of Swedish inner territorial waters, except where the neutral route passed through them. Nor were they allowed to stop or anchor, except briefly to take on or put down pilots or naval officers. If they did they would be compelled by force if necessary to return to Göteborg.

Binney called a meeting of the British captains on the morning of 30 March. The discussion centred on routes and the advisability of dispersal. The plan was on, provided it was foggy. On reaching Vinga, the lighthouse on the coast off Göteborg, three ships, *BP Newton*, *Charente* and *Buccaneer*, would turn south, as if on their way to

Malmö and Copenhagen, and would not turn again until they had steamed for forty minutes. Four ships, *Skytteren*, *Lionel*, *Lind* and *Gudvang*, would proceed northward within territorial waters until they passed the Hallo islands 56 kilometres to the north of Vinga. *Dicto*, *Rigmor* and *Storsten* would put to sea some 32 kilometres north of Vinga.

Once in the North Sea, the course was to be left to the individual masters, but they were told that the German patrols would probably expect them to follow a route along the edge of the deep water at the maximum distance from the Norwegian coast.

The captains were instructed to be ready to sail on the evening of the following day and to remain on board and cut all communication with the shore. A new port regulation helpfully prevented anyone except the captain from going ashore after a ship had been cleared. As some of the Norwegian captains had contrived to circumvent this regulation to spend time ashore with family or friends, Binney decided that the Norwegian captains could not be included in the meeting of captains. Excellent men though they were, he was not prepared to discuss the routing instructions with anyone who had contacts ashore.

A further meeting was held aboard *Dicto* at 4 p.m. on 31 March during which Clark, the meteorological officer brought over from England, explained the weather prospects. He showed the approximate position of the fog area and estimated that thick weather was likely to set in early the next morning. As far as could be judged the prospects for an extensive area of fog were as favourable as could be hoped for.

Binney warned the captains that there was no question of leaving the coast until the fog materialised and that if they put to sea late that night they could not expect aircraft cover at dawn as they would still be well short of the limit to which air cover could be sent. Unanimously the captains decided to leave that evening and to sail along the coast until the fog arrived. Given the longer days, it would not be dark till 8 p.m. when the first ship would sail. It was also a night of full moon, so the onset of fog was all the more vital. The captains expressed satisfaction that everything was in order – the deck houses to be used against fire, the scuttling charges and Lewis guns, and the drugs that would keep the wireless operators going through the voyage. Finally he stressed that this was in no sense a convoy and they must use their individual discretion once they reached the Vinga lighthouse. He then went ashore to carry out the final formalities before sailing and to dispatch messages to alert the naval and air force authorities in Britain.

Returning to *Dicto* at 7.30 p.m., he heard disquieting news. The latest meteorological reports showed that clearer weather was moving rapidly in over the British Isles from the west but that the speed of the cold front was likely to reduce as it moved north-east. Barometers were falling in the northern section of the chart, suggesting that thick weather would arrive even sooner. For the meteorologist, the question – with life-or-death implications for the operation – was to estimate the duration of the bad weather in the light of the cold front. His first reaction was to advise an earlier departure time, but on reflection he felt he could not take such a responsibility when weather developments remained so uncertain. Binney decided that the ships should proceed to the coast pending a further meteorological report at 11 p.m., when he could still cancel the operation using the code he had set up with the captains.

By 2340 hours on 31 March all ships had left harbour. *Dicto* was the flagship, and to facilitate communication with the other ships was the fifth to leave. Shortly after leaving Vinga, *Dicto* passed *Charente*, *Buccaneer* and *Lionel* steaming on a parallel course within a mile of one another. They were accompanied by a Swedish warship. The night was still disturbingly clear with visibility of about 19 kilometres. Off Marstrand, *Dicto* ran into heavy drift ice and altered course until thinner ice was reached, allowing her to continue a course parallel to the coast but probably just outside territorial waters. With the ice alongside her she made an uncomfortably good target, but at least attack could come only from the port side. At about 2 a.m. *Dicto* was rounding the Hallo Islands when a large trawler opened fire, prompting her to turn in to the coastal ice. The trawler sheared off but *Dicto* sprang a leak while cutting her way into the ice. Clearly it was necessary to delay putting to sea until the weather thickened. With a falling barometer, Clark now became concerned that the fog would be clearing and that there would be good visibility long before the ship could reach a point where there would be naval or air protection. Binney therefore decided to break radio silence and warn the other ships of the unreliability of the weather. The signal was repeated at two fifteen minute intervals. Strangely none of the ships appears to have received the message though constant wireless watch was being maintained. This raises the spectre of sabotage.

Dicto now obtained a pilot from the Hallo Islands, providing independent evidence that she was now in territorial waters. Shortly after midday she ran into fog and anchored on the pilot's instructions, preventing her from taking advantage of the very weather she needed. At about 5 p.m. the weather started to clear and *Dicto* was hailed by a Swedish destroyer and a message shouted from the bridge: 'Follow after me to Gothenburg, and if you do not follow I am going to use my guns.' As the ship was anchored on the instructions of an official Swedish pilot this was an extraordinary threat.

Lionel had a lucky escape. She was a 10-knot ship carrying 4,500 tons of cargo, of which about 3,690 were machinery and steel for Russia, with a crew of forty men. At 6 a.m. on 1 April the weather appeared favourable with thick snow flurries, and Captain Kershaw and Captain Schnitler decided to take the ship out to sea. By 6.40 a.m. she was 6 miles out from coastal waters when the weather alarmingly cleared. A German trawler quickly sighted them and approached, signalling *Lionel* to stop. Instead *Lionel* immediately turned back towards land. The trawler opened fire but the shells missed and the trawler now turned to pursue *Buccaneer* 3 kilometres to the south. Heavy gunfire was heard as well as two heavy explosions. Shortly after re-entering the safety of Swedish territorial waters, *Lionel* was hailed by two Swedish destroyers, *Puke* and *Psilander*, which were flying the signal LNL, 'put to sea'. As a protest, Captain Kershaw hoisted his answering pennant to half-mast, indicating that the signal had not been understood.

At this point *Charente*, *Lind*, *Rigmor* and *Gudvang* were near by, accompanied by a number of Swedish patrol boats. One of the patrol boats immediately came within hailing distance and shouted to *Lionel*: 'Proceed west, you may not remain in Swedish waters.' A number of other Swedish patrol boats excitedly hailed them in similar fashion. *Lionel* then asked whether she could proceed to Göteborg and was told: 'Yes, but you will never get out from there again.' Captain Kershaw, who had long experience of this coast, took the firm decision that the weather was developing unfavourably and set course for Göteborg, berthing in the harbour that evening.

MT *Stortsen* had a speed of 10–11 knots. On her way to
Vinga a fault was discovered in the steering gear and the ship
anchored for some hours for repairs. Captain Reeve put to
sea in apparently favourable weather the next morning but
was attacked by aircraft that evening when about 48 kilometres south of Kristiansand, towards the outer limit of the
Skagerrak. The ship's wireless failed to function. She was
torpedoed amidships and disabled. For fear of falling into
German hands, her charges were blown and she sank. The
crew and volunteers, fifty-one in all, took to the boats. One
boat, seeking to reach the Norwegian coast under cover of
darkness, arrived at dawn on 4 April and was quickly
spotted. Eight managed to escape, just two succeeding in
making their way back to Sweden. The other boat attempted
to make the much longer voyage to Scotland. At 8.10 a.m. it
was spotted by a Lockheed Hudson, crewed by members of
the Royal Danish Air Service, about 145 kilometres off the
Naze. Tragically, later search patrols could not find the boat
and all aboard were lost.

Skytteren was a large whaling ship and according to the
Foreign Office report on the attempted escape offered
'exceptional opportunities' for the saboteur. 'Fearing that
the scuttling charges might not in themselves be sufficient to
sink a vessel with so many tanks and bulkheads Captain
Wilson had in mind to set her alight if faced with capture.'
This, SOE believed, could have accounted for the fact that
the ship was seen burning fiercely. Swedish fishermen, however, said she had been attacked by both a torpedo boat and
a U-boat. She was carrying a minimum of cargo but her
crew and supernumaries totalled 103 plus a few approved
stowaways.

Buccaneer had a speed of 12–13 knots and was carrying
a valuable cargo. She was intercepted at about the same
time and place as *Skytteren*. Intense machine-gun fire was

heard on the coast at the time she was being attacked. The Foreign Office report reads: 'The guns on this ship were in charge of Mr J D Lennox-Conyngham, a Finnish volunteer from Ireland. The Germans later complained to the Swedish Government of casualties on some of their ships from our machine-gun fire, and it would seem likely that Lennox-Conyngham and his two Lewis gun crews used their opportunity to advantage.'

Newton was the fastest and second largest of the ships, with a speed of 16 knots. She was on her maiden voyage, having been completed at Kockums' Works in Malmö early in 1940. Her cargo of 5,000 tons was second only in importance to that of *Dicto*. At 6.45 a.m. on 1 April she was 4 kilometres north-west of Paternoster Point, proceeding northward. 'She passed two Swedish destroyers, each of which flew the Swedish ensign, lit by a searchlight. The destroyers fired rockets to westward which were taken as orders to proceed in this direction.' Some five minutes later two armed trawlers were observed approaching from the coast and one approached within hailing distance and shouted from the bridge in Swedish '*Newton*, ahoy, proceed to sea. I have orders to force you out of territorial waters.' *Newton* sensibly ignored this order, calling the Swedish bluff.

Shortly afterwards it started to snow and visibility deteriorated sufficiently for *Newton* to make a bid for the open sea. Four or five miles from the coast, now making full speed, she passed *Lionel* returning to land after being headed off and attacked by a German trawler. *Lionel* warned *Newton* by signal of the danger, but *Newton*'s captain held her course. By 10 a.m. *Newton* was enveloped in fog which held for two hours. Shortly after 1 p.m. she was attacked by a small armed trawler from the port beam, but with her superior speed *Newton* was soon out of range. An hour later two more armed trawlers appeared on the starboard side. Disregarding an order to stop, *Newton* was again attacked. Between fifteen and twenty shells were fired at her. These threw up huge plumes of water but she was unscathed apart from a few machine-gun hits.

At 4.10 p.m. there was a more serious attack from enemy aircraft. She replied with her Lewis guns. An SOS was sent out. A second German plane appeared at 5.30 p.m., followed ten minutes later by a third, which dropped bombs – the nearest landing just 45 metres from the ship. Fierce Lewis gun action kept the enemy at a distance. One plane was seen to be hit, leaving a trail of black smoke. One bomb fell very close to *Newton*'s stern but failed to explode. Enemy aircraft continued to circle the ship menacingly until dusk at 7.30 p.m.

During the night *Newton* made good progress through the minefields without incident. Then at 6.40 a.m. came the glorious sight of a British destroyer on the port bow. Soon after this friendly aircraft were sighted. The next morning she docked safely at Leith. The post-operation report gave special credit to Brian Reynolds for his handling of the Lewis guns. 'In their protest to the Swedish Government, the Germans admitted the loss of aircraft, and accused us not only of the use of machine guns, but of cannon. The latter were ordinary ships rockets released from tubes; they were intended to give the impression that the ships carried heavier armament than Lewis guns, so that hostile aircraft should keep their distance.'

The dangers encountered by *Newton* are made all the clearer by the fate of the gallant *Rigmor*. She put out from the Swedish coast on 1 April at 6 a.m. in apparently favourable conditions but the weather soon cleared, revealing an enemy patrol. *Rigmor* quickly turned back towards the coast, only to be hailed by a Swedish destroyer which endeavoured to force her out to sea again. At about 10 a.m. the weather again appeared favourable and *Rigmor* put to sea. Visibility was intermittent and it was not until after 5 p.m., when *Rigmor* was only 180 miles from the Scottish coast, that one of the numerous German planes scouring the Skagerrak found her and came in to attack at low level. Two incendiary bombs were dropped. One ripped open the centre tank and badly damaged the railing on the storm bridge, the other fell into the sea. The plane continued to circle and made several further attacks until 8.15 p.m., when darkness finally enveloped the ship. Captain Gilling, who was on the bridge, had been shot in the thighs, and the wireless room was damaged. But they sailed on safely through mist and rain until at 9 a.m. they saw first one and then a second British plane. But these had to depart, and shortly after midday a German plane appeared, followed by a second. This time their minimal defences were to tell against them. The planes attacked with machine guns and bombs. A bomb close to the stern put one of the diesel engines out of action. Two further bombs ripped up the starboard side of the ship. An SOS was sent. The ship was now unnavigable and listing heavily, and Captain Monsen gave orders to abandon ship at 1.15 p.m. Two further German planes now arrived, one putting a torpedo into *Rigmor* amidships. Shortly afterwards no less than four British destroyers arrived and picked up the crew. Their guns were turned on the German planes and the destroyer *Eskimo* was narrowly missed by a torpedo. An attempt was now made to board *Rigmor* in the hope of towing her to safety but this proved impossible in the heavy swell. 'After consultation with Captain Monsen and Captain Gilling the Naval Commander decided to sink *Rigmor* as she was drifting down on our minefields. She was consequently sunk by gunfire. Happily Captain Gilling has since recovered from his wounds. There were no other casualties and all on board were saved.'

Lind, a small, recently built coastal tanker, carried merely a token cargo to comply with the legal formula that she was chartered 'for the public use of His Majesty's Government'. Her advantage was that her draught was no more than 8 feet 6 inches, so she was in little danger when sailing through minefields. The intention was that she should be the lifeboat of the expedition. She was the only ship that Binney had agreed could go to the aid of other ships, the reason being that if one of the larger ships was mined in the North Sea other deep-draught ships could be jeopardised in going to her rescue.

Shortly after 6 a.m. on 1 April a light haze reduced visibility to little more than a mile, and *Lind*'s two captains decided to proceed to sea. When an enemy patrol boat was spotted *Lind* turned back, but at about 7.20 a.m. two Swedish patrol boats, a trawler and what was thought to be a minesweeper fired warning shots and ordered her out to sea. At about 8 a.m. two Swedish destroyers and another warship gave the same order. Shortly after 9 a.m. *Lind*, now with *Rigmor* and *Lionel*, decided to return to Göteborg. Swedish patrol vessels accompanied them, keeping to landward. 'It is difficult to understand why the Swedish warships should have found it desirable to use the ships as a shield within their own territorial waters, when it was their duty to protect them from attack,' said the FO report. At 9.50 a.m., in yet another change of weather on this fateful day, a heavy fog bank rolled up from the south and after ten minutes both *Lind* and *Rigmor* bravely turned north. Visibility was no more than 365 metres – the very conditions they had hoped for – though all too soon the fog broke again. *Lind* steered a course down the centre of the Skagerrak without incident until at about 6.15 p.m. a plane was observed 3 kilometres to port, flying almost at sea level. As it approached *Lind* it veered out of control into the mist and suddenly a sheet of flame was seen, suggesting it had crashed before it could attack.

The night passed without attack, though patrol vessels were spotted and avoided. The next day at noon a German aircraft appeared and started to drop flares prior to making a torpedo attack. Captain Trovik zigzagged violently to prevent the enemy establishing a steady run-up to his target while Captain Nicol manned the Lewis gun mounted on the roof of the galley. From his tracer fire he appeared to be hitting the enemy repeatedly at a range of 275 metres but without apparent effect. At 12.30 a British plane arrived and with one short burst prompted the enemy to withdraw. No sooner had the British plane departed than a second German plane appeared and released two torpedoes at 550 metres. The aim was good, but thanks to the shallow draught of *Lind* both passed harmlessly under her. *Lind* finally arrived at her rendezvous off the Scottish coast at 3 a.m. on Good Friday, 3 April. Several hours later, at 1 p.m., she received air cover and was escorted into Methil Roads by a destroyer the following afternoon.

The final tally was grim. Six of the ten ships had been lost, either sunk or scuttled. Two had returned to Göteborg with their cargoes intact. *BP Newton* and *Lind* had reached Britain. Statistically 34 per cent of the total tonnage had been lost through enemy action. But *Newton* was carrying 27 per cent of the cargo by value (and 20 per cent by weight) while 45 per cent of the cargo by both weight and value was still safe in *Dicto* and *Lionel*. The greatest blow was the failure to bring through the heavy machinery needed for making ball bearings in Britain – this was still on *Dicto*, which was now back in Göteborg harbour.

The importance of *Newton*'s cargo is shown in figures produced by the Ministry of Aircraft Production on 13 March 1943. Assuming that a sensible selection of types and sizes was made, 100 tons of ball bearings would be sufficient to cover 75 per cent of the airframe work on 1,200 Lancasters and 60 per cent of the airframe work on 1,600 Mosquitoes, the remainder of the bearings being available from stock. The cargo of Operation Rubble in 1941 had been just under 25,000 tons. *Newton*'s was a fifth of this but still a powerful boost to fast-increasing armaments production.

The human toll was also painful. Though the crew figures on the lost ships are complicated by a number of approved stowaways, it seems that of 471 taking part in the operation 234 were taken prisoner. The greatest losses were the seventeen who disappeared on *Stortsen*'s lifeboat, the captain of the *Buccaneer* and a stoker on *Skytteren*. A further forty-three were tragically to die in the brutal conditions of German prisons in Norway.

The Germans were quick to represent the operation as a failure. The *Voelkischer Beobachter* weighed in with a leading article on 4 May 1942, accusing Binney of cowardice in returning to Göteborg and asserting that the crews of the scuttled ships had been saved only thanks 'to the self-sacrificing readiness' of German naval forces. It also claimed that Norwegians taken prisoner had said they had been made to enlist by threats.

The Norwegian government-in-exile was deeply dismayed at the loss of both ships and men and questioned why better support had not been provided by the Royal Navy and the RAF. The Foreign Office report set out to address these points. 'It was not considered a practical operation of war to send surface forces into the Skagerrak . . .

Arrangements were, however, made to meet the escaping merchant ships with a force of destroyers in the centre of the North Sea as they passed through the supposed gap in the minefields . . . on the second day following sailing [2 April]. In addition, arrangements were made to provide air cover with all available aircraft from four long-range fighter squadrons.' On 1 April continuous sorties were flown throughout daylight hours. Aircraft were flying at the extreme limit of their operational range so that 'each successive sortie could only remain in the area for a comparatively short time'. Seven successive sorties were flown without any sighting of the ships. On the eighth and last sortie *Stortsen* was sighted at 18.27 with no sign of life on board and an empty raft alongside. 'Between noon and 1600 our aircraft destroyed one enemy aircraft, damaged three and drove off six other enemy aircraft at various times. Throughout the daylight hours on April 2nd our aircraft operated for a total of 147 flying hours.' During the whole operation three enemy aircraft had been definitely destroyed and five damaged.

In Sweden, as in Germany, a storm broke out over the news that the Performance ships had been armed. Though it was not illegal for merchant ships to carry arms for their defence, in this case it was clear that the arms must have been smuggled on while the ships were in port in Sweden. The news escaped the censor when the *Daily Express* published a front-page article on 'the men of Hell Passage', quoting one of the seamen who had made it to Britain. 'We were spotted by a lone German plane. He swooped down over the top of us, raking our deck with his guns. We gave him a surprise when we opened at him with our two Lewis guns – the only guns we had – and gave him a lot of lead.'

Though this was pure self-defence it was seized on by elements of the Swedish press and by the Swedish government as a means of diverting attention from the lamentable role Sweden itself had played in delaying the ships' departure and then virtually forcing them on to waiting German guns.

Back in Göteborg Binney visited Admiral Akemark to complain of the way in which the Swedish Navy had behaved and reported 'While he was non-committal on this aspect, he had admitted that he had himself protested to Stockholm that the regulations covering our departure were too severe, but that he had been over-ruled'.

On 24 April, Mallet was called to a meeting with Christian Günther, the Swedish Minister for Foreign Affairs, who said that the Swedish cabinet demanded the withdrawal of Bill Waring, Binney's key assistant, and the vice-consul, Peter Coleridge, who they believed had arranged for the machine guns to be smuggled on to the ships. Mallet defended them firmly, and countered by complaining about the tone of the editorials in Swedish papers, saying that the British press were likely to retaliate 'by attacks on Sweden for allowing troop-transits and transport of German war material to Norway'. Günther piously replied that 'the case was not similar because Swedish law had not been broken'. Mallet added that subsequently Boheman, the secretary-general, had admitted that 'Swedish behaviour was far more damaging to us than our smuggling of machine guns could be damaging to Germany'. As Binney said in his report, 'For Rubble we were [able to] retain the element of surprise for our dash, but for Performance we were methodically stripped of every shred of cover'.

When, on 14 May 1942, the Swedish minister in London went to Eden to protest further about the 'considerable' number of machine guns on board, Eden replied firmly that twenty light machine guns could hardly be so described and that 'only a minor breach of Swedish Law had been committed, for which the two captains had already been fined'. He reminded the minister that the Swedish government had prejudiced British interests by rushing legislation through the Riksdag – to which, significantly, the minister made no reply.

Mallet reported to Hambro on 16 April that 'the heroic element in what most people here regard as a tragedy is well appreciated'. He quoted the eloquent words of Professor Segerstedt in *Göteborgs Handels* (a newspaper) on 8 April: 'No one could be left in doubt that the Germans would do their utmost to prevent the ships from reaching Britain. Those on board knew what risks they were taking. The fate which awaited them if they did not succeed ... was drowning or being made German prisoners. To be a German prisoner is not the same as to be a British prisoner ... There is no doubt on whose side the moral forces are. The outcome of the struggle is a foregone conclusion. If any proof were needed it is supplied by the voyage of these boats. A people whose men throw their lives and more than their lives into the struggle for their country's freedom can never be crushed.'

The great unanswered questioned is whether sabotage played any role in the German success in intercepting the ships. In Göteborg the wireless gear had been sealed up by the authorities, and the wireless operators had no access to their sets until the ships were at sea. The Foreign Office report on Performance states:

The Marconi inspector in Gothenburg had tested the sets before the ships sailed and certified that they were in proper working order. He was a Dane well known to our Security advisors and approved by them. It is also curious that no SOS messages were received from *Skytteren*, *Buccaneer*, *Charente*,

Gudvang or *Stortsen*. On the other hand messages were received both from *BP Newton* whose wireless gear had not been inspected by the Marconi inspector Mr Storm (the Captain having made his own arrangements) and from *Rigmor*, whose set Mr Storm had examined.

The report continues:

The radio operator on *Dicto* was a rating from HMS *Hunter* (R. Brown). He was satisfied that his instruments were working satisfactorily, and that, according to the indicators the message was transmitted. The only corroborative evidence that the message was transmitted comes obliquely from the Swedish steam trawler *Mats*, which was fishing three or four miles away. It was later ascertained from those on board that on three separate occasions that morning she was stopped and examined by German U-boats. On each occasion they searched her systematically for wireless transmitting gear and for the presence of Englishmen or Norwegian among her crew. The inference is that the Germans intercepting the message had secured a fix on the ship's position and were lying in wait for her. It is not beyond the lengths of possibility that an expert could contrive by readjusting the mechanism and dials to delude an operator into supposing that he was transmitting on 600-metre wavelengths when, in fact, he was transmitting on another pre-arranged wavelength on which the Germans were tuned.

Chapter 4

BEN COWBURN – A CLANDESTINE LIFE AND SABOTAGE IN TROYES

The governing principle is to cause the maximum damage and confusion to the enemy in the shortest possible time. This however does not give you unlimited authority to blow up everything at sight, since it is obvious that small acts of sabotage which irritate but do not vitally affect the enemy are to be avoided. In every case the importance of the objective must be weighed against the possible consequences of the act.

Target briefing to Major Cowburn, 9 March 1943

Few SOE stories illustrate the extreme and constant danger faced by agents and the French men and women who worked with them than Ben Cowburn's third mission to France in 1943, which took him to the cathedral city of Troyes – Rabelais's '*ville sonnante*' of peeling church bells.

Cowburn was a tough Lancashireman who had lived in France and come to the attention of SOE thanks to his knowledge of the country's oil industry. Born in 1909, Cowburn had moved to Paris with his parents when he was eight and studied at a British school at Boulogne-sur-Seine and then a *lycée*. After attending two schools of electrical engineering he had spent two months with an American firm, Foster Wheeler's, building distillation

94

plants for oil refineries. Later he travelled all over France, superintending the installation of machinery at refineries.

One of Cowburn's assets was that he did not stand out in a crowd. 'Height 5ft 7in. Weight 160lbs. Eyes green. Hair light brown,' reads SOE's file description. Nonetheless he was decidedly good looking with a high forehead, almond eyes, a strong nose and a broad, rounded chin with an attractively creased smile. Generally he made a favourable impression on his instructors. 'Very good man. Slow in speech and manners . . . very precise in his work . . . Has kept the party cheerful with his knowledge of funny stories,' reads a report of April 1941.

His first mission had been to report on the state of the oil industry after the fall of France. Large stocks of crude oil and refined products had been built up in the country by May 1940. When the Germans broke through at Sedan, and it was clear that northern France was likely to be overrun, the British sent demolition parties to Honfleur, Cherbourg, Brest and other places along the coast. Several thousand tons of aviation spirit had been sent to Donges and Nantes for safety. A British demolition party had made all the arrangements to destroy them when the British officer in command, for reasons left unexplained, refused to let destruction proceed. In Bordeaux arrangements for destruction were also cancelled at the last minute by the British authorities. As a result, said SOE, 'the Germans were able to draw on these stocks at the very end of their long lines of communications at a time when their transport arrangements were strained to the utmost'.

Cowburn was parachuted into France for the first time on 6 September 1941 as a sabotage organiser for Pierre de Vomécourt, SOE's Lucas. When he came back in March 1942 de Vomécourt reported: 'he is an absolutely reliable fellow. His real drawback is that his French, though much better than it was, is not perfect . . . when he remains in a place, people begin to notice his accent. In the South that would not be noticeable at all'. This handicap, which affected another top F Section agent, Harry Ree, was not to hinder Cowburn on his Troyes mission, during which the other quality mentioned by Lucas came to the fore. 'He handles all types of men very well, engine drivers, engineers, etc.'

Cowburn was sent on four missions to France, surviving them all, thanks to exceptional sangfroid and a highly developed sense of security. In 1960 he wrote one of the best early books on SOE, *No Cloak, No Dagger*. This was not, he said, 'a complete account of my war experiences', but rather a vivid description of clandestine life in France. Now the story can be filled out dramatically from his bulky personal file, which is especially rich in detail on his third mission, to Troyes, a major sabotage venture partly intended to avert bombing raids that could have caused heavy civilian casualties.

Cowburn wrote: 'there is a tremendous amount of gossip in a provincial town of 50,000 souls and rumours fly fast. It was soon whispered among the resistance people and others that there was an English agent in the town. What was important was that the enemy should not learn who my contacts were; some of them . . . were well known in the town. If I alone were spotted I could hope to hide but my recruits were tied to their houses, businesses, farms and families and were very vulnerable'.

By way of preparation Cowburn had been sent in February 1943 to Brickendonbury (STS 17) to take the Standard Basic Course in Industrial Sabotage, covering steam power stations, electrical power transmission systems, railways, telecommunications and engineering factories. His report from Lieutenant Colonel Rheam, the commandant, states: 'A very good student with a considerable industrial and technical knowledge ... His personality made him a little difficult to handle, but he should do very well when he is his own master. Is very determined and should make a good organizer.'

Cowburn's file includes his briefing instructions as well as his own reports of his mission and his debriefing on his return, and provides descriptions of his recruits and operations under constant threat of exposure as a result of the heavy German presence.

Cowburn dropped near Contres, 22 kilometres south of Blois, at midnight on 11 April 1943 with his W/T operator Honoré, who he described as 'the most expert radio operator, good friend and brother that any organiser could hope to have'. Honoré was Flight Lieutenant Dennis John Barrett, who was later parachuted in March 1944 to the Minister circuit, where he once again proved extremely capable.

They were told that six containers would be dropped with them. In fact there were only five, and half the night was taken up in a vain search for the other. 'This sort of thing is entirely unforgivable,' Cowburn complained to SOE later. The reception group consisted of three members of the large Prosper circuit – Pierre, a Corsican and 'a very fine fellow indeed,' and two farmers, Théo and Eugène. 'We threw the empty containers into a well. Next morning we had a tremendous breakfast at Eugène's house.' Then a light lorry came and took Cowburn and Honoré and their luggage to Theo's farm, where they met the SOE courier Yvonne Rudellat (Jacqueline), the first British woman agent to be sent to France, who had arrived by boat the previous summer.

Cowburn's mission was to form a new circuit, Tinker, in the Troyes area, using contacts provided by Henri Garry, who had been named Cinema thanks to a likeness to the film star Gary Cooper (when London heard this they changed the circuit name to Phono). Cowburn's team was locally recruited in Troyes, not sent from England. His lieutenant, or number two, was Pierre Mulsant, field name André, who had been recruited in March 1943 by Octave Simon of SOE's Satirist circuit in the Sarthe.

André managed the business of his father-in-law, a Mr Stein, 'a pure blooded Lorrain' and 'quite an important person in Troyes'. Stein had a vast warehouse with building materials and had built the only scientific charcoal-making plant in France. This charcoal was supplied for the large number of cars fitted with charcoal converters or gazogenes owing to the acute shortage of petrol.

André, said Cowburn, was very valuable for a number of reasons. He was new to the game, and was not suspected in any way. He could make his time his own. He could provide two or three motor lorries, two motor cars and two light motorcycles for transport purposes. Cowburn continued:

he is about the keenest Frenchman I have ever met. He is quite fearless and a great admirer of England and all things English . . . He is a keen horseman and swordsman and entered the cavalry. He was overwhelmed with rage and grief when France capitulated. He has always belonged to patriotic organisations and even before the war did a lot of street fighting. He is the Royalist representative (Comte de Paris) in Troyes . . . He is perfectly obedient and applies to the letter the rather rigid discipline I imposed for security reasons. All the people he found for me have been splendid and he can be relied on to provide everything. He is, of course, wealthy and in any case will not accept any money for services for what he considers a sacred duty. I gave him presents of cloth, tobacco and so forth which came in the containers and these produced a splendid impression.

André's wife, Raymonde, was also a great lover of all things English and one of the prettiest women in Troyes.

She had been seriously ill, however, and had only recently recovered from an operation that had nearly cost her her life.

Cowburn's courier, Yvonne Fontaine, field name Nenette, was another ardent patriot, 'quite fearless and ready for anything'. She worked in a laundry, and for her SOE work he paid her 2,000 francs a month. Thanks to Nenette, Cowburn did not feel in need of a woman courier from London. Next came Edouard Balthazar, field name Frascati, a mechanic who looked after Stein's garage. He was an Alsatian, aged about forty-five and of great physical strength. 'He does our heavy transport and has rigged up secret hiding places under the floor of one of the lorries . . . He has even managed to reconstruct some lorries by going and dismantling tyres, wheels and various parts off German vehicles while the Germans were not looking. An extremely tough and valuable man. I pay him a salary of 3000 francs per month and give him odd presents of cigarettes.'

Frascati was often assisted by his future son-in-law, Legoix, field name Le Gendre. Legoix was the chauffeur of a German officer and had 'the cheek to transport some of our stuff in the German officer's car'. These were small parcels containing a couple of Sten guns or explosives. Cowburn reported: 'this officer believes that his chauffeur . . . is running a small Black Market in meat and eggs and has regularly been supplied with eggs and meat by Legoix, and he allows the boy to carry mysterious parcels in the car and thinks it is a grand joke!'

Buridan, field name Tenace, provided a safe house for reception committees at his farm at Nogent-sur-Aube, where he lived with his wife, son and daughter. Tenace had been called for three medical checks to assess that he was suitable to be sent to work in Germany. He had managed to fail them all, by taking a preparation that made him ill. As he remained in his village the local Gaullists had tried to recruit him, and when he refused, unwilling of course to say that he was already working for the Resistance, he began to be looked on locally as a shirker or collaborator, which worried him greatly. The Bourgeois family, who ran a café and tobacconist's at Dierrey-St-Julien, near Estissac, also made their premises available as an arms depot and emergency W/T station.

Through Nenette and André, Cowburn had two crucial police contacts. First was a M. Vassart (Procureur), with the French police, who frequently warned Cowburn and his colleagues of impending trouble. The second was a Russian, Araknovski, who acted as interpreter for the Gestapo in their dealings with the French police. Through Araknovski, Honoré had been warned when his radio had been pinpointed through direction-finding. No less important, they had advance warnings of 'raffles' – heavy house-to-house searches.

By contrast, there was a constant threat from informers. André later gave SOE an example – the village of Jiraudot, in the Troyes area, with a population of just 400. Here the *garde-champêtre* (an official of the Mairie), two young prostitutes and a young woman at the prefecture were all in the pay of the Germans.

Another key contact was Madame Mielle, the owner of the most famous restaurant in Champagne, La Bonne Fermière at Précy-Notre-Dame, east of Troyes near Brienne-le-Château. The notorious Pierre Laval, head of the Vichy government, had eaten there. 'The most amazing thing is that she passes for a collabratrice in order to cover her patriotic activities. She is a grand woman. She has found us a safe house in the neighbourhood and when Honoré and I want to disappear from Troyes we can go to Précy-Notre-Dame, rest and get most excellent food there.' She also introduced him to a schoolteacher who acted as secretary to the Mairie and provided them with several sets of ration tickets every month. Later Madame Mielle was awarded the MBE for her work for SOE.

Another valuable contact was Martinot, a house agent in Troyes who arranged for Cowburn to rent houses 'without our names appearing anywhere. He settles all electric bills and so forth, so that we can stay in a house without any trace of our identity, false or otherwise, being recorded'. Cowburn lived as a 'shadow man', with papers issued in another part of France. If questioned as to what he was doing in Troyes he would say he was travelling or on holiday, depending on the circumstances.

On 15 April, four days after they had landed, Cowburn and Honoré, equipped with ration tickets supplied by the Mairie at Contres, had set off for Paris, leaving their two radio transmitters behind. In Paris they went as instructed to visit Madame Monet, at whose premises a woman courier, Germaine Tambour, came to see them and arranged for them to meet Prosper, the head of the large, fast-growing Paris circuit which was to be savagely broken up by the Germans later that year. Cowburn then went on to Troyes to look round the town and find somewhere to live. Here Martinot provided the upper storey of a villa, 2 Avenue Marcel Dupont at St André-les-Vergers. 'Unfurnished and very isolated,' said Cowburn. When he returned to Paris disaster had struck. Germaine, who lived in the same house as Mme Monet, had been seized by the Gestapo. Honoré, who was in the house at the time, had to make a rapid exit, going to his *cachette* (hiding place) at Bois-Colombes.

Cowburn's problem now was to get a radio set to Troyes. Honoré had already been stopped several times and had been made to open his bags. Cowburn was luckier – during the whole of his stay he was never once asked for his papers or made to open his cases. He decided it was too dangerous to bring such an item through Paris. The problem was that cross-country transport was virtually non-existent. By taking buses and slow trains and walking part of the way, Cowburn brought a radio to Brie-Comte-Robert, on the road from Paris to Troyes. Here, for the first and last time on this mission, he stayed for a night in a hotel. The next morning Honoré arrived, ready to hop on to one of André's lorries on its way back from Paris.

On his arrival in Troyes, Honoré had stayed first with André, but had to move to a hotel for a night when André was expecting some relations. He went to the Hôtel de France, which was partly requisitioned by the Germans. Deftly, arrangements had been made for the *fiche*, or arrivals form, which he had filled out, to be destroyed the very next day by a contact at the prefecture.

Cowburn had meanwhile gone back to Paris to arrange a place to stay on future visits. When he arrived back in Troyes they both stayed with André until their apartment was ready. On May 8 their first attempt to make radio contact with London failed, but two days later they succeeded in sending a message requesting delivery of stores. Cowburn had found a suitable dropping ground near Vulaines, west of Troyes, and less than a week later, on 16 May, they set out for the reception area.

The drop was impressively accurate, right on the middle light. The contents of the containers were less satisfactory: 'a weird mixture, including such items as 66 grenades, which I had not asked for . . . but not a single pistol and a ridiculously small amount of Cordtex'. They threw the empty canisters into the bushes and ferried the stores to his safe storeroom in Vulaines. 'Two days later there was a terrific hullabaloo. The German patrols were searching houses in Vulaines and stopping all cars on the road and we were told that the empty containers had been found, but this proved to be quite wrong. Apparently there had been a parachutist scare which had nothing to do with our operation.'

Nonetheless, as a safety precaution, he now moved the stores to Troyes, to a garage Martinot had found at an empty house, 16 rue Nungeser in the suburb of Ste-Savine. This was to serve as both arms depot and manufacturing workshop. 'As I did not want my friends' cars or motor lorries to be stopped with the stuff in them I bundled it in a trailer on a bicycle, making several trips with André going ahead to signal if any Feld-gendarmes were stopping people, and we got everything safely there. I then started manufacturing the railway charges.'

To move about, Honoré used a bicycle that had been obtained on the black market through friends in Paris for 4,000 francs. His cover was originally intended to be a form of work connected with the cloth trade, but when the necessary certificate could not be obtained Cowburn suggested changing his *métier* to the petrol business. Honoré developed this story with an old gardener who worked at the house where he lived. The gardener asked him to procure 10 litres. Honoré promptly stole it from the Germans. Unlike some agents, Honoré had no complaints over the clothes SOE had provided. Indeed Honoré said he looked 'more French than the French themselves, many of whom affected an English style of dress, tweed jacket and flannel trousers, which they had managed to obtain on the Black Market'.

As always, small details could give an agent away. Never hang up an overcoat in a cloakroom by the loop, Honoré said. And always have a ready excuse. When the shoe cleaner commented on his good English shoes (even though they had presumably been made to a Continental pattern in the SOE workshop), he immediately said he had had them since before the war.

Cowburn had been given two classes of target. 'A' targets were part of a larger plan and were to be reconnoitred and agents kept in a constant state of readiness until orders were given to attack. Other targets were for immediate action. Oil was a high priority, and Cowburn was told to survey the area for oil dumps and regular road routes used for oil transport. When oil was transported by rail, fire was the preferred method of destruction with derailment a second best. He was also told to encourage 'workers in your area to resist, by all means short of bloodshed, being sent to work in Germany. For those whom you may be able to use yourself you should offer financial assistance on a discreet scale, to their families. Those who go to Germany should be instructed to encourage a slowing down of production'.

One key target Cowburn had been assigned was the transformer station at Creney on the outskirts of Troyes, which carried the current to Paris. Cowburn reported that this was extremely heavily guarded, largely a result of indiscretions on the part of the local Gaullists, who had been heard boasting that they would blow it up. As a result it had been given a heavy all-German guard. This consisted of three ack-ack batteries, a searchlight post, a sentry at the main gate and a sentry on the roof of the control building who could and frequently did switch on the floodlights. In addition there were dog patrols inside and outside the railings (which were electrified), two sentries within the blast walls of the main transformers, and electric alarm bells on the only two doors in the blast wall. These were 6 metres high and impossible to climb. Within the station was a twenty-two-man guard post, with a whole company stationed near by. While this tied down an impressive number of German soldiers it made attack almost impossible, even though Cowburn had obtained a key to one of the doors in the blast walls.

A night attack, climbing over the railings, unlocking the door and placing the charges, could not be carried out without the alarm being sounded. A brazen daylight attempt would be foiled as the guards demanded to see the papers of anyone entering, and anyway knew the workers well.

André had nonetheless found a man in the ideal position to do it. Part of the man's job was to check the transformers fifteen minutes before his shift ended at 5.15 a.m. Their plan was that he should lay the charges just before he left. The man would then catch a 6.30 a.m. train which would whisk him to Paris by 9 a.m., two hours before the charges were set to explode. But though they offered money and even a passage to England, the man was too scared to do it. So Cowburn prepared and stored all the charges in wooden boxes, with 3-pound plastic charges, primers, Cordtex and time pencils, in readiness for an unexpected opportunity.

To his irritation, Cowburn had to radio for a second drop to obtain the explosives he now needed as there were vital omissions on the first. He had asked for twenty-eight pistols yet received none. On the second delivery he received six. These were Lugers. He had wanted .32 Colts. The German pistols, he said, were far too big for close-range work. He required a small weapon that could be drawn out of the pocket at a checkpoint. Incidentally, he had no experience of silencers and was concerned at the extra bulk.

At Troyes there were two roundhouses – engine sheds of the traditional type with a central turntable allowing a number of engines to be stabled inside. One contained a few locomotives awaiting repairs. The other held 'all the big main line engines which come in and go out. In the middle of the night there are also three or four of the big locos on the transfer lines near the round houses. The locos in these positions are either of the mountain type 482 or the pacific type 462 and are amongst the biggest locomotives in Europe'.

When Cowburn had first arrived in Troyes, André had introduced him to a Dr Mahée, 'a most excellent man'. Unfortunately Dr Mahée had agreed to serve under the local Gaullist organiser Wauthers, who was described by André as *'le roi des crétins'*. His indiscretions were legendary, said André. When Wauthers later went into hiding, he found he had left behind a table napkin autographed with the names of 800 persons sympathising with the Resistance which he had kept as a souvenir. He went back to his flat and retrieved it under the noses of the Gestapo. 'He was a brave man, but incredibly stupid,' said André.

Cowburn noted testily: 'I understand that this Gaullist organisation had had a number of receptions, getting 15 containers a time and I believe the vast majority of all this stuff has been captured by the Germans ... I believe a number of these receptions failed and the last one near Géraudot was a really disgraceful show. They went, I understand, with the delivery van of the Fromagerie Graf ... It was a really cheerful party which was interrupted at the right moment by the Germans, who had surrounded the place.'

At Dr Mahée's house Cowburn met Lieutenant Barbarousse, who had worked with F Section's Peter Churchill. Barbarousse, he said, was 'a fine man but too military ... thinks an operation should be laid on by a colonel followed by a couple of captains, sundry lieutenants, sergeant-majors, etc, whereas my idea of a gang is a couple of fellows assisted by the servant girl if necessary'.

Barbarousse offered Cowburn a ready-made gang. Cowburn went to see them but they cried off, saying the operation was impossible. He later learned that Wauthers, who was by then on the run and in hiding in Paris, had forbidden the operation. 'Not only had he been incapable of doing anything himself, but he was trying to stop me working,' reported Cowburn with chagrin, continuing: 'the very next night I made my own reconnaissance and found that what they had said was a pack of lies and that the operation, though difficult, was possible'.

He consulted Mahée, who said he had a better man called Senée. Cowburn went to see Senée and found him 'very valuable indeed'. Through Dr Mahée, Cowburn had also been introduced to a M. Thierry, who took him on a visit to the railway depot and introduced him to the chef. Their cover story was that Cowburn was the manager of a football team and had come to visit the football ground near the depot with a view to arranging a game. After that a quick tour of the roundhouses aroused no suspicion.

Cowburn describes them as being about 100 yards in diameter. 'As we wandered about in the great caverns he pointed out the most valuable types of engines and then led me out by the route he commended for entry by night. This was through a lean-to which contained an old locomotive boiler being used as a steam generator. It had two doors, one to the round house, another to the yard.' He added: 'I was able to examine the locomotives closely in broad daylight and found that the outside high pressure cylinders are insulated all round. The only possible way of ensuring permanent destruction was to go underneath and place charges on the inside low pressure cylinders.' The armed sentries, Cowburn learnt, would be both in the yards and inside the roundhouses. 'It appeared that by getting in via the steam boiler it should be possible to creep along the wall and get under the locomotives without being seen from the turntable.'

Reflecting afterwards, Cowburn decided that his demolition team should spend no more than one hour inside the roundhouse so there would be time to get home before daybreak.

Cowburn then made an audacious night reccy, putting on a typical French suit of blue overalls and rubber-soled gym shoes. His route led down lanes and back alleys to a little road that crossed the railway outside the town. Here he was confronted with a strong lamp brightly illuminating the level crossing. He waited in the dark until he saw two other figures in overalls walking towards the crossing, and fell in behind them. Back in the dark on the far side of the line, he found the wicket gate into the railway yard and walked up a cinder track to the boiler house. Feeling his way past the hissing cylinder, he slipped into the roundhouse.

He had entered the depot unobserved, and climbed down into the pit under one of the engines. Crawling forward, he found he could look out under the wheels. The central turntable was illuminated and a number of men, including guards, were chatting.

Turning back was a different story. 'I found it very difficult to feel my way about in the absolute blackness. However, by feel I located within the mass of piston rods, guide slides, valve gears, etc the two places where the charges should be placed. I stayed inside about 50 minutes, then got out again and studied the line of retreat to my arms depot at Ste Savine without going through Troyes.'

He had observed that the guard consisted of a patrol as

well as the guards on the turntable. There was also a guard post near the engines which were standing on the transfer lines. With the enemy just yards away, Cowburn's extraordinary cool-headedness is apparent, as well as his ability to move silently in the dark when there was every chance of treading noisily on a piece of metal. He continues: 'Fortunately the engines in the round house stand with their heads to the wall. These French engines are quite colossal . . .'

The next day he went to see Dr Mahée and said the job could be done. The doctor asked whether he could take five men with him instead of just two or three, as it would be good training for them 'to do their first job under "expert leadership"'.

Cowburn now manufactured forty-eight 1-pound plastic charges, each with a primer and a length of Cordtex. The timing was a very delicate problem as all the charges had to be placed within forty-five minutes between 1.30 and 3 a.m. – the only time the engines would be motionless with no drivers coming to get them. Finding that there was some explosive to spare he put 4 pounds on some of the engines 'to make an extra big bang'.

Cowburn explains in *No Cloak, No Dagger*: 'the plastic explosive had to be kneaded into small cubes. In each was buried a conical piece of solid explosive called a primer. Through a hole in the primer was threaded a short length of silver-coloured detonating cord whose ends protruded from the cube so that detonators and time-pencils could be attached. The bomb was then wrapped in black cloth secured by adhesive tape'. Cowburn often thought that, working at the table in his shirtsleeves, with piles of hand grenades and incendiary pots, and rows of Sten guns and pistols along the walls, he must have looked almost the perfect picture of an anarchist preparing to blow up the grand duke of Moldavo-Slavonia in a pre-1914 play. 'I only needed a pair of false whiskers,' he wrote.

Senée's team included a saddler called Chastre, a former schoolmaster and two other local men. Cowburn gave them two lectures on handling the explosives and fixed the operation for the night of 26 June. Then came bad news. The guards had been changed and strengthened. Thierry, however, who had first taken him into the roundhouses, was able to brief them on the latest situation and the attempt was laid on for the next Saturday night, 3 July, Saturday nights being the best time.

Cowburn and Senée set out that night from his arms depot at 11 p.m., each carrying a small rucksack with the charges and a pistol. They had not gone far when they met a German patrol. It was too late to hide – they were just 6 metres away. Cowburn was preparing to fire just as they passed unchallenged. (His rule was 'police within ten yards, shoot; more than ten yards, run for it'. He considered it extremely unlikely that the police could hit a man in the darkness if they opened fire.)

Reaching the rendezvous under a bridge on the canal at midnight, they found the other four, who had come from town. At 1.15 he took them into the depot by way of the secret route he had used before, the men walking in single file up the cinder track.

'I then took each group of two men under the engines and showed them where to apply the stuff. There was a good deal of fumbling – the difficulty of struggling about underneath the mechanism of a big engine in the absolute pitch darkness has to be experienced to be believed. However, I finally assigned a certain group of engines to each one of the three teams and we got to work.'

Cowburn added: 'there were guards on the turntable all night whilst the team worked. Noise did not matter, as there was a natural background of whistles, steam, clanging etc.' Cowburn and Senée tackled three engines themselves before moving outside to attend to others on the sidings and transfer lines. When the time for withdrawal came they still had a few spare charges to set but could not risk staying longer.

After forty minutes they left, each team going home separately. 'We had to cross the tracks to get away and, by a stroke of luck, the floodlights which were located at one of the level crossings must have been out of order as they were off. At La Chapelle-St-Luc, Senée and I very nearly walked slap into a Feld-gendarme. This meant a hurried retreat across the fields.'

They had been going for about half an hour when the first charge exploded. Cowburn continues:

We had set two-hour time pencils and this one prematured. We hurried on our way home and the bangs began to succeed each other at the rate of one every ten minutes or quarter of an hour. There were thirteen explosions. As soon as the first one occurred, all police and German garrisons were called out and invaded the depot. They rushed about, snatching open doors and poking machine guns into them. They did not realise more than one locomotive had been attacked. When the second explosion occurred they hurriedly ran out of the depot and surrounded it from a distance. Then, as the other explosions succeeded, they began to realise it was a wholesale job and they kept quite clear of the round houses.

Cowburn and Senée arrived back at his arms depot to the satisfying noise of continuing explosions. They tried as best they could to clean off the grease and dirt picked up in the engine shed, all the more difficult as they could not use a light. The sparsely furnished house was not blacked out. Nor was there a bed, though they were far too tense to sleep. Instead they waited till daylight, when Senée went home while Cowburn stayed on till André's driver, Balthazar, brought him some food. On his arrival, he told Cowburn the bangs had been heard all over the town.

A little later Cowburn took out his bicycle and rode to Précy-Notre-Dame to have a well-earned lunch at Madame Mielle's. During the meal a man arrived from Troyes with the news that the '*rotondes*' had been attacked and thirteen locomotives were beyond repair. The job, he said, must have been done by a specialist who had put bombs in the cylinders. Nobody had been hurt and the saboteurs had not been caught or even seen.

Returning to Troyes, he heard further reports. The figure of thirteen was correct and they had had a great piece of luck – a goods wagon had derailed in the marshalling yard, drawing guards out of the roundhouse at the critical moment.

Afterwards Cowburn decided that the reason why the first charge had exploded prematurely was that 'some of the engines were hot, and the pencils are greatly affected by the heat.' On the advice of Faitout who was in charge of the locomotive depot, they had been placed on the low pressure cylinder under the engine between the piston rods – though each engine was different. Cowburn added that they were much more complicated than the engines on which he had been taught sabotage in England. The charges had been tied on with tape. The cylinders were split, and the double charges blew right up through the boilers.

Cowburn also learnt that in the early hours of the morning Oberst von Litroff, the German military commander at Troyes, had arrived to rebuke his men for their nervousness. He climbed on one of the engines on the transfer lines – neither he nor anyone else was aware these had been primed too. No sooner was he on the footplate than the engine next to him blew up. This brought a prompt end to his heroics as he sprang off and scurried back to his waiting car.

The depot was now sealed off until the Germans were sure the explosions had ended. Then came the interrogations and arrests. They began with the people in the roundhouse at the time, but these were soon released. Finding a charge that had failed to explode, they concluded it was the work of specialists and that a British agent must have directed the job. 'The population were quite delighted with all this business, as nobody had been put in gaol for it,' said Cowburn. The people at the Chapelle-St-Luc had been ordered to evacuate because of fear that the RAF would bomb the engine depot. Now they concluded that the British had decided on sabotage to avoid injury. 'Everybody was happy,' said Cowburn.

A new wave of arrests began. Thierry, careful though he was, appears to have been denounced. One day as he was leaving home, he saw twenty Feld-gendarmes walking towards him from the top of the street. He managed to slip away but saw them surround his house. His wife later appealed to Cowburn, who gave her 10,000 francs.

Dr Mahée had long lived in fear of arrest. One day, Cowburn said, 'As I was leaving Mahée's house, I noticed the streets around were full of SS motor lorries and cyclists, driving around with 'Fahrschule' notices on them. I thought this rather a poor disguise and sure enough the very next day Mahée was arrested together with about 200 people up and down the department, including about two dozen at Troyes.'

After his arrest, Dr Mahée's behaviour was magnificent, said Cowburn.

Through Procureur [their police contact] it has been possible to have communication with him . . . He is . . . apparently hauled out for 'interrogation' every Monday, but he has not talked and I think we may count that the Germans will get nothing out of him at all. In fact, at one time there was a scheme for getting him out, but he refused to come out of jail, saying that his escape would probably cause martial law to be imposed in Troyes, which might cause trouble to myself and to my people. How is that for a good soldier and a great gentleman?

Mahée, thought Cowburn, could either have been denounced by his recently divorced wife or by the wretched Wauthers, who Mahée had recently visited. Wauthers was then living in a Paris hotel with 'a mass of the organisation's archives which he kept in a brief case. He was frequently drunk'.

Cowburn had taken the precaution of always visiting Dr Mahée, who was a practising oculist, in consulting hours so he was taken for a patient. 'I am rather amazed that I have never been followed, but this can certainly not have been the case, as I was always most careful to watch for it and nothing ever happened to me.'

The constant risks they all ran were starkly apparent when André himself came under suspicion. One of his cars had simply stopped at a house to pick up a suitcase containing clandestine material and passers-by had promptly reported this to the police, suspicious that black marketeers were at work. Although the car had been to the house only once, it was reported that it 'was always outside the house'. The house was accordingly watched at night and André's father-in-law, the owner of the car, was called before the prefect of police. Making the most of his leading position in the town, he succeeded in brushing the matter aside. Cowburn, meanwhile, removed all the material in the house unobserved to the shop of a nearby joiner. Martinot then promptly relet the house and no more was heard.

Cowburn had a room with a M. Arnauld at 7 rue de la Montée des Changes. Honoré lived separately at 2 Avenue Marcel Dupont, but his address was kept an absolute secret – even Nenette did not know it. Nenette, however, had found a 'nice, safe restaurant where they could get meals without tickets', ironically named the Paul l'Allemand, opposite the town theatre. Eating out was essential as generally there was no fuel for cooking at home.

By contrast Cowburn's strict discipline forbade visits to cafés. Morale was boosted two or three times a week by a visit 'for a real meal' at a black market restaurant, though they took care not to be seen as people with money to burn. One of these was the *salon particulier* at the Buffet de la Gare, where they 'were accepted as a piece of occasional furniture without arousing any suspicion whatever'. Another was a 'real black market place', La Cloche on the canal, where they would go no more than once a fortnight, saying they were engineers who had come to Troyes on business.

Cowburn noted: 'We are never seen in town in company with André, as he is a well-known person and if we got pinched he could be picked up as having been seen with us. If Honoré and myself, or Honoré alone, happened to be at André's home when other visitors came, Honoré was packed away into the top bedroom so that no-one should see him.' Honoré had to keep his windows closed even on the hottest days when listening to the BBC. Much of his time was spent indoors, with two or three visits to 'the wretched cinema' in Troyes and the cycle ride 34 kilometres each way to Mme Mielle's.

In August Honoré had learnt through Interpreter, the Russian who worked for the Gestapo, that the Germans knew that both he and another operator were transmitting. The other operator had been arrested – caught,

Honoré heard, while on air. After this Honoré stopped transmitting from Troyes as operators 'were posted all over the town to listen for him' and direction-finding (DF) vans were on his trail too. For a month he used his country sets, cycling by side roads to Dierry as the main roads were constantly patrolled. Once he passed a stationary DF car in which he saw four men all with earphones. Three were in army uniform and one in plain clothes. Nenette had also seen a car with uniformed operatives. Only when he heard that they had left town did he resume transmissions. He did so partly as he felt that in the country, where houses were isolated, there was a greater danger of being traced. Earlier in June Cowburn had obtained a further wireless set from Dr Mahée following a drop to the Gaullists. The price agreed for the set was ten hand grenades, and Honoré later regretted that he had not taken over the other two sets that had been dropped as both of these were later discovered.

'I cannot recall a single act of carelessness on Honoré's part, but he is naturally feeling the strain,' wrote Cowburn. Later he explained to SOE that the Germans could start the DF from Germany, moving closer as they located signals. There were four fixed DF stations in Troyes, at the cardinal points of the town, and three mobile ones mounted on cars disguised as tradesmen's vans.

Further threats of arrests loomed as the Resistance stepped forward to rescue increasing numbers of airmen shot down as they flew across France on bombing missions to Germany. On one night Cowburn reported that 100 Fortresses had flown over Troyes on their return from bombing Stuttgart. Over the town they had been intercepted by thirty German fighters. Local people looked on as seven Fortresses were shot down. About thirty of the airmen who baled out were caught and a number killed, but eighteen others were rescued by local people. Cowburn's colleagues ended up sheltering a dozen, and André coolly drove them round in his car. Cowburn's object was to send them on their way as quickly as possible, and Nenette found a contact in the secret police willing to help them get to Switzerland. But soon after this the contact was himself arrested. By the time Cowburn left, the remaining Americans had been moved on, some to stay at a seminary under the auspices of a local priest. Cowburn himself went to the rescue of a flight sergeant from a Halifax which had been downed on a dropping operation. He sent him to Biarritz in charge of a very good contact called Baudet, but Baudet was arrested as a result, though the airman escaped. Finally arrangements were made for the airman to return on the same Lysander flight as Cowburn. Even then there was nearly a problem due to the blanket of secrecy over Lysander operations. The Lysander pilot agreed to take the flight sergeant back only because he had flown out on an agent-dropping operation and was therefore somewhat 'in the know' already. (RAF bombing crews would not have known of Lysander operations, and would not have been allowed to use the Lysander route.)

With every day that passed Cowburn himself was in greater danger of arrest – as he knew from his contacts in the police. 'I was unfortunate enough in being known to some of the local Gaullistes. A number have been arrested, and have talked,' he told SOE. One of them had offered to contact Cowburn 'and give me up in return for his liberty'. The Germans, continued Cowburn, 'know not only my field name and description, but have also exhibited my photograph to Mme Hulet [whose husband was a friend of André's], when she was questioned'. Cowburn's photograph had also been shown to an assistant of Chastre, one of the men who took part in the attack on the roundhouse. Has your employer met this man? he was asked. 'There can now be no doubt whatever that I could not have survived long in Troyes, and that I was lucky to last so long there, or in France for that matter.' Meanwhile Cowburn had heard that Nenette was in danger as the Gestapo had been seeking information about her private life after Dr Mahée's arrest.

Cowburn's troubles now increased. His main mission complete, he had gone to Paris, hoping to get a Lysander home. Here he visited Octave Simon, who had initially recruited André. Simon, however, 'was completely blown and on the run'. Returning two days later, Cowburn found Simon's wife, 'who said that not only was she blown but the day before the Gestapo had called at the place where she was hiding and she had had to slip out by the side door while they entered at the main door. I gave her 50,000 francs. She told me Simon had unexpectedly flown back to England the day before'.

Cowburn now spent a week in Paris at a flat in Neuilly, taking Honoré with him. Then, on Friday, 17 September, he learnt that he could leave that very evening. Hastening to a landing ground near Angers, he took one of two Lysanders which landed that evening, reaching Tangmere early the next morning.

On his return to England, Cowburn provided further details. The Gestapo had taken photographs of the damage to the locomotives. These had been seen by Interpreter, the Russian Araknovski who described to Cowburn the damage he had seen. There had been no reprisals, probably thanks to the one charge that had not exploded and had been diagnosed as British. In his debriefing Cowburn continued: 'If it were somehow possible to indicate to the Germans that *all* sabotage was being done by British agents, the local people would feel safer, although as it is, they do not complain.' The townspeople, he added, believed that British paratroopers had been dropped in the town especially to blow up the locos, and several people were found the next morning who had actually witnessed the paratroops landing.

Less than a month later the fearless André was also brought back to England for training prior to setting up his own circuit. He received a glowing report from Brickendonbury, where he had been sent for further sabotage training. 'A first class man – keen, interested and enthusiastic, he worked well throughout the course and learnt a great deal. Fit for leadership and organisation. The best student on the course.'

In England André reported on another enterprising piece of sabotage carried out by the Tinker circuit. The director of a textile factory making shirts and singlets for German submarine crews had put an itching powder in the underwear intended for the crews and had also made false returns of his stock, supplying one singlet in three to a French customer.

After D-Day André's men carried out highly effective sabotage on railways and telephones. By the end of June he had 500 men. Tragically André was caught when he went to assist an SAS party that had landed in a heavily patrolled area. They had left by the time he arrived, but the SS were there in force and André was arrested, and taken first to Fresnes and then to Buchenwald, where he was executed on 14 September 1944. Buckmaster recommended him for the Military Cross.

For Cowburn himself Buckmaster reserved his highest accolade. Proposing a bar to Cowburn's MC, he wrote in November 1945: 'The GOM of the Section. Tough and reliable – inclined to be biting and prickly, at first, he mellowed with added responsibility and set an example to the younger men of which we are very proud. His sense of discipline and loyalty is exemplary. A grand officer, whose fame in France is legendary, and whose sense of clandestinity is 100%.'

Chapter 5

GUS MARCH-PHILLIPS AND THE KIDNAP OF THE DUCHESS

SOE's Operation Postmaster is straight out of the pages of a novel. It takes place in a sleepy Spanish colonial port that is pure Graham Greene and which is awoken one night by a piratical raid as dashing as the climax of Daphne du Maurier's *Frenchman's Creek*. Its success boosted SOE's reputation at a critical time and demonstrated its capacity to plan daring, difficult, commando-style secret operations and deal robustly with the political consequences.

The operation originated with one of SOE's many great characters, the Buchanesque Gustavus or Gus March-Phillips, who, like many of SOE's best agents and officers, had joined the organisation because he could not stand conventional military life and was determined to find his own way of making a personal contribution to the war effort. 'He had a complete contempt for small regulations that sometimes make life in the army tiresome . . .' said the SOE agent Peter Kemp.

His comrade Geoffrey Appleyard wrote: 'He's the first Army officer I've met so far who kneels down by the side of his bed for ten minutes before he goes to sleep,' adding that March-Phillips had a violent temper, turning white with rage when people disagreed with him, or stammering very badly.

Another contemporary, Gordon Winter, listed some of his qualities: 'impatience with anybody who was slow or dithery, the importance of getting on with something quickly, importance of doing whatever you did well, and a kind of built-in dislike of any sort of slackness . . . And a great scorn of anyone who was carrying an ounce too much weight'.

To many, including my mother, who knew him before the war, March-Phillips was an archetypal English hero, good looking, an all-rounder, keen on sport, a countryman, but literary minded and above all incredibly brave. Years later, in a radio interview, his wife recalled: 'he looked frightfully conventionally good-looking, if you got him at the right three-quarters, and very beaky if you got him at the wrong one, and this marvellous scarred, beautiful mouth'.

March-Phillips had the guts and the derring-do to carry off great coups, as well as an engaging ability to admit his own fears to others. But while courage was his greatest attribute it was also to be his undoing, for at times it veered into foolhardiness. On occasion, impetuosity clouded his judgements and prevented him from weighing risks as a commander should.

His success was due above all to his ability to motivate his men, and to forge a team in which rank played little part. All worked together with total commitment, pitching their physical strength, stamina, quick wits and resourcefulness into a series of pioneer commando raids intended to show in the desperate days after Dunkirk that Britain was still on the attack. The approach appealed to Churchill, who said memorably: 'there comes out of the sea from time to time a hand of steel, which turfs the German sentries from their posts with growing efficiency . . .'

In operations that depended on careful preparation and rehearsal, intense fitness, superb morale and swift execution, March-Phillips was a brilliant leader, able to delegate tasks to others and giving all the sense of playing a vital role. Some found him exasperating, and could never have served with him, but those who did gave him their complete loyalty and trust.

Geoffrey Appleyard recalled lying by the beach at Dunkirk and 'thinking this is it'. He then heard a voice: 'I say, I f-feel a b-bloody coward – h-how about you.' It was March-Phillips. Appleyard also said, 'He's a keen naturalist, a great lover of the open air, of country places, and above all of this England of ours and all its unique beauty and life.'

During commando training in Scotland, when it was pouring with rain, March-Phillips set his men the task of writing an essay on 'How to win the War'. One of them, Jan Naysmith, penned a piece about keeping troops in enemy territory by making them wholly independent in terms of food and shelter. 'That's exactly what I was trying to think of,' March-Phillips told him. Soon the paper was on its way to Gubbins, who was in charge of SOE's training and operation.

In the early days of SOE, boats were seen as the principal clandestine means of ferrying men to France and a base was needed near the coast. Appleyard described how 'Gus and I drove down to Dorset to spend a day house hunting. We located a magnificent house about seven miles from Wareham and ten from Poole. It's a large and very beautiful Elizabethan manor, and in every way ideal for our purpose, very much in the country, in an excellent training area with beautiful gardens. The head gardener is staying on, and we shall, when not training, give a hand in the grounds and gardens. Initially there'll be about thirty of us living there, nearly all officers.'

This was Anderson Manor, just off the road from

Dorchester to Wimborne Minster, approached along an arrow-straight avenue of limes. A bridge across the narrow River Winterbourne leads to a gem of Elizabethan architecture, all picturesque gables and bay windows but symmetrical in every detail.

March-Phillips wrote to his wife: 'I wish you were here. It's really a marvellous place, and the weather is perfect. Every morning I ride out through woods full of primroses and bluebells and violets with the dew still on them, and the sun shining through the early morning mist. I think when the war is over we must settle down here, perhaps in this house if we're very great people then. It's one of the most perfect gardens I've ever seen.'

Peter Kemp told how he heard first hand of March-Phillip's new venture, the SSRF, the Small Scale Raiding Force. 'He told us his plan which was to mount a series of small raids across the Channel, to attack German strong points, signal stations on the Brittany coast and the Channel Islands, with the idea of . . . scaring [the Germans] and secondly causing them to divert more and more troops to garrison duties to prevent these raids, and in this way hoped eventually . . . to mount raids all the length of occupied Europe from Biarritz up to Norway.'

In Poole harbour they found the *Maid Honour*, a 65-ton Brixham trawler. 'Gus decided she would be excellent for training and a voyage to west Africa.' They kept it in a remote inlet, sailing her day and night in all weathers.

In 1941 March-Phillips set sail for Africa with a crew of five. Geoffrey Appleyard, his second in command, had sailed in advance while Prout took the rest of the party on another ship. All were to rendezvous at a camp near Freetown. The mission followed reports that German submarines were using the river deltas in Vichy West Africa for refuelling. *Maid Honour* was to reconnoitre remote estuaries and lagoons. Though no secret German bases were located they used the time for hard training. From the camp on the beach near Freetown Appleyard wrote: 'we have been getting a tremendous amount of exercise while on shore and I am now really fit and getting a lot of the fat off which I had accumulated in the first month out here. I get a half mile swim and a half mile run every day before breakfast . . . we wear nothing all day but bathing trunks and sand shoes'. In the tropical heat they all drank a gallon to a gallon and a half a day, after which there was just half a cup of fresh water with which to brush their teeth, shave and wash.

Though spartan, March-Phillips always took trouble to ensure that his men were well fed. For this purpose, he had recruited Ernest Evison, who came from a long line of cooks, including both his father and grandfather. 'As it is his profession he takes a real pride and interest in his job. He is only a young chap of 23,' wrote Appleyard. Trained in France and Switzerland, Evison spoke good French and German.

Meanwhile careful preparations for a major coup were being laid by SOE's Africa mission. They had targeted two vessels in the port of Santa Isabel on the Spanish island of Fernando Po. This mountainous, well-wooded island, 70 kilometres long and 25 broad, lies in the delightfully named Bight of Bonny or Benin, at the very point where the long West African coast suddenly turns south. Here Nigeria bordered with Guinea, today the Cameroons. Guinea was then a British protectorate, but Fernando Po, though just 30 kilometres offshore, was part of Spanish Guinea, more than 160 kilometres to the south.

The story of Operation Postmaster is told in fascinating detail in SOE files, notably in the end-of-operation reports by March-Phillips and several of his comrades. All SOE personnel had code names. WO1 was March-Phillips. W4 was Captain Laversuch, SOE's man in Lagos, who found the target and laid the plans and preparations. His key contact on the island was an anti-Fascist Spaniard referred to in the files as AZ.

The first of the two ships targeted, lying in the harbour of Santa Isabel, was the *Duchessa d' Aosta*, often referred to as an Italian liner but in fact a large merchantman built in Trieste in 1921 and owned by the Lloyd Triestino line. The second was a powerful German diesel tug, the *Likomba*, in which German personnel on a plantation in the British Cameroons has escaped just before the outbreak of war. With this had come a smaller diesel-driven barge, *Bibundi*. The *Duchessa*'s radio, left unsealed by the Spanish authorities, was considered a threat to Allied interests with the potential to provide damaging military and naval intelligence from West Africa. The *Likomba* had attracted interest in June 1941 when she took on 2,000 litres of fuel and all the Germans on the island gathered in Santa Isabel with the apparent intention of embarking – later a number were to depart instead by plane.

The ships had been kept under observation by Leonard Guise (W10), during his frequent visits to the island as diplomatic courier, and in August a plan was put forward for seizing the *Likomba* and immobilising the *Duchessa* by destroying her propellers. On 25 September 1941 Guise reported on the *Duchessa*: 'She is lying with her stern within 50 yards of the western end of the quay. She is very slightly down by the stern where she appears to be drawing 17 feet.' Her cargo included over 3 million pounds of wool, 316,610 pounds of hides and skins, 1.3 million pounds of tanning materials, 400,000 pounds of copra, 544,660 pounds of crude asbestos fibre and over 1.1 million ingot bars of electrolytic copper. The cargo loaded at Zanzibar, Beira, Lourenço Marques and ports in South Africa was estimated to have a value of £250,000. The greater part was destined for Genoa and a quarter for Marseilles.

Strangely the first page of the manifest was missing and, when the local shipping company requested this, the captain refused to hand it over, prompting suspicions that munitions or armaments were aboard.

SOE now had help from the local English chaplain, the Reverend Markham, who slipped on board during a party, mistaken for a Spaniard. He was able to spend nearly an hour wandering about and talking with the officers and crew before he was found out and had to leave in some hurry. He told Guise he had seen no preparations for departure and learnt that there were now eight officers and thirty-five crew on board. Regular watches were kept, but there was a general impression of indiscipline. No one he spoke to had shown the slightest inclination to leave the island and become involved in the war. Astutely he observed that some of the ship's brass fittings had been removed and sold by the crew.

He also struck up conversation with the ship's carpenter, who made model ships and promised Markham delivery of a particularly fine specimen in six months' time. Guise noted:

'Ship has been in for 14 months, and monotony and isolation have not improved morale. The Captain has returned to Europe and the ship is under the command of the Chief Officer. He appears an efficient man with control of his crew, but both junior officers and crew are apt to be a nuisance when on shore. Local Spaniards complain of their behaviour. Apart from two incidents when bottles were thrown at the British Consulate, the crew does not seem intensely anti British. Rumour has it that many are opposed to Fascist Regime . . . At least 4 have been sent to Spain sick and a large number suffer from venereal disease.

The only onshore guard was an occasional patrol. A more serious problem was the twenty-four-hour guard on the barracks overlooking the harbour from the east, which was equipped with 4-inch guns. Consideration was given to sinking the ship, but the harbour was so shallow that this was unlikely to destroy the cargo, even though considerable damage to the hull could be effected by a small explosion.

Crucial to the whole operation was the attitude taken by the British naval and military authorities. Caesar, the head of SOE's African mission, whose real name was Julius Hanau, telegraphed on 1 October 1941 saying gloomily that in London the Admiralty were indifferent to the *Duchessa*, feeling that the ship 'is unlikely to be of much practical value as a result of long disuse'. As for the *Likomba*, SOE had not even approached the Foreign Office, feeling that any proposal would have met with certain refusal.

Caesar continued: 'I hope you are not regretting having directed us to go ahead with the "Maid Honour". We feel ourselves that even if the ship does not prove entirely suited for operational purposes . . . you will find her crew of value to you for training agents and [for] land operations. She was, of course, approved by the Admiralty who had full knowledge of her destination and the type of work she was to undertake.'

In November Louis Franck, the head of Neucol, the Neutral Colonies Organisation, succeeded, while in London, in winning Foreign Office approval for a cutting-out operation (clandestine seizure) of both vessels in Fernando Po. Approval came from the Admiralty on 20 November and a signal was sent to Admiral Willis, C-in-C South Atlantic, requesting him to offer all possible assistance.

Laversuch was now charged to submit plans to local naval

and military commanders, the governor of Nigeria and the vice-consul in Fernando Po. Caesar wrote:

the principal factor . . . was the avoidance of any concrete trace of British complicity. Speed and surprise were therefore the chief considerations. It was proposed that the raiding party should enter the harbour on a moonless night in a powerful tug and, [a] launch . . . The whole operation from the boarding of the ships to the moment of departure was timed for 15 minutes. The ships were to make as if for Cotonou until intercepted at an agreed rendezvous by one of H.M. ships. To diminish the opposition it was hoped to arrange for the majority of the Italian crew to be entertained ashore.

The strength of the raiding party was fixed at thirty-two, to consist of eleven from the *Maid Honour* and four local SOE staff, with the remaining seventeen recruited from local military personnel. A major blow came when General Giffard, GOC-in-C West Africa, declined to authorise the loan of military personnel on the grounds that the operation was bound to be ascribed to the British and might jeopardise certain unnamed plans that he had in mind. Worse news followed on Christmas Day with a signal from Admiral Willis stating that he had decided to suspend the operation in view of General Giffard's objections. Four days later the Admiralty, supported by the Foreign Office, replied, saying suspicion of British complicity was inevitable: what counted was the avoidance of any tangible proof.

As tensions mounted Laversuch and March-Phillips left Lagos by air for Freetown on 3 January 1942 at the invitation of Admiral Willis for a meeting with him and General Giffard. After three days of suspense the desired telegram arrived; authority for Postmaster had at last been obtained. Willis had detailed the corvette *Violet* to intercept the captured vessels while ostensibly en route for Douala.

One obstacle remained. General Giffard still felt unable to comply with the request for personnel. At this moment the spirited governor of Nigeria, Sir Bernard Bourdillon, intervened, personally authorising Laversuch to seek volunteers from the colonial administration.

The Liverpool shipping firm of John Holt had an office in Santa Isabel and one of SOE's staff, Richard Lippett, was put on the company's books and made the crucial preparations on the island. Lippett had not been able to cross back from Douala to Santa Isabel until 18 December 1941. To get the ferry to sail that day he had to pay for twelve native passengers.

On my arrival I met my man AZ and made an appointment with him for early next morning. I told him that I had been approached by a shipping company in Lagos regarding the entertainment of officers and men of the D de A at Christmas as there was international sympathy between shipping companies at that time, and the owners did not want their men to feel neglected. I of course could not take an active part as we were at war with Italy, and if it came to the ears of the British Consul he would report me to the British Government and it would be very bad for me. He readily agreed and he suggested he would get the Governors Pilot to assist him also Dr Sola. He went to Luhr who was the Agent for the ship, and at 9pm he told me all would be ashore except eight or nine men on watch.

It then transpired that Luhr had himself invited the ships' officers to his house for dinner on Christmas Eve. Another dinner took place on 27 December. Attended by thirty people, it was held at the casino, lasting until 4 a.m. Lippett continued:

The next day the 28th many of the crew were ashore in the evening at the bar Rosario and were very drunk, in fact keeping up the party spirit . . . On the 6th January the Officers of the ship gave a return party on board, the people who attended the Casino party being invited, this party lasted till 2a.m. and it was noticed that some of the wines etc., sent on board for the crew on the 27th were used. Much useful information was picked up such as the actual numbers of the officers and crew, the general watch kept, etc., which left me in no doubt that if on the night 12 officers who could give an order, were off the ship little opposition would be encountered . . . Once the date became known, it was left for us to fix the time, and together with W51 [the British consul] it was decided that 11.30 would be suitable. Mrs Luhr's services were enlisted, and she chose the restaurant Valencia as being the less conspicuous, but two days before the date, the owner called the dinner off, as his wife was ill, the dinner was then arranged for the Casino . . . Some days prior to the Day AZ asked me quite frankly if there was any danger in the matter, as if there was he was prepared to leave SI [Santa Isabel] by canoe and take his chance in Nigeria. I gave this good thought, and also consulted W51 and it was decided that, knowing the Falangists as I do it would not be too healthy for either him or myself if he remained, and without giving him reason, advised him to leave, he then arranged for his canoe. AZ then confided in me that the reason why he was assisting was that he was certain that the British would win the war, and the Spanish Government would have to change, and when that time arrived, he would then go back to Spain, in a better position than he previously held, furthermore he could help his country more than he was now doing by being assistant manager in a hardware store. Although I was never in any doubt as to his sincerity I checked and re-checked him and he came through every test with flying colours.

Meanwhile the call for volunteers from the colonial civil service had produced an immediate and impressive response. At midday on 10 January, reported Guise, 'as choice a collection of thugs as Nigeria can ever have seen

was assembled . . . None of these volunteers had any accurate idea of what they were to do, and guesses varied from
blowing up objects in Dahomey to the kidnapping of the
Vichy Governor. Some of them, in fact, convinced that they
were going to trek for hundreds of miles, had been practising walking in thick boots for the previous twenty four
hours'. When the party assembled at 32 Cameron Road in
Lagos they were told nothing in detail but were briefly
addressed by March-Phillips and Laversuch and given an
opportunity to step down, which no one took.

At 10 p.m., when the stores had been loaded, the party
was taken in groups to the marine tug *Vulcan*, which lay at
Apapa wharf with the launch *Nuneaton* beside. 'By now the
forty thieves were slightly convivial, but by midnight the
decks of the *Vulcan* vibrated with snores, and 560 lbs of the
Administrative department were fast asleep on Nuneaton
sun deck.'

The two tugs had been provided by the Governor of
Nigeria and were crewed by some fourteen African stokers
and trimmers. *Vulcan* was an excellent, reliable vessel, but
Nuneaton was a constant source of trouble, repeatedly
jeopardising the expedition. In recognition of this,
Nuneaton was towed alongside *Vulcan* when they left
Lagos harbour at 5.30 a.m. on Sunday morning, 11 January
1942. As they crossed the bar she was slipped on to a long
tow, 'dancing along behind like a naughty pup on the end of
a lead', said Guise. Though the swell subdued, the small tug
made a bad tow and on the Monday morning after a particularly violent sheer she was slipped and told to proceed
under her own steam.

Intense training now began on both vessels. The Folbot
canoes, to be used for boarding the *Likomba*, were rigged
up and painted grey. The hawser party, charged with cutting
the steel cables or hawsers of the *Duchessa*, was instructed

by the tugmaster, Mr Holden, who also made a plan of the Italian ship based on aerial photographs. Charges were assembled and equipment decided on for each member of the assault parties. The crew of *Maid Honour* kept the deck watches and 'magnificent food' for the entire ship's company of forty men was provided by the splendid Evison, ensuring a happy ship, said Guise.

He provides a vivid sketch of *Vulcan*. 'Decks were clean, bedding and baggage stowed away and everything ship shape. Immaculate officers from *Maid Honour* strolled the bridge, our three tame Spaniards were peeling onions . . . an opulent DO was washing dishes, and a prominent Treasury official with the air of a retired Field Marshal was shovelling coal.'

After twelve hours of steaming *Nuneaton*'s engine began to cause trouble and she had to halt to repair it. The small-end bearing had been running hot. Within two hours this was repaired and an attempt was made to take her on a short tow, but this proved unsuccessful and she was again told to proceed under her own steam. Remarkably, in view of later events, she gave no further trouble on the outward voyage.

After dark the raiding party on *Nuneaton* under the command of Graham Hayes carried out an exercise, lowering the Folbots and boarding *Vulcan*. This proved a considerable success. The Folbots were able to approach within a few yards without being seen. Action stations in full equipment were practised on *Vulcan*, and manoeuvres were carried out to simulate the approaches to the targets the next night.

With the compass out by 10 degrees but corrected by azimuth, navigation and timing were crucial as the ships were slowly brought into position for the attack the next night. As dawn broke on 14 January they found themselves farther east than expected with a view of Tom Thumb Peak in the Cameroons and the 2,850-metre Santa Isabel Peak. They now had to reverse their course, but fortunately visibility was bad and there was no fear of being seen from the shore.

'We had to dawdle on Wednesday morning ... Explosives were made ready on both ships, and a cold lunch was served on *Vulcan* because the galley stove was occupied by an earnest figure boiling and moulding plastic' (a reference to the plastic explosive frequently used by SOE). Torches, pistols and tommy guns were issued, and that afternoon, when the island was sighted, everything was ready. Strangely the commanders were not aware, as Laversuch was, of the crucial hour's difference in time between Lagos and Fernando Po – a reflection of the difference between English and Continental time in the mother countries. It took him the best part of an hour to convince them on this vital detail.

Towards evening the weather cleared, and as they approached Santa Isabel an east-by-south course was set so that they appeared to be steering for the mouth of the River Cameroon on the mainland. At dusk a new course was laid for the light of Cap Formoso, held until the lights of Santa Isabel came into view. At 11.15 *Nuneaton* moved ahead and began very slowly to creep towards the harbour. Suddenly March-Phillips's familiar voice sounded through the darkness: 'Will you get a b-b-b-bloody move on or g-g-g-get out. I'm coming in.' This risked entering the harbour while the lights were still on. Guise later recalled: 'Gus himself struck me as completely intrepid, almost to the point of overdoing it, because this was not really a military operation. It was a burglar's operation and burglars don't go in shooting.'

Nuneaton's skipper responded decisively by swinging

across *Vulcan*'s bows and stopping dead. After further furious comments *Vulcan* sheered off into the darkness to wait.

At 11.30 both ships were in position about 180 metres outside the harbour lights, with *Nuneaton* leading. As expected the lights of Santa Isabel went out, leaving only the flashing buoys, a light on the pier and a light on the fore part of the *Duchessa*. Guise continues: 'Very dramatically the blackout arrived, and what had been a well-illuminated display became utter darkness. There was no moon, but the DA could just be seen, and the *Likomba*'s position was known.' *Nuneaton*, with Captain Hayes's boarding party, passed between the flashing buoys and stopped 90 metres inside to lower her Folbots. Ten minutes later *Vulcan* drew alongside *Nuneaton*, and together the two tugs made very slowly and quietly for their objectives. Onshore, to avoid a precipitate departure of the *Duchessa*'s crews back to the ships, AZ had arranged for Tilley lamps to be available, ensuring that the dinner would still be in full swing as the raid began.

At this point command and navigation of *Vulcan* were taken over by Mr Coker, the tugmaster. The boarding party were armed with coshes – 12-inch bolts covered with rubber – and had the strictest orders to avoid the use of firearms. They assembled on the mess decks and lower deck behind the iron bulwarks, awaiting the order of action stations, when they were to file up on to the bridge deck and to stand on boarding planks, which had been built out over *Vulcan*'s sides. Though the light on the *Duchessa* now picked out the tug, there was no movement on the big ship and Coker manoeuvred the tug in a wide sweep to lay his port side alongside the *Duchessa*'s starboard side. As the tug approached a few lights shone from the portholes and figures could be seen on the after deck, but they appeared to take no notice. As they came closer a torch was shone towards them but no challenge was made, though one of Vulcan's Spaniards stood ready with a reply to gain the vital extra seconds of time. The action stations order was now issued to give the boarding party time to ascend to the main deck. Two Bren guns on the roof of the tug's bridge covered the operation in case of a major mishap.

Meanwhile *Nuneaton*'s canoes had glided silently across the harbour. Hayes and Winter in the first canoe noticed a window above the darkened town in which the light was repeatedly dipping and flashing, which they read as a signal of 'OK OK'. As they drew close to the *Likomba* the watchman challenged them and flashed a light as the first canoe came alongside the *Burundi* – the barge attached along the starboard side of the *Likomba*. They made non-committal noises in reply and the watchman came forward with the painter (rope) under the impression that it was the captain coming back on board.

A letter was proffered, with an intimation that it was for the captain. The watchman replied that both officers were ashore. The men from the other canoe had now also boarded, armed with revolvers and tommy guns. The watchman and a colleague who had appeared immediately took fright, sprinting forward and jumping overboard to swim the short distance to the shore. Coolly Hayes decided to let them go.

Now that they were convinced no one was aboard, orders were given to lay explosive charges on the anchor cables and the hawsers, while one man went below to search and another stood guard against any approach from the shore. The *Nuneaton* drew alongside the port side of the *Likomba*, a difficult operation as the German tug was moored only 60 yards from the shore. As the two tugs came together Guise came aboard the *Likomba* to reinforce the others. The tow rope was made fast on the 'bitts' (fastening posts) ready for the tow.

As there had been such trouble with the *Nuneaton* on the outward voyage, it had been decided to blow the cables on the *Likomba* as soon as the charges were set, rather than waiting for those on the *Duchessa* to be primed. This, of course, risked alerting those onshore to the operation before the main prize had been secured. As soon as the cables blew the *Nuneaton* started to gently tow both *Likomba* and the lighter out of the harbour.

Meanwhile, across the harbour, as the *Vulcan* touched the *Duchessa* March-Phillips and the first five men jumped aboard. *Vulcan* had hit the *Duchessa* hard, and recoiled. Again she touched, and another six men boarded. Another recoil, and this time she was too far forward to attempt to come close again. The remnant of the striking force, including the doctor and his medicine chest, were obliged to board very precariously over 8 feet of bamboo ladder.

The boarding party encountered, said March-Phillips, 'no resistance worthy of the name', though one of them was sent sprawling in the darkness by a pig kept on deck at the back of the ship. Both fore and aft the explosive parties reached their positions unchecked. The charges were laid. Other groups rushed through the cabins and engine rooms collecting prisoners. March-Phillips had gone straight to the bridge, and when he was told the ship was in his hands blew one long blast on his whistle.

The crucial task was to take the tug's hawser or towing cable on to the *Duchessa*, and bend it round the bilts to secure it, a very difficult job even with ten men on the messenger (cable). It was done by the formidably strong Dane Anders Lassen, later to win a VC leading an SAS raid in northern Italy which cost him his life.

On *Vulcan*, the chief engineer was understandably

concerned about the reaction of the African stokers to the large bangs – trapped as they were below decks. SOE's Prout was stationed below to offer them reassurance, as maintaining steam was crucial to the whole operation.

Guise describes the blast on the *Duchessa*'s cables as 'a titanic roar and a flash that lit the whole island [as] the *Duchess* lost the principal lace to her stay'. But one of the forward charges had failed to ignite. Appleyard's clear voice was heard: 'I am laying another charge.' Realising that the whole success of the operation depended on him, he had dashed forward and laid a new charge with a very short fuse on the huge anchor chain. Now his voice rang out again: 'I am going to blow.' Unable to get back to proper shelter, he crouched behind a nearby winch. A blinding flash and a huge explosion followed immediately. The *Vulcan* promptly took up the tow, and the *Duchessa*'s bow immediately started to swing to starboard. *Vulcan*'s performance, said March-Phillips, was miraculous. 'She gave the *Duchessa* two slews, one to starboard, one to port, like drawing a cork out of a bottle, and then without the slightest hesitation, and at a speed of at least three knots, went straight between the three buoys to the open sea, passing *Nuneaton* and *Likomba* a few cables length from the entrance. This operation, the most difficult in my view, was performed with amazing power and precision. Mr Coker, the Tugmaster, and Mr Holden and Mr Duffy, the chief and second engineers, are worthy of the highest praise. The black firemen behaved magnificently.'

After the second explosions, bugles were sounding on the shore, the town lights had come on again and people had gathered at the pier head. But the clamour ceased very suddenly with the noise of the final fierce blast. Shouts of '*Alerta*' were heard and March-Phillips guessed that those on shore believed an air raid had begun.

The dinner for the crew of the *Duchessa* had proceeded without a fault. AZ had provided Lippett with the precise details. It was held on the top terrace of the casino, which overlooked the bay, but the officers were placed with their backs to the ships. Twelve attended from the *Duchessa* and two from *Likomba*, with twenty-five sitting down – the governor's pilot being in Moka with his plane. Just before the town lights went out Lippett learned that AZ 'had excused himself on the plea of going for a Petro Max [a lantern] and he did not return'.

Lippett himself had taken every possible measure to avoid being directly implicated in the attack. At 7 p.m. he had gone with Ruiz the bank manager to play a Spanish game Piloto, and at 9 p.m. they went to settle their accounts. The manageress told them there was a dinner party for thirty Germans and Italians. When the bank manager asked who was giving it she said she did not know, but thought that it was a party of friends just like the other one, as the dinner had been paid for in advance and a lot of drinks ordered and also paid for. This, said Lippett, was his last check on AZ. 'He had carried out my orders to the letter.' They then continued to his hotel for dinner.

Afterwards, following a precedent he had established about two weeks before, he took a walk with Ruiz after dinner, saying he could not sleep on a full stomach. When they parted he walked to the Colonial Guard, finding 'there were no preparations of any kind, in fact several of the sentries were sleeping'. As he walked down to the front overlooking the bay no one stirred. When he returned to the hotel, there was no one about and he went up unobserved to bed. The night, he said, was dark with periodic flashes of lightning lighting up the sky.

The next morning at 5.30 another Spanish friend Mrs Montilla woke him to play badminton, a routine he had established some weeks before. They went to the court behind the consulate but found the place surrounded by soldiers who would not allow them to play. The soldiers told them that two ships had been taken the night before from the harbour, by a fleet of battleships. Mrs Montilla then turned to Lippett and said, 'Well done, the English are very smart.' He replied, 'No, the English would never do a thing like that, especially in a Spanish port,' to which she responded, 'Just wait and see.'

Rumours now increased with the news that AZ was not to be found. Muross, the manager of the store, where AZ worked was arrested. Collinson, the consul, then heard further highly satisfactory rumours – for example, that AZ was seen slipping the mooring ropes of the *Duchessa* (actually steel cables, of course) and then going off with the ship. He also said that AZ had supplied the members of the party with so much drink that when the incident happened no one could do anything, and when they left the casino they could not walk.

W53 provided further details. He had been sitting in the consulate which faced the bay with W51, waiting for the bangs. In the still immediately after the first explosions they heard a very Oxford voice saying, 'I . . . am . . . laying . . . another . . . charge.' Fortunately they were the only ones.

Innocently, they went outside.

Down in the square, trying to look dazed, we asked passers-by what was happening. Nobody had the remotest idea. But most of the men were rushing up to the Guardia Colonial to arm themselves with rifles . . . Spaniards and Africans alike were highly amused by the incident, to judge by the laughter and excited chattering that came up from the Plaza below. Our last visitor that night was Herr Specht [the captain of the *Likomba*] . . . [he]

was very drunk and quarrelsome. He was told to get out. In reply
he struck me in the face, which gave W51 and myself the excuse
that we wanted. Between us we knocked the stuffing out of him
. . . My steward boy then handed the dilapidated Specht over to
the police.

The captain of the Colonial Guard was seen rushing all
over the place, saying, '*Qué pasa?*' (what has happened?).
When the alarm was sounded some of the soldiers turned
out undressed, some with arms, some without – a sorry
mess and clearly quite unprepared. Lippett wrote: 'The
Governor it is said did not give the order to fire because he
was afraid it would draw the fire of the BATTLESHIPS – at
least five were reported to have been seen. But the real facts
were he had nothing to fire except an old gun at the HQ of
the Colonial Guard, which is used for saluting purposes,
which was used some days after the incident, and from the
sound of the explosions it appeared to me to be a two
pounder, and a very old one at that.'

W53 continued: 'The following day was full of rumours
. . . Free French, Vichy, USA, British and even anti-Falange
Spanish pirates were all equally possible culprits . . . admiration and amusement for the way in which the job was performed and timed was shown openly by many Spaniards
but when some . . . were detained and others questioned by
the Military Tribunal . . . the smiles fell from Spanish faces.
People invited to drinks at the Consulate did not turn up;
and nor were we invited to go out . . .'

W51 learnt at an interview with the governor that he
seemed satisfied concerning Lippett's innocence but
nonetheless he was not allowed to leave. W53 continued:
'Every scrap of incriminating evidence that could be
destroyed was destroyed before the 14th. Telegrams and Re-
cipher pages have been burnt immediately they are received

or dispatched. In making this report . . . I have no notes to refer to.'

Out at sea March-Phillips had made sufficient progress by the evening of Thursday, 15 January to set about establishing a routine of both ships' and prisoners' watches. The twenty-nine prisoners, including three engineer officers and one stewardess, were put under strong guard in the dining room. The stewardess was allowed to remain in her cabin – she had fainted at the sight of the boarding party. Watches were organised on the masthead, forecastle and poop and the Bren guns taken to the boat deck in case of any pursuit by small boats, but none came.

The two tugs had hardly left the harbour when trouble began. The *Likomba* and the *Burundi*, lashed together behind the *Nuneaton*, were starting to break each other up. *Nuneaton* stopped and *Burundi* was detached and made fast at the end of a 45-metre hawser. But within half an hour the rope had started to fray. The intrepid Anders Lassen rushed to the rescue. 'With a heaving line tied round his waist he swarmed across the fraying tow rope. The strain of the tow threw him alternately into the sea and high into the air. He gained *Burundi*, and in the light of the torches from *Likomba* hauled aboard unaided the new rope and made it fast.' On *Maid Honour* some of the astounded onlookers thought it was the bravest thing they had ever seen. After five minutes' rest he started the return journey, heaved exhausted back aboard the *Likomba* by his colleagues.

At dawn the *Nuneaton* was making only 1 knot and alarmingly still in view of the island, just 8 kilometres from Punta Formosa lighthouse. During the morning *Nuneaton*'s engines started to give trouble and she stopped for repairs. March-Phillips decided the *Vulcan* should steam on with the *Duchessa* to the rendezvous. By 2 p.m. *Vulcan* was within 3 kilometres of the rendezvous so he decided to leave Appleyard in command of the *Duchessa* and went back on *Vulcan* in search of *Nuneaton*, as there was no sign of the naval corvette coming to meet them. When *Vulcan* reached *Nuneaton* Hayes requested a tow but there was a strong wind blowing and March-Phillips was concerned that he might lose the *Duchessa* in the dark if she made a lot of leeway. So he departed at full speed back to the *Duchessa*. According to Guise 'the island was looming larger every moment', and Hayes understandably felt that having taken two hours to come back to them March-Phillips could at least have spared another hour to pull them clear of danger. But March-Phillips calculated that the tides would take *Nuneaton* clear of Fernando Po even if the engines could not be started.

Nuneaton's engines finally started again at 7 p.m. but they failed again twice during the night while, said Guise, 'the lighthouse still looked infernally near. On Friday morning No 1 cylinder head had to come off, another two hours gap. No shipping appeared, but the view of the peak and the north west coast of Fernando Po was magnificent, if ill timed'. The island remained in view all day, and though they started to tow again the strain on the hawsers was such that they had to be changed twice. Fresh water was in short supply and unpleasant too as the tank had recently been lined with cement which had not fully set. There was, however, at least a large supply of tinned beef aboard.

During the Friday night watch a large blacked-out ship passed dangerously close but did not see *Nuneaton*. On Saturday the engines recovered and the island was at last out of sight, raising spirits hugely. The next night a large, brightly lit liner passed on the port bow, thought to be the Spanish MV *Domine* bound for Fernando Po from Las

Palmas. On Sunday the two men on the *Likomba* were relieved, with a tense moment as the Folbots manoeuvred between the two vessels. The next day the Nigerian government collier *Ilorin* passed, not stopping, but agreeing by semaphore to telegraph Lagos on arrival at Port Harcourt. Only on the Tuesday afternoon were they finally sighted by the British corvette *Ajassa* and taken in tow to Lagos.

Meanwhile the Duchessa had been 'captured' at sea by HMS *Violet* and was escorted, towed by *Vulcan*, making a triumphant entry into the harbour at Lagos. The governor, it was reported, was standing at the end of his landing stage with whisky and soda in his hand, cheering loudly as she came in. She berthed beside *Nuneaton*, which thanks to her fast naval tow had just arrived.

In Santa Isabel the arrests had begun on the 15th and 16th. As soon as Alcorn, the pilot, touched down on his return from Moka, soldiers rushed on to the airfield and did not give him time to alight. All those at the dinner, or who were friends of AZ, were arrested. All, however, were released, except Dr Sola and Alcorn, who were held for court martial.

Lippett was now in an awkward position.

I was treated as usual in a very kind manner by everyone but after the 16th they all cooled off except Montilla and his wife . . . Ruiz the Bank Manager asked me to call on him on the 17th. He asked me point blank if I had anything to do with the ship business. I assured him on my honour that I had not, and he held out his hand and said Ricardo I believe you. You must understand that I cannot openly be the same to you as I have been because we have a Falangist Government and you do not understand what that means to us, but you are and will be always my friend, I have been asked by everyone to say this to you, but I cannot disobey the Government orders.

Bigger tests were to come. On the 17th Lippett had returned to the hotel after work and had just finished his bath when at 5.30 the secretary of the police arrived and told him his presence was requested at the Falangist HQ. 'I dressed and went with him. I was shown upstairs to a small room ... Captain Binea the head of the Colonial Guard said sit down. Miguel Llompart chief of police said "How do you do, Mr Lippett?" and shook hands, this put me at my ease a bit, although I was outwardly calm.'

Lippett was then put on oath, and was warned that if he told any lies he would be sent to a fortress in Spain for a major period. 'I replied that it had always been my desire to visit Spain but not to be shut up in a fortress, and as I did not like lies I would not now, being 45 years old, start telling them. This brought a smile to Captain Binea's face ... A soft light was duly adjusted on my face, which I did not notice, but whenever I moved it was re-adjusted. With his arm stretched out and the Hitler finger pointed at me not so far from my face he asked "How much money have you spent on the Officers and Men of the *Duchessa d'Aosta*."'

Lippett replied, 'No money whatsoever.'

'What are you doing on this island?' asked Binea.

'I thought everyone knew that, but I am here on behalf of John Holt's,' Lippett responded.

'Why have you stayed here six months?' barked Binea.

'Because the work justified my remaining.'

'Why did you go to Lagos on 27th November?' continued Binea.

'Because I was called for a conference.'

'For no other purpose?'

'No.'

Binea returned to the attack. 'Do you mean to tell me that you did not spend any money on the entertainment of the Italians?'

'No, we are at war with them and I never did like them, and if I had any money to spend I would spend it on Spaniards, whom I like very much.'

After further questioning came a break and glasses of water were brought in. 'I smelt mine just to annoy Binea,' wrote Lippett.

Just before they resumed he asked how long it would take as he had been invited to the consulate for dinner. Binea replied: 'as you are suspected you may be kept here till we are satisfied, which might take days'. At that moment a Falangist came in to say that the consul's boy (servant) was outside and could he come in. Binea said yes. The boy came in with small chop and whisky and soda, which Lippett sent back, asking for sodas instead.

As the days passed SOE became concerned about Lippett. 'We have been informed that there is no proof of his complicity. Nevertheless he has been refused an exit permit by the local authorities. Certain local Spaniards are it appears being court martialled in connection with the affair.' About 27 January the British vice-consul on Fernando Po lodged a protest against Mr Lippett's detention with the governor. This proved fruitless, the governor refusing to release him without formal authorisation from Madrid.

Laversuch cabled from Lagos on 9 February: 'He is still held by Spanish authorities. Telegrams are being deliberately held up. His early departure would appear to be imperative ... he has been ill and under doctor for eight days. Our impressions are [that] he is losing nerve and it would be better from every point of view if his departure could be hastened.'

On 1 March 1942 the Foreign Office wired Madrid with better news: 'Tired of waiting for exit permit Mr Lippet [sic] has left Fernando Po surreptitiously by canoe and arrived safely in British territory. You need make no further representations.'

Hugh Dalton, the minister responsible for SOE, wrote an ecstatic report on Postmaster to Churchill, quoting a telegram received on the ships' arrival in Lagos: 'Casualties our party absolutely nil. Casualties enemy nil, except a few sore heads. Prisoners, Germans, nil; Italians, men, 27, women 1, natives 1.'

Dalton continued:

there is reason to suppose that the Spanish authorities are aware that a large tug of unknown nationality entered the harbour and took the vessels out; but that is probably all they know. We do not believe they will be able to *prove* that the tug was British, and the greatest precautions have been taken to see that no information leaks out at Lagos. Thus, all the SOE personnel engaged have now been dispersed and are safely out of reach of interrogation; while the crew of the vessel have been sent to an internment camp 150 miles inland. Although as you know the incident has given rise to a rather violent press campaign in Spain, it is not yet certain that the Spanish Government will protest officially . . . Further I have a shrewd suspicion that, though they may protest, neutral Governments are not unimpressed by such suspected manifestations of force, which they tend to interpret as meaning that His Majesty's Government feels strong enough to disregard legal formalities in the prosecution of total war.

This last sentiment was over-optimistic: there was fury in Spain at what was seen as a gross invasion of neutrality. Serrano Suner, the pro-German foreign minister, took the lead with an article published widely in Spanish newspapers. He described the operation as an 'intolerable attack on our sovereignty . . . No Spaniard can fail to be roused by this act of piracy committed in defiance of every right and within waters under our jurisdiction . . .' Do not be surprised, he added, 'if we return the answer which the case demands – that of arms'.

In Germany the *Volkischer Beobachter* ran an article on 21 January, 1942 under the headline '*British Denials- Admiralty Lies on Act of Piracy.*' German radio said that a destroyer had come into the harbour and dropped depth charges which blew up anchor cables while the crew on board were shot.

Taking advice from Commander Ian Fleming of Naval Intelligence (the famous creator of James Bond) a communiqué was issued at midnight on 19 January:

In view of the German allegations that allied naval forces have executed a cutting-out operation against axis ships in the Spanish port of Santa Isabel, Fernando Po, the British Admiralty considers it necessary to state that no British or Allied ship was in the vicinity ... As a result ... of the German broadcast, the British Commander-in-Chief dispatched reconnaissance patrols to cover the area. A report has now been received that a large unidentified vessel has been sighted, and British naval vessels are proceeding to the spot to make investigations.

Fleming himself, not surprisingly, had initially proposed a further spin to the story – that the crews of the two Axis vessels had mutinied and were attempting to reach the Vichy French port Cotonou. His draft reads: 'One of the crew stated that the ships had been lying in Spanish territorial waters since 1939 and explained that owing to dissatisfaction with their living conditions and lack of pay, they had decided to take advantage of absence of their senior officer to raise steam and slip out to sea under cover of darkness. This story throws an interesting side light on low state of Axis morale abroad and also emphasises once more unceasing vigilance of Royal Navy.'

On 22 January General Giffard wrote: 'for reasons which

148

I was unable to explain you I felt I had to oppose your project. It does not lessen my admiration for the skill, daring and success with which you have succeeded'.

The stewardess of *Duchessa* provided a testimonial: 'I confirm, with the following members of the crew of the *piroscafo Duchessa d'Aosta*, that we have recently disembarked in an English colonial port. We are in good health and no one is in need of medical treatment. We are all pleased with the treatment we have received, and no one has suffered any unnecessary *ordeal.*'

March-Phillips wrote to the director of Marine Lagos on 23 January stating his appreciation of the crew of the tug who 'worked almost without sleep for a whole week, under difficult and dangerous conditions with the utmost cheerfulness and disregard of themselves'. The tugmaster, Mr Coker, was 'a brilliant seaman ... and at times an inspired one'.

Caesar, head of SOE's African Mission, wrote pointedly on 26 January 1942: 'We hope that SOE will be permitted to demonstrate that what was possible in Fernando Po is possible elsewhere: perhaps on the next occasion, it will not be found necessary to preface twenty-five minutes' compact and decisive action by over four months prolonged and desultory negotiation.'

A jubilant message was sent to Gubbins: 'The name of the show [SOE] is good in Lagos (again, of course, largely due to Postmaster), and for this W4 is principally responsible. Everybody in Lagos realises that Postmaster's success was principally due to W4 and two principal qualities, thoroughness and pertinacity. He runs his office well. They all work hard, the morale is good and there is absolutely no nonsense.'

The brilliant planning and preparation were evident above all in the timing. The time taken from entering the harbour to leaving it with both tows was just thirty minutes

– and to blowing the cables precisely the twenty-five minutes planned. Apart from bruises and a few small scalp wounds there had been no casualties. Three watchmen, two from the *Likomba* and one from the *Duchessa*, had escaped by swimming ashore. Though they were the only eye-witnesses to the dramatic events and were presumably known to the ship's officers or agents, they appear never to have been questioned – perhaps, very sensibly, they simply laid low.

Chapter 6

GRAHAM HAYES – COMMANDO RAIDS, ESCAPE AND BETRAYAL

'the hand of steel that plucks the German sentries from their posts'

Churchill

Many SOE operations took place at night – but while agents and arms were dropped when there was enough moonlight to spot lights set out by reception committees, marine operations took place at the opposite end of the cycle, on moonless nights when vessels nearing the shore and human figures creeping up the beaches were least likely to be seen.

The most tantalising part of Operation Aquatint – especially for families of those involved – was the years it took to piece together the story of what happened. The saga of Graham Hayes, who survived the night, also sheds fearsome light on another constant danger facing SOE operations, that of penetration by ruthlessly effective German counter-intelligence.

The mission was straightforward. March-Phillips, fresh from his success with Operation Postmaster, had set his Small Scale Raiding Force (SSRF) at full throttle on a series of operations aimed at probing German coastal defences. These were the subject of a report from Lord Mountbatten, Chief of Combined Operations. The first,

Operation Barricade, on the night of 14/15 August 1942, saw a party of eleven land 5 kilometres north of St-Vaast, attack a German patrol, killing three and wounding six, and withdraw without loss. The second, on the night of 2/3 September, was a spectacular success, with a force of twelve men landing on the Casquets lighthouse off the coast of Alderney, the most northerly of the Channel Islands, occupied by the Germans in 1940. Here March-Phillips and his men spirited off the entire German garrison – surprised in their sleep wearing hairnets, much to the amusement of their captors. The SSRF took their radios, dumped arms and ammunition into the sea, and left no trace of whence the attack came. The third, on the night of 7/8 September, was a reconnaissance raid on the tiny island of Burhou off Alderney. Again there were no casualties. The Aquatint landing on 12/13 September was different. Not one of the eleven-strong landing party returned that night.

March-Phillips took with him the cream of his SSRF, including three captains, Graham Hayes, John Burton and Lord Howard, a lieutenant, Tony Hall, and a Frenchman, Maître Desgranges. With them came a company sergeant-major, Tom Winter, a sergeant, Alan Williams, and three privates representing the diversity of the Allies now fighting the Nazis – Jan Hellings, a Dutchman, Abraham Opoczynski, a Pole known as Adam Orr and Richard Lehniger, known as Leonard, a Jewish Sudetan German. Geoffrey Appleyard, who had been March-Phillips's second-in-command on Operation Postmaster, remained on the motor torpedo-boat (MTB) as navigator because he had injured his leg during the raid on the Casquets.

The MTB left from Portsmouth, passing the Needles at 2012 hours, and set a course to avoid the enemy minefields that stretched across the Bay of the Seine to Barfleur on the Cherbourg peninsula. The night was unusually dark and there were patches of fog off the coast. Nonetheless the MTB made good progress and rounded Cap Barfleur at 2210 hours. To avoid the minefields the MTB had to pass within 4 miles of the cap, along the shipping route between Cherbourg and Le Havre. As they passed the cap, speed was reduced to 12 knots for about three-quarters of an hour to minimise the risk of being heard onshore. Owing to the fog no land could be seen. A direct course was laid for Ste-Honorine, following the main shipping route. Although the fog had lifted, land could not be made out until they came within half a mile of the shore – even though the cliffs here are up to 30 metres high. During the last 10 kilometres soundings were taken with a lead line every 3 kilometres to ascertain depth and thus distance from the shore. The final approach towards the shore was made at 0005 hours using the auxiliary silent engine.

The plan was to land half a mile east of Ste-Honorine and scale the cliffs at a point identified in aerial photographs. March-Phillips's commandos were to attack a small group of houses near the sea from the rear, taking prisoners and returning down the cliff. It was a bold, even rash, plan given the proximity of other houses and the likelihood of the alarm being raised.

The very dark night made it impossible to locate the point at which the cliff could be climbed even from only 350 metres. This was the second night they had attempted this operation. Hall later recalled: 'we couldn't find this ruddy kink in the cliff . . . so we went again the following night, and we still couldn't find it. Then Gus said: What do you think chaps, shall we have a bash?'.

So in total darkness the MTB silently anchored some 250 or 350 metres offshore in 3 fathoms of water at 0017 hours.

Though they were unaware of it, they were a full 4 kilometres west of their intended destination.

Three minutes later the landing party of eleven set off in a collapsible landing craft known as a Goatley. The craft would have taken no more than five minutes to reach the shore. No sound was heard until half an hour later when tommy-gun and pistol fire broke out at the foot of the cliff. Then followed fifteen to twenty flashes and explosions thought to be German stick grenades and a great deal more small-arms fire. The Germans set off Verey lights to illuminate the beach and the sea at intervals along the bay while coastal defence guns were heard booming out to the west. These were followed by long and continued bursts of machine-gun fire on both east and west flanks. On the MTB, Appleyard's assessment was that jumpy gunners were firing at shadows on the water, or trying to frighten off a supposed attack in force.

Appleyard also noted an attempt to get a searchlight working on a cliff to the left. Each time it flashed on and began to sweep out to sea it fizzled out abruptly before the beam reached the MTB. At 1.20 a.m. there was renewed machine-gun fire, apparently from the top of the cliffs down on to the beach. A few minutes later it appeared that the MTB had been spotted – Appleyard came under machine-gun fire as the Verey lights were directed out to sea. Simultaneously he heard a voice onshore calling 'Come back'. Suddenly he caught a glimpse of the landing craft broadside on, almost under the sea wall. There was no one near it. A voice was then heard, thought to be that of March-Phillips, followed immediately by that of Captain Hayes hailing Appleyard by name. The rest of his words could not be distinguished but were thought to be an order to the MTB to withdraw. The beach was now brightly illuminated and enfiladed by machine-gun fire. A gun now opened on the MTB, which appeared to be clearly visible from the shore. Six or eight shells whistled overhead and fell in the sea. The anchor was cut and the main engines started at about 1.30 a.m. Now it was discovered that gunfire had damaged both the transmission gearbox and the ignition of the starboard engine, rendering it virtually useless.

A course was set out to sea for 3 kilometres and the port engine gradually throttled down to give the enemy the impression that the MTB was on her way home and gradually passing out of earshot. No further shooting was heard. Appleyard assumed that the party must have split up and attempted to make their way inland as previously arranged in the case of such an emergency. After about ten minutes no more was seen or heard except the occasional Verey light. The MTB again bravely headed inshore at slow speed on silent engines, showing an infrared contact light on the masthead until within a kilometre of the coast. Here she remained for three-quarters of an hour. During this time there was no further gunfire, though occasional Verey lights went up. Attempts were still being made to get the searchlight going. Nothing was seen of the pre-arranged signals that the landing party were to give if they wished to return or needed assistance. Nor was there now any sign of the landing craft.

At 2.25 a.m. a series a shells suddenly burst over the MTB from the north-west, landing towards the shore and indicating that they were under fire from a patrol boat. Immediately afterwards a shower of more than a dozen shells came from a second craft to the north, one landing within 6 metres and deluging the boat with water. The MTB had been spotted from out to sea against the light of the flares on shore. With the enemy closing in and all hope of picking up the landing party abandoned, Appleyard set a course to the east and after a mile to the north. As the return had to be made at greatly reduced speed, Appleyard decided to set a course directly through the minefield rather than attempt the much longer passage they had used on the way out via Cap Barfleur. The gamble was successful and the MTB was located by Allied air cover at 0645 hours, docking at Portsmouth just under four hours later.

The first news of what might have happened onshore came from the German Official News Agency, which stated that during the night of 12/13 September 'a British landing party, consisting of five officers, a company sergeant-major and a private tried to make a footing on the French Channel coast, east of Cherbourg. Their approach was immediately detected by the defence. Fire was opened on them and the landing craft was sunk by direct hits. Three English officers and a de Gaullist naval officer were taken prisoner. A major, a company sergeant-major and a private were brought to land dead'. What the Germans did not know at this stage was that the landing party had consisted of eleven men and four were still at liberty.

A further account with additional details was issued by the German Supreme Command the next day, stating again that the landing party had been spotted as they ran towards the shore. 'Coastal guards immediately opened fire with anti-tank guns and rifles.' The report added that the boat turned round, leaving behind several members of the crew, with the implication, predictable in propaganda terms but not actually true, that those in the boat had taken fright.

An accurate description of what happened onshore did not materialise until Winter returned at end of the war and filed his report.

As soon as we touched down on the beach we saw that we were too near the houses to be able to leave it with safety. We pulled the boat 200 yards to the East away from the houses and then hauled it up above the High Water Mark to the base of the cliff. There we left Captain Lord Howard in charge of the boat and the rest of the party made their way just East of the houses . . . We went inland and made a good recce . . . After that we made our way back to the beach again to commence operations from there. We had just reached the back of the beach when we heard a patrol coming, which consisted of about seven to eight men. They came along the track at the top of the cliff from the East. We were inland of the track [in] a small depression and well under cover and would not have been discovered had it not been for the dog which was with the patrol . . . We intended to try and get back to the MTB and get away, but the dog scented us.

He continued: 'We tried to fight our way out, but unfortunately the Headquarters of the German Detachment was not very far in one of the houses, and the alarm was raised. We managed to disperse the patrol and succeeded in getting 100 yards out to sea in the Goatley. Verey lights went up and they soon located us and started firing but we were not in a position to return the fire.'

He then said: 'We had all got away except Lieutenant Hall who was left on the beach, presumably dead, with a terrible wound in the back of his head, caused by the base plug of a stick grenade. Captain the Lord Howard was wounded whilst assisting the party to re-embark, but we managed to get him away in the boat.'

Next the Goatley was caught by machine-gun fire and sunk. 'We had to swim for it, trying to make for the MTB but we could not see it. It was, of course, very difficult swimming because the tide was still on the flow and we could not make much headway. The Germans were firing at us all the time and Major March-Phillips shouted "Go back" (not "come back" as stated by Captain Appleyard).'

Winter came ashore on his own and was challenged and fired upon at very short range. Fortunately he was unwounded. 'By that time I was rather exhausted and the Germans had to drag me along to the Headquarters.' Inside he saw Howard lying on the floor and also Desgranges. While waiting for a more senior officer to arrive they were made to put all their possessions on the table. When the officer arrived he told them they would be shot as commandos – this prefigures Hitler's notorious Commando Order of October 1942, denying treatment under the Geneva Convention to commandos and 'sabotage troops' even when they were in uniform. Meanwhile they were to wait for an intelligence officer from Caen to interrogate them.

The next morning, said Winter, only 'Desgranges and I were capable of carrying out the sad task of bringing Gus's body to the top of the beach. It's been said he had drowned but I don't think so. I am certain he died of his wounds'. They also had to retrieve the bodies of Leonard and Williams. 'They filmed the operation and used it in propaganda film *Midnight at Cherbourg* I believe.'

The bodies of the three soldiers, he was told – correctly – by an intelligence officer, had been buried in the cemetery at St-Laurent-sur-Mer. Meanwhile Howard had been taken to hospital, along with Hall, who, despite his grave injuries, was still alive. Winter and Desgranges were driven to Caen, separated and subjected to a very stiff interrogation. The area general came down to question them. Over eight days Winter was dragged out at all hours while repeated attempts were made to extract information from him. But his cover story was the most plausible – that he belonged to the Royal Army Service Corps and knew nothing as he was there only to carry stores for the others. His regimental number confirmed this. The interrogators nonetheless proved more thorough in some ways than the Gestapo. After the first day their clothes were taken away and replaced. They found the maps hidden in the epaulettes but did not divine the use of the two buttons that could be put together to form a compass. Nor did they discover the secret codes they had for the purpose of sending messages to England.

While at Caen, Winter was taken to the hospital to see Howard, who was quite comfortable. Hall, however, was still unconscious. Two days later Winter was sent to Rennes, the Brittany capital, and after three days Burton, Helling and Orr arrived. Winter was put in a cell with Burton while the other two were placed in a cell opposite. All three had managed to escape the deadly fire on the beach. Their story was related by Burton's wife, Anne, who married him in 1946 after his release from POW camp. The 'raid seems to have been an absolute disaster. The Germans had the whole area very well defended . . . John . . . a Pole and a Dutchman were swimming towards the boat when it had to leave because of the heavy gunfire. The three of them swam down the coast for a bit and then went ashore'. They were hopeful of walking to the Spanish border, but found out afterwards that they had been going round in circles. Local French people gave them food and clothing. Then one night they were caught by German parachutists carrying out man-oeuvres. The SS said they would be shot but changed their minds. Burton was sent to a prisoner-of-war camp in Germany. The other two were taken with him on the same train as far as Frankfurt and then handed to the Gestapo for further interrogation.

The French inhabitants of St-Laurent naturally heard the shooting on the beach and saw the prisoners being put into a German car. One of them, probably Desgranges, the Gaullist, was heard to shout, 'Don't worry, we will be back.' Others witnessed the burial of the three commandos on 15 September, hidden behind a wall. This ceremony was attended only by the German major, his secretary and the Chef de Brigade de Gendarmarie from Trevières. To prevent anyone else approaching a machine gun had been set up 50 metres from the cemetery.

The bigger surprise was the sight of a German patrol dog a few days later wearing a medal on his collar. For detecting the Allied commandos, it had been awarded the Iron Cross. This quixotic gesture, showing a decided sense of humour, is recorded in German archives. A German report written on 13 September reads: 'Until 2 a.m. the night was completely peaceful. As the sky was completely overcast, it was so dark that one could scarcely see five paces. The sea was calm, and the tide had just turned and retreated five metres . . .' Two German privates were on patrol when their 'watchdog sprang forward and growled. At this moment Wichert and Kowalski heard suspicious noises and shouted at the same time "Halt! Who goes there?"'. Hand grenades were thrown, an enemy boat was seen by the wire entanglement on the shore. Kowalski was seized and pulled on to the beach. The darkness made it impossible to see how many the enemy were but Kowalski was able to grab a hand grenade, pull the pin, throw it at his opponents, tear himself free and return to his comrades behind the wire entanglement. As firing continued the MTB was spotted out to sea. The rest of the report confirms the heavy exchanges of fire and the taking of British prisoners, with carefully drawn maps showing the Goatley and the position of the bodies of the three slain men found on the beach. Most telling of all is the diagram showing fire from three machine-gun posts above the beach. This demonstrates that almost two full years before the D-Day landings the Germans had concentrated and well-manned defences capable of delivering withering fire on this one 300-metre stretch of beach.

Hayes, who had also tried to swim out to the MTB, had become separated from the others. He sought to distance himself from the shooting by swimming nearly 3 kilometres to the west to an unguarded section of beach close to the village of Asnières-en-Bessin. The coast here in 1942 was full of abandoned houses and Hayes was able to hide. After resting for a while he decided to risk approaching a farmer, who turned out to be a friendly man named Marcel Lemasson who took him to the owner of a local chateau. This was the Château d'Asnières-en-Bessin near Vierville-sur-Mer, where Hayes was very well received. As the owner, M. de Brunville, was mayor, and there were numerous Germans in the neighbourhood, it was considered unsafe for him to remain.

He was given civilian clothes and de Brunville's son bought a rail ticket and put Hayes on the train for Lisieux, a beautiful small town then still filled with splendid medieval timber houses, destroyed alas in an Allied bombing raid in 1944. On the train Hayes was accompanied by M. Septime Humann of the Château de Juaye at Juaye-Mondaye. From Lisieux Graham was taken to the house of Mme Septavaux and her nephew M. des Georges, in the village of Le Pin in Calvados. Here he was cared for over six weeks, having injured his knee, which had previously been operated on for loose cartilage. He was tended by a local doctor, Dr Hautechaud.

A plan was now set in motion to smuggle Hayes back to England via Spain. He was provided with a fake French *carte d'identité* and placed in the care of a man named Ortet, alias Aymand, who took him by train to Paris.

The story of Hayes's arrival in Paris and journey down to Spain shed frightening light on the extent of German penetration of the Resistance and SOE. The Germans went to extraordinary lengths to maintain the deceit. The first sign that Graham was alive after the Aquatint raid came in a letter of 27 October 1942. This was received through the Red Cross on 3 June 1943 by Miss Jean Dreyer, a FANY who was working in SOE's southern African mission. The letter read: 'All is well here. Do not worry. Graham sends his love also.' It was standard practice for SOE agents to be given an address, usually in a neutral country, for messages of this kind, couched in innocent pre-arranged sentences, but this is more direct. Miss Dreyer immediately cabled London with the news that 'Graham was well and sends love'. SOE was also informed.

The letter had been sent intially by Winifred Davidson of 245 Grand Rue in Garches near Paris. A year later, after the liberation of Paris, an SOE staff officer, Captain Planel, was able to visit her. She told him that Hayes, in excellent health, had visited her at her house at the beginning of October 1942; that he was brought to her by a man who was a member of the Resistance and taken away after a short stay by this same man, who later informed her that Hayes had reached England safely. Following a second visit to Mrs Davidson, Planel set out his findings in a memo of 23 October 1944.

These were that Hayes had been brought to Mrs Davidson by Hortet, with whom Hayes was staying near by in Garches at 38 Avenue Foch (there was a sinister link here as 83 Avenue Foch in Paris was the headquarters of the SD (the Sicherheitsdienst, or security service of the SS), where many SOE agents were taken). Hortet had first been to visit her in 1940 to see whether, being English, she could help him contact London as he wanted to work for the intelligence service.

Hayes, she said, was dressed in civilian clothes and had a fresh scar of his face to the left of his chin. He left early in October accompanied by Hortet as far as the Spanish frontier. En route they stopped at Limoges to gather information for Hayes to take with him. On his return Hortet had described the frontier crossing as easy. He said they had taken the train to a small frontier village, gone to the house of a priest and stepped out of the back door on to Spanish territory. This is so very different from the usual arduous crossings of high passes in the Pyrenees that it is suspicious, but two months later Hortet told her that Hayes had arrived safely in England. Yet a letter she had given him, addressed to her father in England, never arrived.

Planel's suspicions had been aroused. He subsequently heard back from SIS of two Hortets or Ortets. The first was a Charles Ortet of 11 Avenue de Celle, Paris, who was in touch with the Overcloud escape organisation and had a good record. The second was a Jean-Louis Ortet, curiously also of the same address, who had an 'unfavourable trace' and 'is supposed to have worked as a "penetrator of allied organisations" and was tied up with the Prosper Circuit in Paris which was completely blown. If this man and the Hortet mentioned in connection with Graham Hayes are one and the same, it would explain the reason for Hayes' disappearance', concluded Planel.

A month later Planel wrote again, having investigated Ortet at the St-Cloud commissariat, talking to an inspector who had dealt with his case as well as a neighbour in Garches. Ortet, he said, had been born in Algeria, fought in the First World War as a captain in the French Foreign Legion, and had been wounded and decorated.

His wounds impaired his mental facilities and he was liable to act in a reprehensive way, as happened in 1938 when he appeared in an Assize Court and was acquitted on these grounds. He used to live an irregular life, living with a certain Madame Hemon, having dealings with shady people who frequented his flat. His employment was supposed only to be a cover for his other activities, as he used to travel considerably. He was employed by a German shoe firm and he used to boast he could get all he wanted from the Germans.

Ortet's body had been found in a pond in the Indre on 1 September 1943. 'He had been assassinated,' wrote Planel.

Mrs Davidson had meanwhile given some further information to Hayes's parents. Hayes had asked whether there was anything he could do for her on his return to Britain, and Mrs Davidson had replied that one thing they badly needed in Garches was a radio transmitter. Hayes said he thought he could obtain one. It arrived in the spring of 1943 and was taken as a sign that Hayes had reached safety. This would indeed have been a clever ploy by the Germans, and was possibly effected using one of the SOE radios they had captured – some of which they continued to operate without SOE suspecting that its agents had been arrested.

Hayes was now incarcerated in the notorious prison at Fresnes where so many SOE agents were sent. By 18 January 1945 Graham's parents had learnt more. Lilian, his mother, wrote to M. Paul de Brunville:

In June '43 a young English Airman came down in France and was captured by the Germans who took him to Fresnes prison. He was put in solitary confinement in a cell under our son who used to shout Good Morning and Good Night and then signal in morse. He told him very little about himself but said he had been in a raid which did not go according to plan, but he escaped and eventually got into Spain. There the Spaniards handed him over to the Germans who brought him back to Spain. They put him into solitary confinement but promised they would eventually send him to a Prisoner of War camp. The Airman on getting back to England wrote to us and said our son seemed to be in high spirits . . . a few weeks later he got no response to the usual greeting and so he concluded that Graham had at last been transferred to a POW camp.

This, alas, was not the case. Graham had been taken out and shot on 13 July 1943. He was buried in the special section of the cemetery at Ivry set aside for prisoners executed by the Germans. In this case they did not have the usual excuse that he was a spy or 'terrorist', as they liked to call SOE agents. He had landed in France in uniform and was simply seeking to escape to Spain like so many other Allied servicemen. To them, however, he was a commando liable for execution under Hitler's Commando Order.

The fate of others involved or caught up in Aquatint was equally grim. While in Paris Graham wrote to Dr Hautechaud to thank him for all his care and attention and gave the letter to another Resistance contact, Raoul Kieffer, to give to the doctor. Raoul photographed the letter and passed it on to the Gestapo. He also obtained a copy of the photograph taken for Graham's false papers and gave this to the Germans. Dr Hautechaud was now arrested and accused of helping a British soldier. This he denied, until he was confronted with a copy of Graham's letter to him. He was promptly deported and died at Buchenwald. His wife was also deported. Nothing is known of her fate but she never returned. If Hayes had attended the training courses given to SOE agents sent to France, he would almost certainly never have written such a letter *en clair* with the attendant risk of it falling into enemy hands. But Dr

Hautechaud was a leading member of the Lisieux Resistance and may already have been under suspicion. When Mme Septavaux and M. Humann were arrested and confronted with Hayes in Fresnes, he denied all knowledge of them. Humann was released and Mme Septavaux spent four months in solitary confinement at Fresnes.

Winter was more fortunate. He had been sent on from Rennes by train with Helling and Orr to Germany. At Frankfurt, he said, they had been taken to Gestapo head-quarters for further questioning. He had proceeded to prisoner-of-war camp Stalag VIII B. There he had worked in the post office. 'I used to go out on cover jobs distributing Red Cross Parcels and managed to do a bit of sabotage work and bribed Czechs to do the same, teaching them how to use the weapons etc. The Germans found out about my part time job and put me in detention but we had to move to a camp near Belsen and my detention was termi-nated when the Allies were nearing the camp. An officer and I got through to the Allied lines to call for help for other prisoners.'

At this distance in time Aquatint has a sense of futility. Every man was captured or killed – all fine men, all highly trained and supremely capable, and all squandered on a mere pinprick against German might. But that is not how it seemed then or seems today in Normandy, where this gal-lant sacrifice is seen as a first raising of the flag on occupied soil. The graves of March-Phillips and his colleagues in the little cemetery at St-Laurent are proudly decorated with Allied flags.

There is another reason why so many details of this story have finally been unearthed and pieced together. On the day following the raid a 22-year-old student was cycling back from the village of St-Côme-du-Mont at the foot of the Cherbourg peninsula, where his aunt lived, to Caen, where

1. Bill Sykes, said by many to look like a bishop, was one of SOE's leading instructors in unarmed combat and silent killing and could draw and fire a pistol in a third of a second.

2. George Bégué was the first radio operator to be dropped in German-occupied France and conceived the system of personal messages broadcast nightly by the BBC to the Resistance.

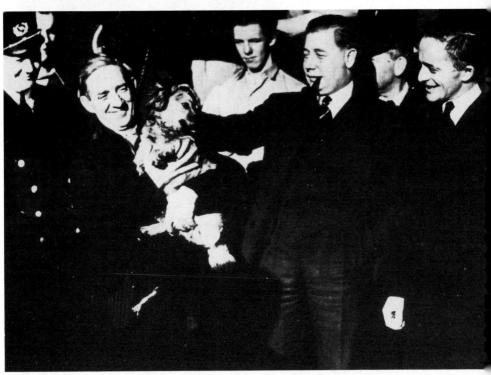

3. In 1941 George Binney's Operation Rubble brought a whole year's supply of ball bearings needed for tank and aircraft production from Sweden through the German blockade of the Skagerrak. German fury was such that when he mounted his second operation, Performance, the Swedish government passed a bill through the Swedish parliament in a secret session arresting all his ships.

BLACK-OUT ZERO HOUR TO-NIGHT UNTIL 6.52 A.M.

MOON 2.49 RISES A.M. | MOON 11.45 SETS A.M.

Daily

No. 13,060

THE OCEAN Jap fleet with aircraft carriers out in Bay of Bengal attacks shipping, sends bombers against two Indian ports.

INDIA Cripps likely to receive new instructions today from the British War Cabinet, aiming at meeting the Indian demands on defence.

AUSTR base at harbour

JAPS RAID IN

'SHAPE COURSE FOR ENGLAND .. AND GOD SPEED OUR SHIPS'

THE inspiring Order of the Day reprinted below was issued by the flagship captain just before the ten British-chartered Norwegian ships made their perilous 700 mile dash for freedom—from the Swedish port of Gothenburg—defying German mines, warplanes and warships to reach Britain. . . Of the ten vessels—ranging from 800 to 12,000 tons unarmed but for a few machine-guns—two were sent to the bottom, some were scuttled and others are now in British ports.

ORDER OF THE DAY.

Today at long last we are going to England determined, come what may, to render a stained account of our voyage, as befits Norwegian seamen. Indeed we run a risk, but what of it? If we succeed, these splendid ships will serve the Allied cause and with their cargoes we shall aid the task of war supplies.

To sink our ships and cargoes rather than to see them captured by the enemy is of course our duty, and on your behalf I have taken such measures as you would wish.

Should we encounter misfortune at sea, remember that in our homes and among our countrymen it will be said with simple truth that we have done our best for the honour and freedom of Norway and Britain; but I, for one, have never held with this blockade and look once more to our success, believing that before many days have passed your laughter will resound within a British port.

So let us Merchant Seamen shape a westerly course in good heart counting it an excellent privilege that we have been chosen by Providence to man these ships in the immortal cause of Freedom. God speed our ships upon this venture.

Long live King George.   Long live King Haakon.

GLIDER SWOOP ON SUEZ?

Express Military Reporter
MORLEY RICHARDS

AIR GENERAL STUDENT, leader of the German paratroops, has joined Field Marshal Karl Kesselring, in joint command of Axis air operations in the Mediterranean.

Some weeks ago it was reported that Student, Luftwaffe organising General, had left his headquarters in Germany, which had directed earlier airborne operations.

Desert landings

THE MEN OF HELL
PASSAGE

They defied bombs, bullets and warships

F.D.R. TO HANDLE VICHY

---

4. Order of the day issued by George Binney to the crews of the ships taking part in Operation Performance.

5. Gus March-Phillips. 'He had a complete contempt for small regulations which make army life tiresome,' said a colleague.

6. The *Duchessa d'Aosta*, the Italian cargo liner, in the port of Santa Isabel on the Spanish island of Fernando Po, which March-Phillips and his comrades seized while the officers were being lavishly entertained on shore.

7. Graham Hayes was the only member of Operation Aquatint to remain free after a night landing on a Normandy beach went disastrously wrong. The Resistance group that organised his escape to Spain was unaware that it had been penetrated by the Germans.

8. The graves of March-Phillipps, Williams and Leniger at the St Laurent cemetery.

9. (*left*) Percy Mayer, the Mauritian agent who cut the vital telephone wires enabling the Allies to make an unopposed landing on Madagascar and take back the harbour at Diego Suarez just as the Vichy government had agreed it could be used by German and Japanese submarines.

10. (*right*) Percy Mayer's wife Berthe, who sent the Allies vital intelligence, often on an almost nightly basis.

11. (*left*) Accident-prone Denis Rake, an actor turned radio operator and a homosexual determined to prove he was as brave as his comrades. 'He is a man who, although not a soldier, has all the qualities one would like to find in a soldier,' said an American lieutenant.

12. (*right*) Guido Zembsch-Schreve was sent to France to organise an escape line from Lille to the Pyrenees. When captured he was sent to Dora, where prisoners were used as slave labour to build V2 rockets deep inside a mountain. He escaped just as the war ended, persuading Russian officers to allow him and his comrades to cross the River Elbe and seek aid from the Americans.

13. (*left*) Harry Ree, a schoolmaster and former conscientious objector who persuaded the Peugeot family to agree to a systematic programme of sabotage in their factory, which was being used to supply transport and tank parts for the Germans – thus avoiding major RAF bombing raids which would have caused heavy loss of life.

14. (*right*) Charles Skepper, after enduring horrendous treatment in a Japanese prison, joined SOE and led a highly effective circuit organising sabotage in Marseilles until betrayed to the Germans. He is one of the few SOE agents whose fate has never been clearly established.

5. Amédée Mainguard, though refused a commission in the army, joined SOE, where he rose to the rank of major and was awarded the DSO at the age of twenty-five.

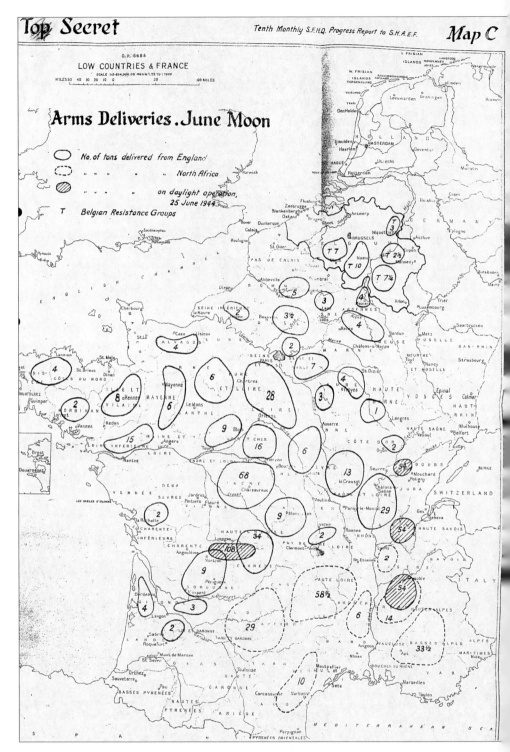

16. Map showing arms deliveries by SOE in June 1944.

his parents were. Near Carentan the marshes can only be crossed by a causeway over three consecutive bridges that have seen battles in every war on this coast. The Germans had established a roadblock and the soldiers were distinctly nervous. They stopped the young man, questioned him and tried to pull out the books in the basket hanging from the handlebars, but they were packed so tight they would not come out.

The young man quickly explained that they were textbooks. He would have been in trouble had they looked further as they were almost all English books, including Kipling's *Kim* and a dictionary. He asked them what the matter was. '*Tommy débarque*' – English landed – was the reply. He laughed, believing it to be a joke, but they impressed on him that it was serious. He found this hard to believe as there had been no rumours and no announcement on the BBC. It was only years later when he heard of Aquatint and checked the date that he realised the coincidence.

A few days later in Caen a friend of his, a medical student, told him to go to the hospital and get in touch with two Englishmen who seemed to be in trouble. He was told how to avoid the sentry by approaching through a back yard. Here he saw the men through the window, one lying in bed; the other waved, indicating that he should leave.

The young man was André Heintz, who has devoted his extraordinary energies to researching Aquatint. 'It was only much later that I realised I must have seen Tony Hall for the first time, the one in bed: and the tall one Lord Howard of Penrith who had waved.' M. Heintz's researches led him to a prime seat at the sixtieth anniversary celebrations of D-Day.

The story concludes with another of life's strange coincidences. Graham Hayes and Geoffrey Appleyard had both been born in the same Yorkshire village. The day Hayes was taken out from his prison cell at Fresnes and shot, Appleyard, now attached to the 2nd SAS Regiment, was on a plane with paratroopers who had been selected to take part in the invasion of Sicily. Having seen them drop in the right place, he was under orders to return with the plane to North Africa. The aircraft never arrived and was assumed shot down over Mediterranean, on the very same afternoon as Hayes died. In the village hall in Linton near Wetherby, Yorkshire, their families placed a stained-glass window to commemorate their two gallant sons. There is a poignant portrait of Hayes in a memoir written by his youngest brother H. Austen Hayes in 1997. The family home in the 1920s was Roundhay near Leeds. Close at hand was a 'large Park with lakes and open country not far away . . . Already, Graham was a naturalist and his "den" was an attic room which he made an Aladdin's cave with his collection of animal skins, bones, feathers and skulls'.

On his 20th birthday, 9 July 1934, Hayes had signed up as an apprentice seaman on a Finnish four-masted barque sailing from Hull to Australia. 'He left as a boy and returned very much the Man. Bronzed, bearded, fit and powerful. With him came a fine set of photographs taken in all weathers from the rigging aloft, at sea and in ports of call,' wrote his brother. On his return Hayes took some woodcarvings he had done at sea to Robert Thompson, a furniture maker in North Yorkshire, and was immediately offered a job. Here he was soon making complete pieces of furniture to order.

After two years he went to London to seek work with Green & Vardy, well-known furniture makers who were so struck with his work that they supplied him with his own bench where he could continue to produce fine carvings. Too often these were snapped up by directors' wives before they reached the showrooms. Even so he made such an impression that Mr Vardy offered to train him as his successor.

But Graham, said his brother, 'wanted freedom not money, adventure not regular hours'. Instead he rented some disused farm buildings in the village of Temple Sowerby near Penrith in Cumbria where he started making furniture early in 1939. The outbreak of war put an end to his dream. No one wanted to buy furniture and a promising career was cut short as tragically as that of the artist Rex Whistler.

In the world of double agents there is a still darker figure than Ortet. This is Raoul Kieffer (sometimes spelt Kiffer, and also called Robert), who provided Hayes with the identity papers he used in France. While doing so he obtained a copy of Hayes's photograph, which he was able to send on to Spain to enable the authorities there to identify him. Kieffer was a very capable double agent who had been turned by the notorious Hugo Bleicher of the Abwehr. (He is not to be confused with SS Sturmbannführer Hans Josef Kieffer, head of the SD in Paris). In his book *Colonel Henri's Story* Bleicher describes Kieffer, or Kiki as he calls him, as 'one of my best agents . . . a good dependable fellow he was too, who was convinced that he served his country best by preventing acts of sabotage against the Wehrmacht on French soil'.

According to André Heintz, Kieffer 'must have cooperated fully with the Germans because many people were arrested in the Lisieux–Deauville area. But Kieffer was so clever and cynical that he kept feeding England with information and even organised airdrops'. To preserve his cover he even let agents organise a number of acts of sabotage with the explosives dropped by the RAF.

Kieffer maintained his cover after D-Day. Even when the Allied forces arrived in his area near Orbec in August and came to arrest him he was able to extricate himself within a few days. He did this by means of a little notebook in which he had noted every act of sabotage. By copying them out Kieffer was able to convince his captors that he was an active member of the Resistance.

When Kieffer came under suspicion again he was exonerated in a report submitted on 28 August 1944 by Captain O. H. Salmon. 'Kieffer personally made a favourable impression. He seems to be intelligent, sincere and competent . . . I therefore recommend the release of Kieffer, so long as no adverse information is forthcoming.'

Three months later a further investigation implicated Kieffer. 'This man was first drawn to our attention by a French woman known to us as Victoire.' This was none other than another notorious double agent, Mathilde Carrée, alias La Chatte. Victoire had been a leading member of the large and successful Valenty organisation, built up by a Pole, Valenty, from November 1940 onward. On 18 November 1941 the Valenty organisation had been broken up. Valenty had been arrested along with Victoire. She immediately began to cooperate with the Germans, enabling them to round up other members of the organisation.

Towards the end of 1942 Victoire had been brought back to Britain and confessed her betrayal, giving, says a note by D. I. Wilson, 'a full account of the break-up of the Valenty organisation which has been found to be accurate on questions of fact, except in so far as Victoire endeavours from time to time to give a twist to the facts in order to minimise her own treachery'.

Chapter 7

PERCY MAYER AND THE LIBERATION OF MADAGASCAR

Madagascar has long been a world apart, an island nearly 1,600 kilometres long with flora and fauna that have remained isolated from those of mainland Africa. Largely unexplored until the 1860s, it became a French colony in 1896. In the Second World War, for all its remoteness, it sat astride major shipping lanes from the Cape to the Red Sea and India, and its position in the Indian Ocean was potentially as important as that of Malta in the Mediterranean. While Malta was a British possession, Madagascar remained a Vichy colony after the fall of France in 1940.

SOE played a crucial and thrilling role in the liberation of the island. It is a story in which one brave and resourceful agent and his equally courageous wife played a decisive role in shaping events and preparing the way for Operation Ironclad, the first major amphibious operation of the war, potentially providing lessons for D-Day landings. The aim was not initially to invade the whole island but to capture the naval base of Diego Suarez (today named Antsiranana), a large natural harbour within 32 kilometres of the northern tip of the island.

The French base there had been constructed and fortified about 1900, and even then was seen as a potential threat to the British in India. The harbour was well defended and could be entered only through a narrow passage a kilometre wide. If success was to be achieved and bloodshed avoided, complete surprise was essential.

SOE's key agent, Percy Mayer, referred to in the files as DZ6 (or WK6), had been born in Mauritius on 25 April 1903, the son of Edwin Mayer and Bertha Brown. Photographs show Mayer with keen, alert eyes and a ready smile, extrovert, buoyant and full of energy. He had been brought up in Mauritius, studying at the Royal College of Curepire, but had subsequently gone to London to study engineering at the City and Guilds College.

About 1934 he moved to Madagascar as representative of the family firm, Edwin Mayer & Co., and took French citizenship. He was both ambitious and enterprising, obtaining a pilot's licence and setting up the Madagascar Air Service, to provide internal flights around the island, much of which was inaccessible by road. Such was his aeronautical prowess that in 1937, during a stay in France, he won the first prize in an air rally open to all French colonies.

During a visit to Mauritius in August 1938, he married his cousin Berthe Mayer, eldest daughter of Dr Clifford Mayer and Jeanne de Chazal. Berthe was then a British citizen. Photographs show her as a considerable beauty with dark hair and deep-set doe eyes. In 1936 she had come to London to study at the Royal School of Music, living with her sister Renée in a flat in Redcliffe Gardens, and like all good Mauritians eating the traditional curry with rice at weekends.

In Madagascar the family firm operated a distillery and rice and flour mills as well as a brickworks. Mayer imported refrigerators, radios, cars and bicycles. He ran the Ford agency and garage and handled all kinds of insurance. Being both bilingual and a French citizen, he was able to continue his business in Madagascar without difficulty after the fall of France.

An SOE report of 29 November 1940 assesses the growing problems in Madagascar. British citizens, who previously travelled to the island from Africa, could no longer get permission to land. Restrictions were in force against British shipping. No ship could call without permission from the German authorities in France. A German–Italian Armistice Commission was expected at any moment. The landing ground was being enlarged, presumably to allow heavily loaded military planes to make use of it.

The island's most important export, graphite, was now the subject of earnest negotiations between the Vichy government and both the USA and Japan. A vessel was due to sail from Yokohama early in January and the Japanese were asking for a guarantee that 1,000 tons of graphite would be available. A Japanese trade mission was also en route to the island.

Mayer first offered to work as an agent during a visit to South Africa (then always referred to as 'the Union') towards the end of 1940. SOE files note him as serving with the organisation from November 1940, when he arrived at Durban on the last ship of the Bank Line to sail from Tamatave, the port on the east coast of the island which served the inland capital at Tananarive.

The terms of SOE's Madagascar mission were set out on paper on 10 February 1941. They were, first, to establish clandestine radio communications with the island from the Union through Mayer; second, to introduce 'written, verbal, broadcasting, whispering and pictorial propaganda to the island and finally to undertake subversive activities subject to approval from London'. Mayer was not to be introduced to Free French elements in the Union, presumably to avoid any possibility of him being compromised.

In March 1941 Mayer returned to Madagascar having

arranged for a Bank Line steamer to drop him off in the centre of the Mozambique channel in a small boat he had purchased for the purpose, sailing into Majunga five or six days later. He brought with him a powerful wireless set which was installed in the loft of his house at Tananarive. Berthe immediately took on the role of clandestine radio operator and together they supplied a great deal of valuable intelligence during the spring and summer of 1941. One of the reports Berthe sent was responsible for the capture of five Vichy blockade-runners by the Royal Navy on 2 November 1941.

Following the fall of France the French governor of the island had initially rallied to de Gaulle, but after the British bombarded the French fleet at Mers-el-Kebir in July 1940 he resigned and was replaced by a Vichy supporter. The British consul departing from the island in November 1940 reported that 'the Governor had completely crushed what remained of Free French support in Madagascar'. Thanks to underwater cables that ran from Madagascar to Mauritius the British were nonetheless able to tap the lines and obtain reports of 6,000 troops stationed on the island as well as rumours of the arrival of planes from North Africa.

As tension mounted, Desmond Morton, Churchill's intelligence adviser, wrote to Gladwyn Jebb at the Ministry of Economic Warfare on 30 May 1941 asking 'whether bribery, corruption, murder . . . barratry on the high seas or any other crime in the calendar, excepting the sin against the Holy Ghost to which I will be no party . . . may . . . bring about a change of regime in Madagascar without the external aid of armed force?'. On 30 June the Treasury sanctioned a further expenditure of £4,000 (making a total of £8,000) for SOE's Madagascar operation. Very soon after this SOE sought to increase this to £3,000 a month, allowing the establishment of a similar (but smaller) mission in East Africa to that in West Africa.

A telegram of 4 June 1941 to SO(I) – the political warfare department – in Cape Town shows that consideration was now being given to a *coup d'état* and large-scale bribery: 'dollar pensions obviously cheaper than naval military operation . . . If bribery alone inadequate physical liquidation Governor and other Vichy and pro-Axis extremists clearly indicated, is this practical?'.

In October 1941 Mayer paid another visit to the mainland, to Portuguese East Africa and the Union, ostensibly on a trade mission. While there he had extensive discussions with SOE's East African mission, which appointed him head of mission in the island with the task of recruiting agents.

The outbreak of war with Japan in December 1941, coupled with British and American naval losses, now appeared to make a Japanese descent on Madagascar a very real possibility. In Axis hands the island could serve as a base to attack Allied shipping in the Indian Ocean. There would be a major threat to the large number of ships carrying troops and supplies to India, which had been forced to use the Cape route as the Suez Canal had been virtually shut down following German advances in North Africa. German and Japanese submarines refuelling in Madagascar would also have been a threat to both Aden and Suez and could have prevented American lend-lease supplies from reaching Russia via the Persian Gulf. Oil from the Middle East was also vital to the British war effort, both for British forces in North Africa and India and at home, shipped to Britain round the Cape. The ultimate nightmare for the Allies was that German and Japanese forces could meet at Suez.

Mayer arrived back in Madagascar in December 1941.

Soon after this he made contact with French naval commander Paul Maerten and took a great personal risk in endeavouring to persuade him to arrange a peaceful surrender of Diego Suarez, presumably with the hint of a substantial bribe. Though Mayer met with no success, Maerten appears not to have alerted his Vichy colleagues to the overtures and Mayer avoided being compromised.

A telegram from Durban on 15 January 1942 set out the very serious difficulties facing an Allied offensive on the island. 'If any direct attack on Diego is contemplated it must be borne in mind that it naturally lends itself to easy defence and that under Maerten's energetic leadership its defences have been considerably increased recently and are maintained in a state of complete readiness. Even if Diego operation successful we could look for no spontaneous action by sympathisers in rest of island.'

For a direct attack on Diego to succeed, SOE calculated that preparations had to be in place to sabotage the main defences with reliable guides available to direct demolition gangs arriving on the island immediately before the operation. As well as putting the two heavy batteries at Diego out of commission, SOE considered it essential to destroy all available fighter aircraft and to seize or destroy stocks of aviation spirit and petrol.

A briefing note of 13 February 1942 adds: 'Diego Suarez provides one of the best anchorages in the world and from its geographical position is easily defended. In addition there is an excellent aerodrome at Ivato and many landing grounds, some of which could be enlarged without difficulty.' An internal coup would take at least six months to organise, with the risk that the Japanese might arrive first. By contrast a military operation aimed at neutralising Diego Suarez could be arranged in two and a half to three months.

The fall of Singapore on 15 February 1942 increased the threat dramatically. Japanese occupation of French Indo-China had contributed hugely to Japan's success in the Pacific. By 26 February 1942 the Joint Planning Committee in Washington was involved. The Americans were deeply concerned about the Japanese threat to the island, considering it vital to deny them the harbour at Diego Suarez.

A US War Department report of 16 February 1942 had stated: 'there are [now] only a few Vichy supporters on the island, including Governor Annet and there is no German infiltration. Defence of Island was limited to a garrison of 8,000 men with Diego Suarez as main fortified naval base'. Fixed defences included four 305mm guns, four 190mm guns and four 100mm guns, and a minefield at the mouth of the harbour. Tamatave, the main commercial port, had a garrison of 600 men, while at the capital Tananarive there were five not very serviceable two-man tanks with heavy machine guns. Air strength was limited to seventeen Morane defence fighters at Diego Suarez and eighteen light bombers at Tananarive.

In March 1942 Magic intelligence brought confirmation that Germany was pressing the Japanese to occupy Madagascar. (Magic was the American code word identifying deciphered Japanese diplomatic communications.) To forestall this, British chiefs of staff decided that the naval base of Diego had to be taken.

A meeting at the Admiralty on 15 March 1942 was attended by Major-General Sturgess, commander of the proposed invasion force, Brigadier Festing, his second-in-command, and various naval officers. They discussed ways in which SOE could help. Military assistance included cutting the telephone lines from the landing beaches and batteries at Courrier Bay to Diego Suarez, as well as those from the aerodrome. For the navy it was a matter of primary necessity to have a light at Nossi Anambo Island visible at a distance of 5 miles to aid navigation – the island was 50 kilometres in a direct line from Courrier Bay. Information was also sought about mines and the location of submarines and aeroplanes, notably bombers. SOE was also to provide two pairs of guides to conduct advance demolition parties to the two main batteries defending the naval base. A further proposal was for Mayer to 'arrange suitable entertainment of senior French Officers on the night of the operation' – emulating the success of Operation Postmaster.

Mayer had recruited sub-agents at Diego Suarez, Tamatave and Majunga, but only the latter, his brother, was considered reliable enough for operational purposes.

A cable of 18 March 1942 brought the disturbing news that a party of German experts had arrived safely at Diego Suarez from Portuguese East Africa, and was suspected of establishing wireless communication with the German command.

On 31 March, SOE's trading schooner, the *Lindi*, managed to land arms and stores for Mayer. He relates: 'I was in Majunga [on the north-west coast of the island] attending to the operations of the *Lindi*, from which wireless sets, arms and ammunition had been landed, when I got a signal from my wife saying that instructions received were that I should proceed to Tananarive immediately. I got the message at 11 a.m. and left the same afternoon at 5 p.m. for Tananarive which I reached the following day at noon after travelling right through the night.' At this time he had succeeded in retrieving only one wireless set and a box containing the codes from the beach. These he took with him to Tananarive.

His main task now, apart from supplying the intelligence

requested by Durban, was to provide guides for the proposed advance landing parties and to establish a radio link from Diego to Durban. At this moment he had no contact in Diego as the agent he had sent there, Henri Lejeune, was back in Tananarive for trial on a political charge. To carry out the tasks allotted, all the men would have to be sent secretly to Diego well in advance to give them time to reconnoitre, as none of them knew the terrain.

Mayer noted: 'It is a matter of extreme difficulty to find in Madagascar reliable persons willing to take the risks involved in such an operation. It was fortunate that K.H. Pack, the Managing Director of the Meat Canning Factory at Boanamary, an entirely reliable person, was in Tananarive at that time'. Pack had already helped him obtain intelligence. 'I knew him to be very keen and trustworthy.' Pack, however, did not think he could help because of his obligations to his company, and instead offered four of his best men from Majunga, namely his acting manager, MacPherson, Mitchell, Hudson and Gaddie. Of these four men, Mayer said, only one was totally reliable, and that was MacPherson, but it was impossible to use him as leader owing to his total lack of initiative. Instead he approached a casual acquaintance, Turner, whose record during the First World War was very good and who 'had previous experience in intelligence work as a member of a military mission in Siberia in 1919'. Mayer decided to appoint him as leader. At this point Pack decided he would like to join the party, but though Mayer believed he was the better man for the job he felt he could not go back on Turner.

They left Tananarive at 2 a.m. on 21 April and reached Majunga on the coast at six o'clock the same day. Mayer took Turner with him in his car to have an opportunity to assess him more closely. By the time they arrived he had decided that he had made a mistake. Turner was not just 'wet' but had a slight tinge of 'yellow'. In Majunga, Turner stayed hidden in a safe house until the party embarked on the *Lindi* on 24 April. Here they were joined by a Captain Van Veen, an expert in reconnaissance work sent by Durban, and Legg, the radio operator.

The *Lindi* had sailed from Dar es Salaam on 18 April under the command of SOE's DZ7, arriving off the coast near Ambararata Bay on 23 April. DZ7 now had four days to waste. Mayer had warned him of the danger of coastal air patrols and he decided that 'audacious action might be preferable to long patrol in open water ... I therefore hoisted a French flag and laid a course for Nossi Mitsu', a nearby island. Here he was able to convince the native *chef de village* that his was a French vessel on French service.

Mayer travelled separately. He explained: 'To be able to go to Diego openly I had to imagine a cover as I could not use that of an ordinary business trip, as it was well known that there was no business to be done there that would justify such a trip from Tananarive, especially as I had to take my own car with me for running around the place.'

With the shortage of shipping, there was now a serious problem in supplying Diego with rice, the staple food. Though there were rich alluvial plains in the Diego region, where large quantities of rice were produced, the lack of roads meant that the rice had to be sent by dhows and lighters to Nossi Be and then reshipped to Diego by sea. Adverse currents and winds around Cape Sebastien had so far defeated this. As his cover, Mayer therefore devised a plan by which he offered to transport the rice, using large lighters and tugs, to Ambararata Bay, taking it on by truck to nearby Diego. Mayer telegraphed his agents in Nossi Be to arrange tugs and lighters and buy the rice. He then telegraphed the district commissioner at Diego asking for his support. This justified taking his car, as he would need it to explore the Mahavavy district, as well as securing him the necessary fuel in the face of the very severe petrol rationing.

Pack had arranged for his company ship, *General Pau*, which was due to leave Majunga for the Comares islands, to delay sailing for a week and to divert to Nossi Be, dropping off Mayer and his car. Mayer arrived at noon on 23 April and stayed for a day to make arrangements about the rice with his agent.

While in Nossi Be, Mayer had dinner with both Captain de Chambure, the local military commander, and the captain of the French submarine *Le Glorieux*. From them he obtained reliable information on the forces at Nossi Be and their equipment, as well as news of submarines stationed at Madagascar.

As soon as he arrived at Diego, Mayer called on the district commissioner and mayor, M. Garrouste, who was very enthusiastic about the rice scheme. Mayer then strung out the discussions on the contract, as he put it, 'until the last day'. He also approached Maerten, offering to land the rice at Courrier Bay rather than Ambararata. Maerten strongly objected, letting slip that Courrier Bay was mined. He invited Mayer to lunch and introduced him to Colonel Clarebout, the Diego military commander. 'There were only the three of us and we talked very freely about the possibility of war being carried to Madagascar, etc. Before lunch I had visited the submarine "Bevezier" in harbour with the submarine "Le Heros" lying alongside.'

On 27 April Mayer set off for Ambararata and Courrier Bay on the pretext of studying the road conditions and landing facilities for the rice. In Courrier Bay he met the French sergeant who commanded the defences of the bay. 'We got very friendly, had a drink, and he then showed me all over the defences, position of machine guns, signalling gear, gave me the number and composition of troops, etc, and finally invited me to spend the day there on the following Sunday for a fishing party.'

Two days later, on 29 April, he went again to Ambararata Bay, this time to meet the *Lindi* and find a suitable place to land the wireless gear. Unfortunately the *Lindi* arrived early, while it was daylight, when she was in danger of being spotted from nearby lookout posts. The landing party came onshore at 7 p.m. without any gear and told Mayer they had received new instructions from Durban. These stated that guides were no longer required and that a wireless set and four men could be landed if Mayer considered there was no chance of it being detected before the attack. After a long discussion he decided that one wireless set should be landed with three men, and that he would return in two days' time with up-to-date intelligence for transmission to Durban. Captain Van Veen, who seemed 'the ideal man', was put in charge. Mayer then left promptly, before the gear was landed, fearing that the authorities in Diego might have been alerted to the arrival of a strange ship and might send an officer to investigate. He had left his car on the road about 2 kilometres away and was concerned that this would come under immediate suspicion. As it happened, on his way back to Diego he passed two native soldiers who were taking an urgent message and asked for a lift. He feared the *Lindi* had been spotted but on arrival at Diego he heard no more.

When Mayer returned, as arranged, to Ambararata Bay on the morning of 1 May to use the wireless to transmit important information to Durban, he was surprised not to

find the landing party. After searching the whole neighbourhood he had to conclude that they had re-embarked.
Fortunately he had two days earlier given the landing
party a report providing extensive 'particulars of shipping,
W/T stations, numbers of troops, road bridges, batteries
and defences'.

The sad story of what happened after Mayer left
emerges from DZ7's report. The shore party had decided
that they needed a vast quantity of stores and provisions,
so DZ7 landed every able-bodied man with a view to
speedily hiding the material in the thick bush. 'With much
labour owing to the low state of the tide, the many rocks,
holes and other obstructions, the entire bulk of the
landing party's gear was assembled on the beach: about
half of it was transported with a difficulty I cannot ade-
quately describe through the thick bush up the hill.' As he
went back and forth to the hiding place with Van Veen,
the appointed leader of the landing party, DZ7 was 'more
and more perturbed by his lack of confidence and
enthusiasm, and his general air of despondency. Finally
his conduct caused me to call a conference on the beach
of the entire party'.

He was now concerned about clearing the coast before
daylight as his most important task was to set up the light
at Nossi Ambo. He reminded them of the agreement they
had made with Mayer, but it had no effect 'but to prove to
me that the morale of the entire party had reached a point
where all enthusiasm and courage was lacking and where
the success of the final assault might be jeopardised'. A
unanimous decision was made, and all the equipment
laboriously heaved up the hill was collected and re-
embarked. DZ7 added that if he had had the authority he
would have placed Legge, the radio operator, in charge of
the shore party, as his conduct during the five hours on

the beach and on the *Lindi* could not be 'too highly praised'.

DZ7 was now concerned about being spotted from the air and laid a course for the island of Glorioso, 160 kilometres off the coast. This they found entirely deserted, with the welcome bonus of nearly 8,000 litres of fresh water stored in tanks with which they replenished the *Lindi* while using the time to collect wild chicken and turtles to augment their food stocks. They left Glorioso at 6 p.m. on 3 May, arriving off Nossi Ambo just after sunset the next day.

Mayer had provided SOE with detailed intelligence about the island's defences. Almost all the military aircraft were at Tananarive with just two bombers and six fighters at Diego Suarez. In addition he had provided names of ships in the harbour spotted by aerial reconnaissance, including five French submarines – *Héros*, *Vengeur*, *Espoir*, *Monge* and *Glorieux*.

Meanwhile Mayer coolly continued to gather more valuable military and naval intelligence. 'Although no civilians were allowed on the aerodrome I managed to go there on the pretext of meeting a pilot friend who was landing there from Tananarive, and found out the strength and composition of the forces stationed there.' At Joffreville the indefatigable Mayer was introduced to the local commander, Captain Thomas; he became friendly with him and found out the number of men under his command. Deciding it might be useful to explore the road from Diego to Orangia, he drove out and met an NCO, and, over drinks in the hotel, learned how many troops were stationed there. He was also able to make a sketch of the landward defences of Diego.

As no wireless set was now available, and Mayer was anxious to communicate all his valuable intelligence to the Allied C-in-C, he decided he must try to make contact on the night of the landing. In case he could not meet the C-in-C personally, Mayer prepared notes and sketches which he could hand over.

On 4 May he went again to Ambararata 'on business', leaving there at dusk to return to Diego. At 6.30 p.m., at a point 19 kilometres from the town, he stopped his car and coolly carried out the most crucial element of his mission, cutting the telephone line from the battery at Windsor Castle to defence headquarters at Diego. He then returned to Ambararata Bay to wait for the troops to land. He stayed there until 10.30 p.m., when the moon had risen well into the sky. 'Seeing no signs of anything, and having lost contact with Durban since April 29th, I feared that the date of operations might have been altered in the interval without my being aware.' He was also concerned that the military might realise the telephone line had been cut and send out a repair party. So that his absence was not noted, he returned to the hotel. All was still quiet at 2.30 a.m. so he went to bed. At 4.30 a.m. he woke to hear guns booming in the distance, which he thought must be the Windsor battery. To his surprise no alert was sounded until at 5.35 a.m. Allied planes began to bomb the shipping in the harbour. He dressed, walked to the harbour and watched the sinking of the auxiliary cruiser *Bougainville* and the submarine *Beveziers*. On his way back to the hotel about 7 a.m. he was stopped by a French police officer and sent to the police station to wait for the officer's return. Suddenly he remembered he had in his pocket all the notes intended for the Allied C-in-C.

The Allied invasion force closing on Madagascar was a sizeable armada. A slow convoy had sailed from Durban on 26 April followed by a fast convoy two days later. The combined fleet, under Rear Admiral Neville Syfret, now comprised fifty-seven ships, including the battleship *Ramillies*, the aircraft carriers *Illustrious* and *Indomitable*, two cruisers, nine destroyers, six corvettes and six minesweepers. The landing force was commanded by Major-General Robert Sturgess and comprised two army brigade groups and No. 5 Commando. Admiral Sir James Somerville was providing long-range cover with the bulk of his eastern fleet.

There had been a moment of serious alarm in London at a sudden press campaign demanding the capture of Madagascar. This was entirely spontaneous – there were no fears of a leak. On balance it was decided that the enemy was unlikely to take the press reports as evidence of an imminent attack and they were allowed to persist. The greater danger came from Japanese submarines known to be operating north and south of the island and in the Mozambique channel. At dusk on 4 May the two convoys drew together 105 kilometres from the Madagascar coast.

The night landing at Courrier Bay was a remarkable feat which the French had deemed impossible. It had to be made through shoals and reefs as well as through varying and possibly strong currents, which could not be predicted in advance. Crucial to this operation was the marker light placed by SOE. The *Lindi*, cruising offshore displaying the light, proved all the more crucial as it was found that Nossi Ambo was 2.8 kilometres farther west than charted.

The light enabled the destroyer HMS *Laforey* to buoy the channel and ascertain the conditions for landing craft while HMS *Lightning* placed a fixed navigational light on Nosi Fati shoal – the starting point for the approaching ships. Even so, one of the buoys was either laid incorrectly or dragged and the minesweepers that followed went too close to the shoal and all lost their sweeps. The crew being unaware of these problems, the landing craft were lowered and proceeded to the beach. One of the minesweepers, HMS *Romney*, set off two mines – fortunately the French defence forces remained sound asleep. Complete surprise was achieved with three of the beach landings, while opposition at the fourth was quickly overcome by one of the other landing parties, which attacked from the rear. By 6.20 a.m. 2,300 troops had been landed. From the flagship the position appeared to be that 'our troops everywhere seemed to be advancing, taking prisoners and incurring negligible casualties themselves'. Successful air attacks had been made on both the aerodrome and the hangar and on ships in the harbour. Nonetheless the ultimatum to the Vichy military commander had been rejected and opposition began to stiffen seriously during the morning.

Admiral Syfret's report continues:

'At about 1400 the General arrived on board. He was hot, begrimed and unhappy. Things were not going too well, he said. The 29th Brigade had been held up about 3–5 miles south of Antsiranane since the previous afternoon. The enemy held a strong well-sited defensive position; they were plentifully equipped with 75mm and machine guns. The 29th Brigade in 30 hours had marched 20 miles, and made two ineffective attacks on this position. They were tired and unfit to put into battle again this day. Their casualties were high – 25% over the whole brigade. The 17th Brigade were gradually getting up to the front line, mostly on foot, and the majority should be in position by 1700. He considered that after two hours rest they should be ready to go into battle, and he intended they should make a night attack on the enemy position – zero time being 2000. He was emphatic that the attack should be carried out before the moon rose at 2300, as the position was too strong to be captured in moonlight or daylight in the absence of strong artillery support.'

Syfret now 'offered any and all assistance the Fleet could

give. The enemy's position was outside the range of *Ramillies* and Cruiser's guns. Aircraft bombing up to zero hour was promised'.

The navy agreed to send in fifty marines as reinforcements to create a diversion in the enemy's rear with a landing on the Antsiranana peninsula. The destroyer HMS *Anthony* was called alongside and given instructions while Captain Price of the Royal Marines on *Ramillies* was told to collect fifty of his men and embark on *Anthony*, which sailed at 1530. Syfret continues:

The impression left with me after the General's visit was that the intended quick capture of Diego Saurez was already 90% failure. The night attack, planned in a hurry, to be carried out by tired troops against very strong positions, had only 10% chance of success. Prolonged operations, which we so much wished to avoid, was the unpleasant alternative. *Anthony*'s chance of success I assessed as about 50%, my advisers thought 15%, and of the Royal Marines I did not expect a score to survive the night. The next few hours were not happy ones.

The first indication that the unexpected was about to happen came at 2129 hours with a report from HMS *Anthony* that she had accomplished her task successfully. This, said Syfret, was 'the principal and direct cause of the enemy's collapse'. His belief was that, on hearing the firing in the town, the men manning the enemy trenches 'must have turned their heads and inclined their hearts towards a quick run to the town to look after their homes and belongings'.

At 7.23 the next morning Syfret received a request to postpone bombardment until ten o'clock, and at 9.50 he was asked to postpone it again as chances of surrender appeared good. He continues: 'I was tired of this shilly-shallying and parleying for which I had given no authorisation, and which was keeping the Fleet steaming up and down in dangerous waters, consequently I informed the General that I intended to commence a 15 minute bombardment to encourage the enemy to surrender.' Ten minutes after the bombardment began Syfret received a message that Oranjia had surrendered.

Minesweepers were sent in and on receipt of a signal that no mines had been found *Ramillies*, *Hermione*, *Lightning* and *Paladin* proceeded into the harbour. *Indomitable* followed the next day, being attacked off the entrance by a submarine that was afterwards destroyed by *Active*. *Illustrious* remained at sea to provide fighter support, entering the harbour a day later.

By 24 May Syfret was satisfied that the military and air forces were securely established and the naval base and port facilities running smoothly. The fleet departed, taking the 13th Brigade on to India but leaving a garrison to defend the harbour and the surrounding headland. The decision was taken to remove all the prisoners of war except those of Malagashy nationality, and on 20 May the *Oronsay* sailed for Durban carrying 111 French officers, 836 French other ranks and ratings, 402 Senegalese, 55 Germans and 70 Italians, as well as 26 wives and 44 children.

Syfret drew firm lessons for future engagements with Vichy forces. 'In operations against French possessions, all ideas of using a white flag or dropping leaflets should be abandoned. They do harm and no good and only cause the Frenchman to consider that his military honour is at stake. The only policy that is sound is to exert the maximum endeavour to destroy his air forces, warships and military works from the start of the operation. Stories of what the inhabitants did with the leaflets would surprise their originators.'

Waiting in his cell on the morning of 5 May, Mayer had decided to tear his notes into tiny pieces, hoping the native policemen would not notice. Unfortunately one of them became suspicious and sounded the alert. The police officer rushed back to the station. Mayer was searched and the notes found. He was immediately taken to Defence Headquarters where Colonel Clarebout questioned him and sent him to Naval HQ for further interrogation, following which he was sent swiftly to prison on a charge of espionage. Though the notes were written in English, they had succeeded in piecing enough together to decipher parts of what he had written.

Mayer learned afterwards that he had been denounced to the police by a man he had done business with for the last fourteen years but who, unknown to him, had connections with the Sûreté. Mayer had invited him to lunch with the NCO from Orangia, whom he had pumped for information. The authorities decided he should face a firing squad but Maerten had not had time to attend to the matter. Instead Mayer found himself let out on parole by the naval chief of staff, Commandant Melin, who believed the British had broken through the lines and would shortly be in Diego. Mayer later discovered that his hotel room had been thoroughly searched, but he had burnt all compromising notes here the previous day.

In his report Mayer expressed his pain at his blunder in failing to destroy the notes and his inability to take part in the military action. But SOE and the Allied commanders took a more bullish view. Mayer was the hero of the hour. He had cut the vital telephone wires, ensuring the first landing took place unopposed.

Perhaps because of his embarrassment over his arrest Mayer went on to explain more fully the way he had set out to influence Maerten. Maerten knew that Mayer had been to Africa after the fall of France and had been in touch with the military authorities there.

I was in a position to influence his ideas about what the British would or would not do regarding Madagascar. I have always expressed to him, with very convincing arguments, that the British would never make the first move against Madagascar . . . consequently Maerten was resting on his oars, convinced that the British would not move first. I had confirmation of that from Commander Melin . . . [who] after he had released me on parole became more friendly and in the course of conversation told me they had never dreamt that the British would take the initiative in any action against Madagascar, and that they were completely taken by surprise.

Mayer also explained why the planned drinks party with Maerten and Clarebout – at which SOE hoped he would slip drugs into their drinks – had not taken place. 'The knock-out drops were handed to me by Turner at Ambararata Bay but without any written instructions. The only thing that was known about the drops was that it would knock out the subject for $2^{1/2}$ minutes. That of course was ridiculous, as to be of any use the subject would have to be unconscious for at least 24 hours.' More pertinent still was that he might have found it very difficult to persuade the pair to come in the first place. Indeed, inviting them might just have led to his earlier arrest with possibly disastrous consequences.

A cable from Durban on 10 May 1942 reported that Mme Mayer had 'supplied daily intelligence reports up to May 8th to Admiral Commander-in-Chief. These reports gave details of shipping movements including submarines, aircraft and information regarding reaction in capital and aircraft movement during the operation'. On 30 April, Mayer had supplied particulars of ships in the harbour at Diego Suarez, wireless stations, numbers of troops, and bridges.

SOE had hoped that the invasion force, having established a bridgehead, would quickly take over the rest of
the island. Berthe Mayer had provided a comprehensive
report on the defences at Tananarive for the force commander on 14 May. The Allied force was strong enough
but the decision was taken to postpone the attempt, avoid
further direct confrontation with Vichy forces and play a
waiting game, using the blockade to cripple the Vichy
administration.

The problem now was that the bridgehead was vulner-
ably small. A telegram from Durban of 20 May 1942
reads: 'our head agent in the island is of the strongest
opinion, and we associate ourselves completely with his
views, that principally on economic grounds the present
area of occupation of the Diego Suarez region is inadequate and must be extended'. This was partly because
the area could not produce adequate food and famine
would soon threaten – though large quantities of rice were
growing near by.

SOE's role remained important. Fortunately there were
no disastrous repercussions in the area under Vichy control,
though several agents there had their houses searched and
were put under close police surveillance. DZ61 was
instructed to close his house some miles outside Majunga
and to come and live in the town, where he could be more
closely watched. All British subjects in the unoccupied part
of the island were also kept under close scrutiny.

Even so, SOE was laying plans to move a spare wireless
set to Majunga for use by DZ61, instructing him if necessary to move to a more commodious house where he could
more easily conceal it. 'We now know that the authorities
are getting much more rigorous in their attempts to trace
our secret wireless stations as in addition to their usual
practice of switching off current without any warning in

certain parts of the city while our agents are broadcasting in order ... to locate their whereabouts, they are also using radio directional finding instruments,' read a report of 25 June 1942.

There was a moment's worry on 10 May when Durban lost contact with Berthe Mayer (Madame DZ6 as she is referred to) but the very next day a new cable announced 'wireless communication restored last night but for safety reasons we do not anticipate she will be transmitting to us'. Two days later, on 12 May, came a further telegram saying: 'Madame DZ6 transmitting last night certain shipping intelligence ... She also states that bank accounts of British subjects frozen.' No calls for caution, it seems, could curb her zeal for the Allied cause. A further telegram of 16 May notes: 'Despite messages from myself urging extreme caution and from DZ6 himself advising her temporarily to cease transmitting we are nightly receiving reports of political and military intelligence.' The importance of her work is highlighted in SOE's *Diary of Ironclad*, which notes that on the arrival of the brigadier at Durban on 20 April 'he was supplied with a summary of all relevant intelligence received from DZ6's organization and with answers to the Force Commander's special questionnaire. Subsequent intelligence reports were passed daily to the Admiral C in C, as received from Madame DZ6'.

The same day brought the news that Vichy headquarters 'knew for certain that secret wireless transmitters are operating in Tananarive and neighbourhood. Large reward will be paid for information leading to discovery of culprits and their accomplices who will be summarily dealt with by court martial'.

By contrast the occupation of Diego continued smoothly, and on 18 May Pack wrote from Diego saying:

'very large sums of money were paid into the banks the day they were reopened which shows the confidence paid in the British'.

The navy had been universally praised for its brilliant navigation during the attack – but it was of course SOE's light on the *Lindi* which had made this possible.

The best compliment to Mayer came from General Sturgess in Pretoria, who described Mayer's cutting of communications on the night of the operation as 'the finest bit of Fifth Column work he had heard of this War'. Further commendation came from the brigade major, who said that the successful attack from the rear made on the machine-gun post commanding the landing place in Courrier Bay was the result of a suggestion by Mayer, who had made a personal recce of the post.

Three days later, on 15 May, came a jubilant telegram from Durban congratulating all 'on a grand job well planned organised and carried out and which already has redounded to the credit of SOE and given us strong backing in high quarters for our claim to damage the enemy wherever and whenever we can get at him'.

SOE was now anxious that Mayer should resume his British citizenship. This would allow him to hold military rank – as major. Technically Mayer needed to prove one year's continuous residence in Mauritius prior to his application, as well as an additional four years out of eight spent in British dominions, hardly practical in view of the war and SOE's urgent need of his services elsewhere. This brought the kind of sour reply that faced other distinguished overseas SOE agents seeking British passports. A Colonel Calthorp pointed out that 'when he relinquished his status as a British subject, he did so for his own advantage, and there is nothing to prove that if and when the French take over Madagascar again he will not wish to become a French citizen for the purposes of his business'.

Though the Allies had decided to leave the rest of the island in Vichy hands, General Smuts, South Africa's prime minister, now insisted that other ports be taken as well. Further landings were made at Majunga and Morondava on the west coast on 10 September, followed by others. Eventually, on 5 November, an armistice was arranged and control of the island passed to the Free French. General Paul Legentilhomme was appointed high commissioner and in May 1943 he handed over the island to a civilian governor general.

Percy Mayer went on to become the highly successful leader of SOE's Fireman circuit in France. Landing by parachute near Angoulême with his brother Edmund on the night of 7/8 March 1944, he played an important role in arming the Resistance and harassing German columns hurrying to reinforce opposition to the Normandy landings. For this work he was awarded the MC, in addition to the OBE he received for his valiant work in Madagascar. After the war the Mayers established themselves in Durban, building a fine house at Kloot in the suburbs of the city.

Chapter 8

HARRY REE AND SABOTAGE AT THE PEUGEOT FACTORY

Had it been necessary to rely on Allied bombing to put the [Peugeot] factory out of action, it would have required a large force of bombers at fairly frequent intervals to achieve a similar disruption . . . It was only after a personal visit to this area that HQ officers realised to the full the immense authority which Captain Ree wields in the Doubs and neighbouring departments, where his name is legendary, and the prestige of Great Britain at the pinnacle

Harry Ree was an agent with a sense of humour that shines through all his exploits. Before finally making a successful drop into France he spent three successive moon periods at RAF Tempsford. The first time, in January 1943, he was destined for a reception committee south of Clermont-Ferrand. He describes how he, and the radio operator who was jumping with him, sat on opposite sides of the trap-door 'with our legs dangling, looking down at the land below, and waiting for the dispatcher . . . to shout "Go!". The countryside that night was covered in snow, and looked beautiful in the full moon I remember. We followed a railway line, then a river, wandering about like a bee looking for a favourite flower.' But the pilot couldn't find the lights of the reception committee and he was flown back to Tempsford for a ration of double fried eggs in compensation. A few hours later came a message from the reception committee. 'Who do you think we are? Bloody Polar bears?' They had been waiting all night in the snow and tantalisingly heard the plane, which never came close enough to spot them. He made two further abortive sorties, each time saying goodbye to his wife, 'the only one who knew what I was going to do'. Finally he was dropped near the Pyrenees on the night of 14 April 1943, with the same radio operator, the brave Mauritian, Amédée Maingard. Both had been offered a blind drop but both felt the need for a reception committee. Maingard, though he spoke French well, hadn't been to France since he was a little boy while Ree spoke French with a pronounced English accent.

They dropped surrounded by metal containers and wire cages full of stores for the circuit receiving them. On his descent Ree noticed a container passing just 20 metres from him, only for it to become entangled in electricity lines between two pylons. The two agents found each other quickly after landing but of the reception committee there was no sign, only, alarmingly, a dog barking near by.

Ree later learned from Maingard that the dispatcher had given the instruction to jump in such a low voice that Maingard had not heard it. 'Instead of another turn being made,' he later told SOE, 'the warning was given again,' but by this time they were out of sight of the ground and out of view of the reception committee.

It was impossible for the two of them to gather and hide all the containers but they found Maingard's radio and grabbed another suitcase, which Ree hoped might contain rations, especially the chocolate and cigarettes that SOE often sent out to boost Resistance morale. Then they set off to find a hiding place in the woods, walking in heavy overcoats up a stream for 300 metres to throw any pursuing dogs off the scent. Settling in a thick wood at first light, after struggling with the heavy suitcases for 2 miles, they found nothing but tins of machine-gun oil inside.

As the next day dawned they could see the Pyrenees rising in the distance, providing some assurance that they had been dropped as intended near Tarbes. After lying up for a day in the woods, Maingard set off to a nearby village, pretending to be going to mass in case anyone was suspicious of his smart clothes so early in the morning. There he saw signposts to Tarbes. They had been given two addresses in the town and it took Maingard the whole day to track down their contact. The first address was the Hôtel Normandie, which he found on arrival had been taken over by the Gestapo the week before. But at the second address he was received with jubilation by a lady who fed him and summoned the reception committee.

Ree, meanwhile, was becoming increasingly worried and hungry. Late in the afternoon he heard someone walking through the undergrowth and then a dog bark. The dog quickly found him but it was a mongrel – not the sort of dog a German patrol would have, he thought. A man in faded blue overalls appeared, looked at him and quickly said, '*Je vous ai pas vu*' – I haven't seen you.

Ree decided to take a chance, saying that he was an escaped English soldier making his way to Spain. The man – a farmhand – replied, 'You must be hungry,' and came back in an hour with a bottle of wine, some hard-boiled eggs, a loaf and some thick slices of ham. Ree now spent a night on his own, but Maingard returned the next morning with his contact and a spare bicycle for Ree to cycle with them to a safe house in Tarbes.

Ree had been born in Manchester on 15 October 1914. Though his parents had British nationality he joked that he was not English at all. His father's family were Danes who had settled in Hamburg. His mother was born to an

American father whose family came from France. He described his father as a manufacturing chemist, 'one of those neo-Victorians who retired very early and went into public life in Manchester, sitting on committees and boards . . . he was President of the Chamber of Commerce'. Ree was educated at a prep school known as 'The Craig' at Windermere, and at Shrewsbury. He then went to St John's College, Cambridge. After taking his degree he became a schoolmaster at Beckenham County School, teaching French and German. He had married just before the war and had a small daughter about two years old.

Ree had signed the peace pledge at Cambridge and was a conscientious objector with decidedly left-wing views. When called up in 1940, he volunteered for minesweeping, which he felt was a suitably pacifist occupation. Just before the fall of France, he said, 'I realised this was much more than just a capitalist war . . . the concentration camps and the Jewish business convinced me . . . my father was part Jewish and you couldn't live in Manchester in the twenties without having a lot of Jewish friends.'

He had been to Hamburg to see his relations there in the mid-1930s and his first venture in journalism was an article on Hamburg in the *Yorkshire Post* in about 1937, a big middle-page spread headed 'Where Hitler has German critics'. He now joined the field artillery for six months, which he described as a nonsense – 'guns with wooden wheels' – but found himself with Michael Wharton, author of the famous Peter Simple column in *The Daily Telegraph*. Satirically they invented the Royal Army Tram Corps, 'where I was drilled by Sergeant Cesspit who called me Gonorrhoea . . . all artillery men are gunners'.

Just as frustration began to overwhelm him, he received a letter from his brother, who had been farming in France before the war and escaped at the last moment. 'He said he was looking after the security of people who were going to be dropped into occupied Europe and said if you want an interesting job using languages why don't you transfer.' Ree now enlisted for training in field security, and after several months found himself in the security section of SOE. One of his first tasks was to look after three Russians due to be dropped in central Europe. He was attached to the wireless school at Grendon Underwood, where he had to organise exercises for the trainee wireless operators, finding them safe houses from which they could practise clandestine broadcasting back to base. These he established in the homes of his parents, brothers and sisters. He and his colleagues would play the role of circuit organisers, summoning the trainees to clandestine rendezvous in cafés and giving them messages to transmit, and later descending on the students in the middle of the night like the Gestapo to see whether they had hidden their radios properly. 'I was working with two others, one a Canadian, and we said in the end "we speak better French than these people. We ought to go ourselves".' He put in a request for transfer to active service – learning only after the war that this had been strongly opposed by the head of his section on the grounds that he knew too much about SOE's organisation.

Ree spent the last part of his SOE training at the demolition school at Brickendonbury, learning how to set fire to tons of rubber. SOE's plan was that he should organise a huge blaze in the Michelin tyre factory at Clermont-Ferrand. He now travelled there by train from Tarbes with the SOE courier Jacqueline Nearne. When he arrived the agent in charge (Michel) heard his unmistakably English accent and decided that Ree should leave immediately. There were too many collaborators and Gestapo in the town. Instead Ree was sent to the Jura to help Maquis groups in the hills. Here he organised landing grounds and gave instructions in the use of arms and explosives. After his organiser was arrested Ree took over. His circuit was Stockbroker – ironic for a left-winger, he thought, but a typical SOE tease. His code name was Cesar.

Ree noted that there were 'groups in the small towns and villages who were keen to receive and store arms and explosives from parachute drops and then organise derailments of goods trains or blow up canal locks. This was quite important as the Germans were building small U-boats in Germany and sending them down the canals into the Mediterranean – once we actually sank a U-boat in a lock'.

On 5 May Ree was staying in a little cottage with a family listening to the BBC news. Knowing that his wife was expecting a child, SOE had arranged to broadcast a *message personnel*, *'Clément ressemble à son grandpère'* (or *grandmère*), bringing the good news. That night Ree heard he had a daughter – the news being broadcast on the very day the little girl had been born.

Shortly after this Ree arrived in Montbéliard and made contact with André van der Straten, a foreman in the town's huge Peugeot works who later became his second-in-command. He was also put in touch with another André, a lieutenant in the French army. In Montbéliard Ree lodged with M. and Mme Barbier of 41 Grande Rue Valentigny, 'a marvellous family', he said.

In July 1943 Ree and André successfully destroyed a large stock of 5,000 lorry tyres. These had been removed from the factory to a barn guarded by two Frenchmen. With two others André entered the barn, overpowered the French guards and threw six fire-pots among the tyres. 'There was a tremendous conflagration in which all the tyres were completely consumed,' Ree later told SOE.

Ree also made contact with the Peugeot family, who, he said, lived in big houses in the town but knew their

workmen still. From Rodolph Peugeot he borrowed a substantial sum of money to finance the circuit, using the
familiar SOE technique of arranging for the BBC to broadcast back Peugeot's chosen *message personnel* to establish
Ree's credentials.

On 14 July, Bastille Day, the RAF had carried out a raid
on the Peugeot works, which had been turned over to
making tracks and engines for tanks for the Germans. Ree
had been in Besançon that night, watching the bombers fly
over. The works had not been greatly damaged, although
there were 160 casualties. Ree reported to SOE that there
was no anti-British feeling. At the time of the attack people
had fled into the fields, but the Germans had sent up red
flares which the pilots mistook for markers and a large
number of bombs fell in the fields where they were hiding.

Later Ree set this in context. There were strong hopes in
France that the invasion would take place in 1943. Many
French, he said, felt that the British and Americans were sitting on their bottoms across the Channel, getting ready for
the invasion, and very much taking their time over it. 'It is a
horrid thing to say but what impresses them most is the
death of allied personnel, whether it be bomb victims or
aviators, and consequently they appreciate those who risk
death, like them. This sympathy with the allies assumes
gigantic proportions when they can see with their own eyes
living proof of this common suffering and common risk
taking. Hence the bounteous help to escaping airmen and
the almost embarrassing and fantastic funeral arrangements for the unlucky ones.'

The casualties nonetheless made a deep impression on
Ree, who immediately afterwards made contact with
Rodolph Peugeot. 'I said wouldn't it make more sense to
organise sabotage inside your factory.'

Peugeot replied, 'Of course.' As well as being strongly

pro-British, Rodolph Peugeot did not want his factory flat-tened by bombing as it would then be out of action after the war, with about 60,000 people thrown out of work.

Peugeot said he would put Ree in touch with Pierre Lucas, chief electrician at the works. This was done in a roundabout way, through a local schoolmaster, Roger Fouillette. Ree describes Lucas as a quiet, intelligent man who initially seemed dubious of the success of an attempt to sabotage so enormous a plant. When Ree explained to him how easy it was to damage machinery with small quan-tities of plastic explosive, well placed, it appealed to his mechanical mind, and he became wildly enthusiastic about the idea. Showing exceptional cool-headedness, he lent Ree a pair of overalls and under the watchful eyes of the German guards showed him all the factory machinery in detail. A few days later Ree was woken with the news that Roger Fouillette and many of his other friends had been arrested in a massive German round-up of suspects. Realising he was now in serious danger, Ree set off for Switzerland on 25 July 1943 to obtain fresh instructions from London, accompanied by a *passeur* (who escorted refugees and escaped prisoners), whose name had been given him by one of his contacts at Peugeot. Ree describes his journey as a wonderful early morning walk.

The *passeur* was a village barber with a shop about 10 kilometres from the frontier. 'He was a cheerful little man, sharp and sprightly, and he had an enormous, cheerful Juno of a wife – a blonde, she did the ladies' hair.' He supple-mented his income by heaving tyres across from Switzerland and selling them for three times the price.

The *passeur* knew where the German patrols were and they waited for ten minutes after they had passed before making the crossing. Ree had not received any briefing on frontier crossing and rashly announced to the Swiss border control guards that he was a British officer working with the Resistance in France. He was promptly taken into custody and sent on to Berne to see the general. 'There was only one in Switzerland,' he said laconically. The general told him he would have to be interned but allowed Ree to go to the British embassy, where he met Peter Jellinek, who was himself working on sabotage in Germany and France. Through him he was able to send the first of a series of long reports asking Buckmaster to request that the RAF suspend bombing raids on the Peugeot works. Ree later learnt that this was agreed after a stormy meeting on condition that he provided monthly reports of production figures from the factory. 'It was a wonderful job for an ex-conscientious objector to stop bombing,' he said.

His internment allowed him reasonable freedom and after a couple of weeks the embassy advised him that he could write to the general saying 'Military duty calls you back and that you have escaped'. 'No more will be said,' he was told. He met his *passeur* at Porrentruy, just across the border from Montbéliard, in September, and arranged for all his mail to pass to and from a safe house there via the embassy to London. As couriers Ree now enlisted a series of smugglers and *passeurs*. One, Robert, was called Le Chou, 'a little alcoholic who had been an airman once who was useful for taking messages as he had so many friends he could go anywhere without arousing suspicion'. Another was a smuggler called the Bigame who was said to have a wife on both sides of the frontier. He was a very energetic young man 'prepared to go across in all weathers'. Another was Ree's unofficial lieutenant, Claude, a bank clerk who had been called up for work in Germany and decided to take to the woods with the Maquis.

Ree later remembered how they had been sitting in St-Amour in the Jura after an enormous lunch with abundant wine. It was half past four and they had reached the coffee and cognac stage. 'We ate very well in the country areas, there was no question of starving, or even of rations.' Suddenly Claude said to him, 'You know, Henri, we'll be saying these were the best times of our lives.'

Lucas had explained to Ree that, although sabotage of the factory's main transformer would help considerably, there were sufficient sources of reserve power which could be employed at a moment's notice. In discussion it was decided to attack as many of the smaller transformers as possible, as well as the main turbo compressors. The group selected for the sabotage attack comprised six men in all, factory workmen, and included André van der Straten, who was in charge of the team detailed to attack the *gazogènes* and turbo compressors.

Ree was once again in serious danger. He reported to SOE that on 20 October 1943:

Gestapo made descent in the night, arresting 160 people in the Belfort Montbéliard area, and all but decapitating French organisations. They had names of all *chefs de groupes*. At Besançon they arrested a man who, before July, used to put me up. They said '*Vous logez un certain M. Henri*' ... They did not ask for me elsewhere, and I think they do not suspect that I am where I am. I shall know a little more if they release any of the 160, or if news of interrogations leaks out, as it probably will do. The arrests acted like a *coup de masse* on the morale of the region. We decided, those of us who were left, that it was essential to make bangs and fires everywhere as soon as possible.

The night of 3 November 1943 was chosen for a large attack. André and his group arrived in the evening just before the day shift went off duty with their charges in their pockets – blocks of plastic explosive with a hole in the middle in which to insert the detonator. They hung around in the recreation yard, waiting to go in. Some of the German guards were playing football and invited them to join in. While the game was in progress, one of the Germans shouted to André that something had fallen out of his pocket. He looked round and to his horror saw a block of plastic explosive lying on the ground. He hurried to pick it up, murmuring about electric fuses. The game continued.

At the agreed time the teams set off to place their charges. Ree, who had remained outside, jumped on a bicycle and circled round the outside of the factory, feverishly awaiting the first explosion. When no sound came he went home and waited. Later Lucas appeared. He expressed disgust that nothing had happened, blaming Ree and the SOE charges. After investigation it was discovered that the detonators had been put in upside down. Lucas was now bitterly disappointed at his stupidity and begged to be allowed to repeat the performance the next night.

In the meantime André, in his haste to get to work, had forgotten to bring his time pencils with him, so his group hid their charges under the floorboards and came away unnoticed.

They decided to try again two nights later on 5 November. It was Guy Fawkes' Day in Britain and this time luck was with them. Work at the factory stopped after the attack and an intensive search by the Gestapo for the culprits met with no success. Ree reported jubilantly via Berne that the attack had blown a large hole in the turbo and the leaves were twisted and the bearings pulverised. 'The 2,500hp motor was irreparable.' Destruction of the motor meant 'complete stoppage of the forge shop, drop forge and other power hammers . . . A stoppage of 3 to 6 months is anticipated, during which the forge shop will probably operate at one fifth of the usual output.' Similarly the press shop, which operated on compressed air supplied by the forge shop, was also partially closed. Though an auxiliary air compressor could be installed in about a month the output even then would be only 25 per cent of normal.

The damage to the gas generators of the foundry and machine shops would also have very serious consequences on production. With the core-shop out of commission in the foundry, casting of all cored parts would cease.

A telegram from Berne dated 11 November 1943 brought news of an attack on the Marty gudgeon-pin factory where two transformers and three electric motors were hit. Two transformers, one 500 kilowatts and one 100 kilowatts, were 'pulverised and flying pieces smashed three electric motors, a switchboard and two batteries of accumulators'. As in all attacks against transformers the greatest damage was the loss of transformer oil – here 1,600 litres. Another telegram of 14 November from Berne brought news of an attack on the Elmag works at Mulhouse. This was the Elsassiche Machinenfabrik, formerly the Société Alsacienne de Construction Méchanique. Here Peugeot estimated that the damage to the twenty-five turbo-compressors would take ten to twelve months to repair as moulding patterns for these turbines no longer existed.

Ree obtained further inside details from an official of the Ponts & Chaussées, the highways department. He said that of the two 350-kilowatt transformers that were attacked 'one was completely destroyed and the second can be repaired in 3 months and has been sent to Alathom for repairs. The brick buildings housing these transformers were completely destroyed and a steel door thrown 25 metres'. SOE's technical experts guessed that these could result in a complete shut-down for two months.

Ree never re-entered the factory but continued to coordinate operations from outside. On 25 November, after a large and enjoyable Sunday lunch, he arrived at 4.15 p.m.

at the house of one of his contacts, a young schoolmaster. The door was opened by a stranger in civilian clothes, who held him up with a pistol. Ree thought this was a joke, a hot-blooded resistant pretending to be a gangster, so he told the man to put the gun down. But it soon became clear that he was a Feldgendarme, and that Ree was under arrest.

He followed me all the time with his revolver. For 10 minutes I talked with him, and found out that the proprietor, who I had come to see, had been arrested after a search in which a sten and some grenades had been found: that the house was empty; that the mother and sister had been arrested, and that I was also to be taken for an interrogation at about 6 o'clock. Since I knew that they were looking for a certain Henri, a tall, fair Englishman, in that region, and since I had 50,000 francs on me, I decided not to risk the interrogation, and, after having lit a pipe, and poured out a drink for both of us, I knocked him on the head with a bottle. The blow did not have much result – he emptied his pistol – 6 shots. I think that four hit me, but I believe they were blanks, because they did not injure me.

In a later interview Ree gave further details. 'He was wearing a hat. I didn't hit him anything like hard enough. It was stupid . . . we had a real fight. He pushes me downstairs into a cellar. I pushed back up. He got my head in one of those grips, a sort of half Nelson. I told myself "If you're ever going to see your daughter you've got to get out of this one".' Ree now resorted to one of the tactics he had learnt in unarmed combat. 'I put my hands right back and pushed them up into his stomach and he let go . . . He fell back against the wall and said "*sortez, sortez*". I didn't ask twice.' Ree was too weak to take his bicycle but remembered that the schoolmaster had told him that, if he ever needed to get away, there was a way out at the back straight across the fields to a river. He stumbled across the fields, now soaking wet, and put his hand inside his clothes to see whether the rain had soaked through. It came out covered in blood – the bullets hadn't all been blanks after all.

He swam across the river and reached a village where the grandmother of some friends was living. Knowing that they sometimes went there for Sunday lunch, he went to her little villa and knocked on the door. It was opened by the son, who, horrified at the bloodstained, bedraggled figure appearing on his doorstep on a Sunday evening, quickly beckoned Ree in and put him to bed. A doctor arrived and told Ree, 'yes there is a bullet hole which goes in just above your heart and comes out on the other side and the lung might be affected'.

He was told he had to get to a hospital in Switzerland within a week. Three nights later a group of resistants arrived to take him across the frontier. Once again he gave himself up to the Swiss and was able to contact the embassy, which arranged for him to stay in hospital for a fortnight and then go on to a quiet little skiing hotel above Interlaken where he wouldn't be troubled by the police. Here he stayed from December until May, keeping in touch with his circuit in Montbéliard and passing on to SOE the extraordinary story of continuing sabotage at the Peugeot works.

An armed watch had been placed on all key machinery and SS guards posted at the factory entrances. A poster issued at the Sochaux works reads: 'At any request from the Waffen SS packets must be opened and pockets emptied and turned out.' The RAF's demand for evidence was met in the greatest detail. A boring machine was put out of action for three months and as it was a German one it could not be replaced. A group of Turrot lathes were put out of use for three weeks by a magnetic mine placed inside the gears. These had to be sent back to Germany for repair and in the meantime efforts to find substitutes were unsuccessful. In

March 1944 magnetic mines were placed in the gears of two rectifying machines that had been brought from Germany and were in the process of being set up. A set of lathes that had just arrived from Germany and were standing in the factory yard were destroyed. Further sabotage was carried out on replacements and parts arriving from Germany. A consignment of springs for tanks, which left Germany sealed up, arrived at the factory with the seals broken and most of the contents missing.

Two engineers were in command, and they detailed workmen to carry out each individual job. There was also a team of mechanics who were constantly on the lookout for suitable machines to attack. When these were identified, the team leader took the necessary material from a stock of plastic mines and explosives stored in the factory. After the work had been done a report of the damage was sent. In January 1944, one of the engineers had smuggled 40 kilos of material, plastic explosive and mines, into the factory.

Only the main transformers remained impossible to attack. They were very heavily guarded by twenty Germans. It was decided that the potential loss of life among the attackers would be too great. They would have to force an entry and fight with men armed with heavy machine guns.

Not all sabotage attempts were successful, of course. Ree describes how his group had penetrated a depot containing a hundred new Buicks, about to be converted into army cars. Trails of phosphorus (pinched from the Germans) were laid, linking all the cars to huge piles of cushions by the door, in which two hefty incendiary parcels were laid. 'We only had one box of 12 hour pencils left. We had pressed them 9 hours before. On examination, 3 out of 5 had gone off. We attached the remaining two, taking out safety pins, and retired. They never went off.'

In May the embassy arranged for Ree to go back to England through Spain. 'It was a luxury tour,' he said, 'driven down from Geneva by a journalist to Marseilles. Accompanied from Marseilles by a Frenchman up to Bayonne. Handed over to a pub keeper.' In Spain, after a month in a hotel in Pamplona, he was sent on like so many SOE agents for a spell in the notorious 'concentration' camp at Miranda. 'By this time, at least if you were British, conditions had improved ... the Vichy consul in town would meet us at the gate of the camp every day and we would hand him a list of things we wanted like chickens and sausages. We cooked them ourselves, in fact we hired a French cook and really lived very pleasantly for a month.'

In Pamplona he had the intriguing experience of hearing the Berlin Philharmonic on a propaganda tour playing in the local cinema on D-Day. 'They didn't play very well. There were very few people in the audience and I nearly felt like going forward and introducing myself,' he says with a laugh.

Ree left Spain via Gibraltar, returning to London. Soon after France was liberated he was back at Montbéliard, having a celebration lunch at the Peugeot offices with his original contact. 'He said would you be interested in the V2 rockets. He said a friend of ours has been up to Peenemunde where they're made and he's come back with some drawings of them which he obviously wasn't supposed to bring and we wondered if you'd like to get them through to the British. I said of course.' Ree took the drawings to his contact in Berne and was told to take them upstairs to the intelligence services, where he was informed politely: '. . . if you wouldn't mind keeping out of this sort of business in the future'.

Ree's operations had spared Montbéliard from bombing and avoided many civilian deaths. The human cost was nonetheless harrowing among the families who worked with the Resistance. He had often stayed with the Barbier family, and it was to their house that his replacement, the American lieutenant Paul Ullmann (Alceste), was taken after he arrived in France on 14 April 1944. By a tragic co-incidence the Gestapo came to the house asking after one of the sons the very morning Ullmann arrived. Everything might have been all right had Ullmann not taken fright and attempted to escape by the back door. He was seen by one of the Gestapo and shot while trying to climb over the wall. He was killed instantaneously. As a result the whole Barbier family, consisting of the father, his wife and their daughter, a schoolteacher, were rounded up and imprisoned, though the daughter was released two or three days later.

The Mathis family, who ran a café in Monmorot, a suburb of Lons-le-Saunier, had looked after Ree on his arrival in France. They had been compromised and the Gestapo smashed up the café completely. The Malnatte family, who ran the Café Grangier in Sochaux, suffered a worse fate. The wife and two daughters were arrested by the Gestapo and though Malnatte himself escaped he was later recaptured. The Gruet family at Besançon, with whom Ree had stayed, were betrayed and arrested by the Gestapo. The same happened to the Clerc family, wine merchants at St-Amour. One of the sons escaped but the father was taken in his place.

Ree's greatest anxieties were for the Fouillettes. After his arrest Roger Fouillette had been brought back home from prison in Dijon by the Gestapo. The children were told to leave the room. Mme Fouillette was told that her husband could remain if she did one simple thing. 'You'll make an arrangement with the Englishman Captain Henri to meet him at a café and at the same time tell us of the arrange-ment. Then we will return your husband to you.' She had turned anxiously to her husband and he had said stoically, 'Follow your conscience.'

She then told the Gestapo: 'I did know him . . . but I have heard he's escaped, lost his nerve, gone to Switzerland.' This brought no respite. Her husband was taken to Buchenwald. Ree went to visit the family, now wearing battledress. When the door opened the elder daughter, now fifteen, exclaimed, 'Papa,' thinking her father had returned. Never had Ree so fervently wished he was someone else. Four weeks later, back in England, he received a letter. 'My dear Henri, I am alive. I am at home.'

Chapter 9

GUIDO ZEMBSCH-SCHREVE – BETRAYAL AND ESCAPE

I found Guido living in a quiet leafy suburb of Brussels. Even at the age of eighty-four, bowed by brutal treatment in German concentration camps, he was still self-evidently wiry and well built, retaining a strong trace of youthful good looks and alert bright blue eyes. He treasured his wartime memories and had fitted up his attic with mementoes, including his commando dagger. He clearly loved to tell his story, and had written his own book, *Pierre Lalande*, as well as compiling a 300-page album filling out the story. More than any other agent I met he appeared made for the double life, for interweaving truth with fiction or bluff.

Agents, like other people, have sometimes altered their stories to make them crisper in the telling. This is often a case of simplifying, of dispensing with complexities, rather than embroidering. With Guido, while much of his story is well attested in other sources, there are parts which puzzlingly are not. His SOE PF tells a different story in places from that in his book. But in many ways it is a better story, revealing still more of his cunning and ability to survive. Much of it emerges in two debriefings on his return to England carried out on 30 May and 1 June 1945. Even here certain details differ, as indeed they might if any of us were struggling to tell a complicated story running over many months to a stranger in a consistent and comprehensive manner. And in Guido's case, for all his natural ebullience and belief in himself, there was the added dimension of physical and mental trauma and exhaustion, of bouts of brutal treatment and near-starvation.

Sitting in his living room over coffee and later a delicious cold lunch, Guido told me the story of his life. 'I was a spoiled brat. I was born in 1916 in Berne when my father was fifty and had already retired to Switzerland. We had an English nurse, a German-speaking gardener and two girls in the kitchen from the Ticino, the Italian-speaking part of Switzerland. At school the lessons were in French, at home we spoke Dutch, so I grew up speaking five languages.'

As Switzerland has no official school age, the precocious Guido told me he was sent off to school with his older sister aged four, and as a result graduated from high school aged sixteen. His first job was at the Comptoir Maritime in Antwerp. He then moved to London to work for his uncle Philip van Ommeren in a Pall Mall shipping office. Soon Guido was driving round in a beautiful green MG. 'In the low seats girlfriends always got runs in their stockings so I kept a supply in the glove compartment,' he said.

In 1936 he seized an opportunity to go to America to work for the Holland-Amerika Line in New York, Boston and Philadelphia. By August 1939 he was back in Belgium with the latest Chevrolet. 'I could not be called up as I had been born in Switzerland and saw no useful purpose in donning a uniform,' he told me. Two events, still vividly engraved in his memory, changed his mind. Holland-Amerika had put him in charge of the passenger office in Antwerp to help handle the growing wave of Jewish refugees seeking passages to America. 'When the invasion began there was panic. We crammed 2,800 into a ship made for 800, but when the gangways were drawn up desperate people jumped off the quay and were crushed or drowned.'

He left Belgium on 17 May 1940 after the invasion and headed for Paris, where he registered with the Royal Netherlands Army. He told me: 'From the British I obtained enough petrol for two thousand miles. Outside Noyon, when there were only refugees left on the road, Stukas attacked, wantonly machine-gunning defenceless old people, children and farm animals. Raising my head from the ditch, I saw what total war could do to civilians. At that moment I told myself, "You are the only one in the family who can do something. You have to fight steel with steel."'

He recalled that when his father, a very successful doctor, had heard Hitler's first broadcasts on the radio he had said tersely, 'The man's mad'. Aged just twenty-eight, Dr Schreve had been placed in charge of five Rotterdam hospitals. There he had taken a special interest in mental patients, ending the cruel practice of exhibiting them in cages on Sundays to raise funds for the hospital.

Guido reached Marseilles in the Chevy, where the American vice-consul, Miles Standish, gave him papers according him American status, and allowing him to drive into Spain and on to Lisbon. He arrived practically penniless, but again his luck held. 'The Dutch consul gave me just enough money to send two telegrams to the States, one to my sister-in-law's father, who was president of Shell in America.'

To Guido's astonishment a large limousine drove up a few hours later at his drab little hotel in Lisbon and took him straight to the Palace Hotel in the fashionable coastal resort of Estoril. Then followed an incident he still could not fully comprehend. 'The Portuguese director of Shell invited me for a game of bridge at the casino. I played a fair hand but had no idea of the value of the stake. Though I changed tables three times I won steadily all through the evening and suddenly found myself with enough money to pay not only for my stay in Estoril but the fare for both me and my car to the States. When I arrived in New York I still had five hundred dollars in my pocket.'

Soon after this he re-enrolled in the Royal Dutch Brigade in Ontario, Canada, and arrived in Liverpool in October 1941. In England, he said, he was offered a place at the Officer Training School in Camberley. 'I flatly refused. There were already 211 officers in the brigade and I told the general I had not come all that way to sit on my arse till I could enter my country again waving a little flag.'

Ordered to Carlisle, Guido found himself entering a military detention camp. He was a little happier when he was given the uniform of the Pioneer Corps and sent on, twenty-four hours later, to join the Lovat Scouts (forerunners of the Commandos) at Thurso. Here he embarked on arduous training for a raid on Norway. When this was abandoned he was enrolled with No. 12 Commando and given street-fighting training in the bombed-out streets of Gourock, near Glasgow.

Guido was seconded to SOE as a corporal in the Commandos by the Royal Netherlands Army in April 1943. At this stage he was destined to become an agent in Holland, working for the Dutch section. He was sent first, on 3 March 1943, to Special Training School (STS) 3, at Stodham Park, Liss, in Hampshire, for basic operational training. Here Sergeant Mendes assessed him as 'Intelligent and very determined. Would be a good leader, only he spoils things by a certain affectedness in mannerism and by showing off too much his physical qualifications.' A week later the comments were as follows: 'Natural security mindedness . . . Very good organizing ability, though he tends to put his knowledge over to others in a way which causes them annoyance. He disregards the consideration whether other people approve his actions or not, provided he has satisfied himself that they are the right ones. Temperate habits, perfect emotional stability and mental alertness.' SOE rated Guido as trilingual 'Dutch English French 100% German 75% Spanish 50%'.

By now it was apparent that Guido 'is not suitable to be a leader of his fellow countrymen'. A memo of 26 May 1943 reads: 'I had a special word with this man on the possibility of his being employed in France. He liked the idea and, in fact, said that he would prefer it as he feels more at home in France than in Holland.'

He now came to the attention of L.A.L. Humphreys, who ran SOE's DF Section, which organised escape lines. Guido's training was adjusted accordingly, especially the ninety-six-hour scheme, under which agents had to carry out a clandestine mission in a British City. Guido went to Liverpool. According to a memo of 27 May 1943, he was sent here 'to look into the possibilities of organising the escape of prisoners of war to Ireland'.

Guido tells a rattling tale.

I was sent to Liverpool to find out about a young woman teacher suspected of helping people – such as escaped prisoners of war – to cross illicitly to the Republic of Ireland. I had only her description and the name of a pub she went to.

I found a bed and breakfast and started visiting the pub and making friends, never a great problem for me, and made it known in the greatest secrecy that I was an escaped German prisoner who had been able to don the Pioneers uniform and that I wanted to get out.

He was introduced to Fiona, a beautiful, sweet girl with black hair and blue eyes. 'I have to say I used every method of luring her into my net,' he recalls. Guido moved to the flat below hers, though he never had to sleep there, enjoying nights of passion on the floor above.

'Two days before I had to return to London she told me I would be met at my digs and was to board a ship that would take me to Cork.' Making sure he was not followed, Guido found a telephone box and rang the emergency number he had been given in London. 'In civilian clothes with a duffel bag on my shoulder I was taken to Birkenhead Pier where on the point of boarding we were arrested by a swarm of plainclothes police.'

Back at the police headquarters in Liverpool, he was confronted with Fiona and the barman. Guido's handcuffs were removed. 'As soon as Fiona realised the truth, she spat at me. I know I deserved it and, do believe me, I'm not proud of what I did.' Why did the police take the handcuffs off in front of Fiona? 'To break their spirit,' he told me. Fiona and her companions spent the rest of the war in a detention camp on the Isle of Man.

Guido was dropped near Fontainebleau on the night of 23/24 July 1943 with his wireless operator, Claude Planel (known as John Cornet and Baseball). 'I had chosen the one who spoke the best French – he had been born in Mauritius and looked like a Mediterranean boy. We boarded a Halifax which crossed the Channel with a bombing formation and then peeled off to fly at three hundred metres across France below German radar.'

He continues: 'The hull opened up to drop packages and pamphlets and we were allowed to sit with our feet dangling out of the hold. It was a wonderful sight to see the glitter of the Loire in the moonlight.'

They were dropped in the wrong place and came down in a stubble field, but the packages containing their wireless sets and clothing landed in standing corn and could not be seen. 'There was only one option, to seek help from the farm near by. I climbed over the gate so silently that even the dogs did not hear, and threw pebbles at a first-floor window where there was a light. The farmer came down, followed by his wife, who was obviously expecting a baby. I told them I was a parachuted agent needing help.'

According to Claude: 'the farmer was scared as there was a company of German soldiers in the chateau near the farm, but he finally agreed, after much persuasion, to try and find the two packages, and to keep them until one of the others returned to collect them'. Guido and Claude spent the rest of the night in the woods, and the next day, said Claude, set off to Paris, 'hitch-hiking part of the way and travelling the rest of the way by bus'.

Guido relates that, having no success in stopping a vehicle, he finally stood out in the road and flagged down the next car, which turned out to be a small open Mercedes carrying two German airmen. 'My German was put to use. I chatted about the beauties of Munich and they gave us chocolate as we swept through a series of German control points.'

Guido's contact in Paris was a senior official in Gaz de Paris, Edmond Duquesne (alias Doris). When they arrived at his house they gave the password but found their host still suspicious. It later transpired that he had expected them two months earlier, and the password or catchphrase contained the name of a cousin who had been in difficulties with the Gestapo. Guido won Duquesne's confidence by giving details of contacts in Marseilles which London had provided him with.

That night Guido was driven back to the farm in a Gaz de Paris van by Jean Lesech (Lucien), whom he describes as a fiercely anti-German Breton. The farmer had found one package and hidden it under freshly cut corn. Guido found the other just 25 metres away and also retrieved the revolvers. 'They gave the farmer ten thousand francs to keep his mouth shut,' added Claude.

Soon Gaz de Paris vans (which could pass freely through security checks) were whisking radios and other clandestine material across Paris, and Guido had a set of papers in the name of André Lavigne, a representative of Gaz de Paris canteen management. He also obtained the necessary *Ausweis*, complete with German stamps, allowing him to go to Annecy, his staging post for Switzerland, to negotiate the canteen's meat and cheese allocation.

This enabled Guido to pursue the second part of his mission, which was to establish a means of exfiltrating quantities of precision instruments from Switzerland, including, he said, special crystals made in Zeiss factories in Germany, near Erfurt, which were needed for Allied wireless sets. He explained to me the delicious irony by which 'these goods went concealed in German transport to Hispano-Suiza in Spain'. When they arrived in Barcelona, agents at the factory surreptitiously removed the packages for onward transport, via Gibraltar or Lisbon, to Britain. The service from Switzerland was fortnightly, and Guido also used it to send messages to England. Guido told SOE: 'All couriers carried their goods uncamouflaged, but took the usual precaution of having two suitcases – one of them innocent – and were instructed entirely to disown the incriminating case in an emergency.' No trouble was ever experienced by any of the couriers. According to Planel this line was also used to smuggle in W/T sets from Switzerland, many of which were hidden in Planel's apartment before they were distributed.

In Switzerland Guido was also sent by Humphreys to verify the identity of two agents, Ubbink and Dourlein, who had escaped from Holland with first-hand confirmation that the Germans had completely penetrated SOE's Dutch network and were arresting agents as they landed and then playing back their radios. This was the infamous *Englandspiel*, or English Game, which left SOE convinced that its Dutch circuits were flourishing. Even when Ubbink and Dourlein appeared to be telling the grim truth they remained under suspicion, and Guido, as one of Humphreys' stars, was sent to Berne to make quite sure they were who they claimed to be. But by the time he arrived he found that their evident sincerity had already cleared them.

Duquesne also put Guido in touch with the remarkable Abbé Henri Jeglot (code name Hector) of the Eglise de la Trinité, who, though initially guarded, was convinced of Guido's veracity when the BBC broadcast his own chosen message, 'the Breton Abbé has grey slippers'. Moving in smart society, as well as running an adoption society, the Oeuvre de l'Adoption, the abbé had perfect cover for every kind of contact and was also exempt from the curfew.

A Frenchwoman who rendered courageous service was Suzanne Budelot (alias Simone), secretary to the Board of SNCF (French Railways), who not only provided a safe house for agents in transit but procured train tickets, saving Guido from standing in long queues at stations where he might have been observed by security police.

The abbé, and other priests whom he recruited to help on the escape line, took great risks on Guido's behalf. In October 1945, General Gubbins, head of SOE, recommended the abbé for the King's Medal for Service in the Cause of Freedom, citing 'his determination to do all in his power to assist our organisation and his complete disregard for his own personal safety'. This may have been upgraded to the King's Medal for Courage – the abbé's brief SOE PF is not clear.

The abbé, said Gubbins, had made his church, his house and his office available as a rendezvous for agents, storing secret wireless equipment and funds and extending hospitality, material and spiritual. 'At all times he met every request for aid and took every risk that might be of assistance to the work of the circuit. After the arrest of the organiser, the Abbé continued to give all possible help' to preserve the circuit, 'pending the arrival of a new organiser'.

Both Guido and Claude were highly security conscious. At first they stayed with Duquesne, but early in September Claude moved to Pierrefitte to live with a butcher, Picotin, who had been recruited as his bodyguard. Here he was introduced to the Tettare family, who lived at Ecouen, and made his first transmission from their house. His identity card, supplied by London, had been made out in the name of Jean-Jacques Cornet, unfortunately with the address of a hotel that had been requisitioned by the Germans. Through Mazure, a friendly police inspector, he obtained a fresh identity card with a genuine address. The owner of the house given on the new card was an elderly artist who knew he was a British agent. She had agreed an elaborate story by which she would say, if questioned, that Claude had lived with her for two years as her gigolo, but that the liaison was now over and he was ill and in the country. She did not know his real address but could contact him through a friend of Picotin. He could also warn her by the same means if he was in trouble.

When Claude stayed with the Tettare family he carried a

fake medical certificate stating he had been examined by X-ray and that '*malgré sa bonne mine*' he had TB. The family thought he was *réfractaire* using devious means to avoid Marshal Pétains's call for workers to go to Germany, except for the eldest daughter, who knew what he was doing. When he was with Picotin he also used his medical certificate to show that he was unfit for work in Germany. He would also dress as a butcher, while with Duquesne he played the part of a bourgeois.

At one time Claude had no less than five houses to transmit from. One belonged to an invalid, Mlle Bichoffe, whose nurse was very suspicious of him, so he went there only at weekends when she was away. For a while he also used a villa at Montmorency requisitioned by the Germans but left empty. A friend of his was caretaker there, and he would accompany him dressed in workman's clothes as if he were going to carry out repairs. He also fitted up a mobile transmitting set in the gas company van driven by Lesech and broadcast from the country.

Shortly before Guido's arrest Claude obtained a genuine *carte de travail* through Duquesne as an employee in the gas company. He did this by signing up to work as a manual labourer, then leaving after a week, sending the manager a medical certificate saying he was unfit and required rest. Claude usually travelled with Picotin, using the cover of buying meat for the shop. In the Métro, Picotin 'acted as scout and went on ahead to look for controls'. This enabled Claude to turn back before he was seen by the police carrying out the control. Claude's radio sets had been damaged by damp, but through Duquesne he had been introduced to a radio engineer named Millard (Robert), who repaired the sets. Picotin was paid 3,000 francs a month for services and accommodation, while

Claude paid the Tettare family 4,000 francs a month for his accommodation.

Guido decided to divide his escape route into three stages Lille–Paris, Paris–Perpignan and Perpignan–Spain. The southern part was handled by a Dane, Thorkil Hansen. Guido's system, following Humphreys' intense concern for security, was to set up a reception house, a safe house and an HQ in each town. The agent was taken to the reception house by the guide, who did not know the other two locations. The HQ would then arrange for a new guide to take the agent on to the safe house, chosen because it provided a secure refuge for quite a lengthy stay if necessary. A new guide would then take the agent on to the next town – by this means no guide ever knew more than one section of the escape route. The people in Lille would be advised by London of the agent's description and password and would pick him up on the Belgian side of the frontier.

Many of the recruits came via Jeglot, who often acted as a cut-out so the recruits would not know Guido's identity. When meeting strangers, Guido used passwords and descriptions and occasionally a special sign, usually a particular object held in his hand. Guido told SOE he paid all the people involved with the route in cash or in kind, depending on their social position. Couriers were paid a small retaining fee and a further sum per job. Jeglot refused all remuneration. Anyone with dependants was promised that they would receive an allowance if he or she was captured or had to go into hiding. Money for the organisation was brought in by courier from Spain.

With the help of local parish priests, Guido set up two escape lines over the Pyrenees. The first, the Basque Abbé Usaurgu, said Guido, was horrified at the smuggler London had suggested as a guide, saying he was convinced the man had robbed and murdered several of his charges on the way. Instead both priests arranged their own *passeurs*, who were to be paid only on return, on production of an object, different each time, given them by the SOE receiving agent in Spain.

In December 1943 Guido received instructions by radio to deliver a spare transmitting set to the Tao Bar in the rue Gaillon. To cover himself, when he met his contact he carefully expressed ignorance of what he was delivering but was promptly told it was a wireless transmission set. Guido expressed surprise, saying he would never have brought it if he had realised what it was. His contact nonetheless went on to tell him that he was able to obtain false papers, particularly for Belgium, which he visited regularly.

By the beginning of March 1944 Guido was preparing to extend his line to Belgium, and needed to go there. The Belgian identity papers he had requested from London had not arrived and so he decided to try to obtain them from the man at the Tao Bar. He made contact on 17 March and arranged to collect the papers three days later at the bar. He left his apartment at 2.30 p.m. and went to collect his train ticket from the head office of SNCF – as arranged by Mlle Budelot.

The Tao Bar in rue Gaillon, he says, was 'a place with cosy corners to go with a mistress'. He had hardly arrived when a hostess sitting at the bar whispered, 'Take care, it's a trap.' Swiftly he pressed his apartment keys into her hand. The contact arrived and handed over his new false papers, insisting that he should fill in his address as 32 rue de Souveraine. Later Guido concluded this was a trick, making it easier to pick him up when he presented his papers at the border. Within moments of his leaving the café, four men sprang from a waiting car and pushed him into a doorway.

One was a Frenchman and three were Germans. He was immediately taken by car to the Avenue Foch, the SD headquarters used for the interrogation of British and French secret agents. On the way Guido overheard in German mention of the man from the Tao Bar, presumably coming to identify him.

On arrival Guido was taken to the top floor and subjected to an informal interrogation by the Frenchman. They had taken his still-blank Belgian identity card and his forged SOE French identity card as well as the 38,800 francs he was carrying. Fortunately there was nothing else to compromise him.

Guido was then taken to a neighbouring room and interrogated by a German in civilian clothes. He immediately accused Guido of being a British agent and of delivering a radio set to the Tao Bar. Guido concocted the following story. He said that his French identity papers were false, that his real name was André Berard (a friend whose details he knew well but who had been born abroad so his birth certificate was not obtainable). He gave his own birth date of 17 May 1916.

He said that he had become involved in the black market through a man called Jean Bart. Bart, he said, was an escaped French prisoner of war sending contraband from Switzerland to Paris. Later Guido added that he had learnt that cigarettes could be obtained more cheaply in Courtrai than in France and decided to go to Belgium to acquire some.

When he had left his apartment for the Tao Bar a sixth sense had prompted Guido to take his original false identity card supplied by SOE, not his current one which gave his address. As a result the Gestapo never came to search the premises. When Guido failed to attend a rendezvous the next day Claude found 'everything in perfect order except that Pierre's hat and coat were gone'. They quickly removed all incriminating papers and assumed that Guido had been arrested in one of a series of recent round-ups.

Guido was next taken to the notorious prison of Fresnes, near Paris, and lodged in cell no. 253. Here he was further interrogated, mainly about Bart, and at one point his clothes were cleaned prior to a possible trip to Lyons.

Guido could only see one slip in his story. The rail ticket he had obtained from SNCF had been for the following day, whereas normal tickets had to be obtained from the Gare du Nord and booked at least eight days in advance. Fortunately this point was not picked up – it would have put Mlle Budelot severely at risk, and Guido was not sure how she would have stood up to interrogation. As to the money, no questions had been asked at all, though 800 francs had been returned. He presumed the rest had simply been pocketed by his captors and conveniently forgotten.

During his interrogation he had managed to steal a pencil. He then obtained some scraps of paper from a man in the neighbouring cell – they were able to communicate via the water pipes and air vents. He now wrote a message in code explaining his position, the reason for his arrest and giving the name of the person who had denounced him. Unfortunately the pencil was discovered, leading to a thorough search of his cell, during which his message was also found with other scraps of paper. They were placed on the table in the cell and, while the search continued, Guido edged towards them, grabbed the coded message he had written and swallowed it. As soon as his captors realised what had happened he was severely beaten and given twenty-one days' solitary confinement on half bread and water rations. He was also subject to the *baignoire*, or bathtub treatment, repeatedly held under water till his lungs were bursting. 'I dropped to forty-three kilos,' he said.

To take his mind off the repeated interrogations and beatings, Guido told me, he occupied himself by training fleas. 'They are amazing creatures, and very quickly realise where you are trying to get them to jump.'

He now told his captors that he had informed the man in the cell above him (who had since departed) that he was going to Lyons, and the man had asked him to deliver a message in code which he had passed down the air vent written on scraps of papers. Guido said he had transcribed the message on to one sheet – this explained why it was in his own hand – and put the original slips down the toilet. He had swallowed it because he was confused and frightened. The letter was to be left at a certain place in the toilet in the station. If this was impossible he was to contact the Librairie Fueri in the rue Paradise in Marseilles, where he was told to ask for a book on genealogy by a Dr Morand. He was never questioned about this address and the Germans now appeared to have got bored and left him alone. Though there are numerous small contradictions in the two versions Guido gave, his ability to weave a story impressed his British debriefers too. 'My own opinion is that possibly the first part of Pierre's [Guido's] story owes something to his fertile imagination, but is probably genuine in substance. The second part of his story after his evacuation from Fresnes is so substantial and is coupled with so much documentary evidence that it is almost certainly completely true and anyhow can be easily checked.'

On 15 August, barely a week before the liberation of Paris, Guido and his fellow prisoners were evacuated from their cells at 8 a.m. and taken to the Gare Pantin in trucks, leaving the station late that afternoon in cattle wagons, seventy to each wagon. The guards were not SS troops but thought to be Feldengendarmerie officers from a training school. At the beginning of the trip the guards had asked for German speakers, and Guido had been chosen to be responsible for his wagon and told that ten would be shot for each one that escaped. Escape, he told SOE, would have been easy, but he was afraid of the reprisals. Later he considered 'it would have been much better if he had escaped since they probably all died a lingering death anyhow'. He added that miraculously the French Red Cross fed them on the way.

His party arrived at Buchenwald concentration camp on 20 August and were driven in by guards and dogs. He was 'bitten by the dogs and showed me the scars which still remain on his legs,' wrote the SOE debriefing officer.

Guido entered the camp with the number 77249 under the name André Berard. There were no sleeping quarters. They were given only rags to wear and no shoes. On 23 August Buchenwald was bombarded and they were put to work clearing up.

On 3 September the whole of his convoy was sent on to Dora, a notorious slave labour factory concealed in caves beneath a mountain where prisoners worked, assembling V2 rockets beyond the reach of Allied bombs. On arrival they passed through the registration office. As it was lunchtime the SS themselves were working instead of the usual prisoners. They asked for all those who spoke German. Guido promptly stated that he spoke seven languages and his name was noted for future office work.

At Dora Guido was put on pick-and-shovel work from 4.30 in the morning until six and sometimes eight in the evening. He recalls grimly: 'At Dora twenty-three thousand men lost their lives in twenty-eight months – the dust from digging the tunnels was so intense that it ate away your lungs within six to nine weeks.' In this ghastly charnel house groups of prisoners were hung every day for the smallest infringement. 'Even so the prisoners managed to ensure that half the rockets produced could never fly,' he says.

On Werner von Braun, the German rocket engineer later spirited to America to help develop the American rocket programme, Guido has no doubts. He told me: 'He definitely was a war criminal. I have seen him in the tunnel laughing when prisoners were hanged because of suspected sabotage and I have seen him walk past the heaps of dead bodies gathered every day at the entrance.' Conditions were particularly bad because slave workers were overseen by criminals, all serving long sentences. They 'were completely brutalised', said Guido.

When sheer exhaustion brought him to the point of complete breakdown, a fellow prisoner secured Guido's transfer to the registration department, reminding the authorities that his languages would be useful. According to a report on Guido's personal file, 'the privileges pertaining to this kind of office work were considerable, since the Germans did not like to be surrounded by the miserable creatures [in the state] to which they had reduced the ordinary inmates of the prison'. The hair of these 'trusties' was not clipped and Red Cross parcels that the Germans had stolen were left around, so the prisoners could surreptitiously take food.

As the advancing Russians drew close, Dora was evacuated on 6 April 1945, leaving only eight doctors and 125 invalids in the hospital in an attempt to cast a veil over the brutality that had reigned. Now Guido and his companions travelled in open wagons, 120 packed standing in each wagon. Over three days they were given only half a tin of meat to eat. At Osterode they were evicted from the train and forced to leave what little food or drink they had secreted. Then they were force marched 38 kilometres over the Hartz mountains to Oker. Only the strongest survived the fourteen-hour ordeal. At Oker they were put on another train and taken from camp to camp, searching for a place willing to receive them. After nine days they arrived at Ravensbruck, finally to be given food by the Swedish Red Cross, which had established itself at the gates of the camp. Those with sufficient strength were promptly set to work until Ravensbruck too was evacuated on 26 April.

Guido was now ordered to set off on a forced march to Malchow. On the night on 27/28 April he and five others managed to slip out of the barn in which they were sleeping and climb into the loft above. They waited until the other prisoners had left and then set off eight hours later on the same road. When they met yet another convoy from Ravensbruck they told the officials that they were admin staff, trying to catch up with their party. Here, four men managed to join him from the second convoy. In Steuer, Guido picked up two American POWs, Russell Kay of Dunbar, West Virginia, and Apolinas Jaramillo of Barstow, Texas.

In one abandoned farm they found an ancient road map of the north of Germany dated 1908. Near the village of Vietzen they came to a large lake and found a farm and manor house – he called it a chateau – which at first sight appeared abandoned. They installed themselves in the farm buildings. Then Guido decided to explore the main house. The shutters were closed but a first-floor window was open, and he thought he saw a figure looking at him.

A double staircase led up to the front door. He ascended and knocked. 'The door opened and a woman with grey hair, aristocratic in stature, stood before me. A young girl and two ancient retainers stood behind. I said they had nothing to fear. I was an escaped English officer with fellow prisoners of war seeking to reach Allied lines. We sought only a lodging for the night.'

Having seen the starved appearance of some of his companions, the woman was afraid they might torch the house. He was invited into the salon. The shutters were opened. By now his comrades were asleep or settled into the barn. He sat down to a frugal meal. The retreating Germans had taken almost all there was to eat, but two bottles of wine were produced. The family's main residence had been in Berlin, but they had last been there in 1936 when the woman's son had been taken by the Gestapo. She had never seen him again.

Guido slept once more in a real bed. Early the next morning the baronne and her granddaughter produced some of the clothes she has hoped her husband and son would one day return to wear. A dozen pairs of shoes and boots appeared, 'so the Russians won't have them'.

As the party continued along the lake they became merged in an ever growing stream of refugees fleeing in advance of the Russians. At four in the afternoon 'the news spread like a forest fire. Hitler and Eva Braun were dead. Admiral Dönitz had assumed power. Not a mention was made of other leading Nazis. We were jubilant . . . People were stupefied. Women were in tears. For us the question was simple. Who would arrive here first – the Americans or the Russians.'

On 4 May they reached the River Elbe but the Russians would not let them cross to the American side, even though they could see soldiers in American uniform on the far bank. Then, at Schnackenburg, they met their first Americans, who had crossed the river to exchange cigarettes and chocolate for vodka. While at Dora, Guido had secretly made himself a Dutch army badge, and he now approached a

Russian officer who he said spoke English with a very Oxford accent for permission to cross the river with his party. Guido was allowed to cross with his American comrades, and after talking to a Texan colonel and pleading for his whole group he recrossed the river with more chocolate and cigarettes, having secured safe passage for all his comrades. Guido was now assigned a small Fiat truck and drove his party across northern Germany. Arriving at Hanover, he said, 'we had our first sight of a bombed-out German city. It is true we had seen Magdeburg but only from a distance and the SS would not allow us to look for long. The town had been reduced to rubble standing no higher than a man. We saw civilians emerging like rats from cellars and hastily constructed shelters . . . It was sad to see but after what we had endured we were inured and without pity . . . Minden, Osnabruck offered the same picture of desolation.'

On Guido's file is a permit dated 6 May with the 211th Field Artillery Battalion stamp stating: '2nd Lt G Shreve of Royal Netherland Army, ex POW has been screened by the RAF Police. He is proceeding to Holland in charge of the following ex-POW's (Concentration Camp)'. In his party were seven Dutch, two Belgians and one Frenchman. His harrowing time in prison behind him, Guido arrived at the Dutch border two days later, continuing across Holland to Breda. At Appeldoorn his Dutch army badge was spotted by a young girl and suddenly he was the hero of the moment – the first Dutch soldier seen in the town for five years. Guido completed his odyssey by driving his Belgian comrades and the Frenchman across the border to Brussels, a chauffeur-driven finale to weeks of travel that had begun in the most atrocious conditions imaginable.

The last word goes to Planel, his wireless operator. Guido, he says, 'just disappeared. By sheer willpower he succeeded in keeping his circuit intact. His arrest was followed by no other and it was by his line that I left Paris for Perpignan and crossed the Pyrenees'.

After the war, in Provence, Guido was reunited with the Reynauds, family friends who had helped in the war. He married their daughter Jacqueline, who had served in the Red Cross and carried out dangerous assignments for the Resistance. The citation for Guido's Légion d'honneur states: 'his silence during interrogation was exemplary, allowing the circuit which he had created to continue its activities unharmed'.

Chapter 10

DENIS RAKE – THE ADVENTURES OF A HOMOSEXUAL AGENT

One of SOE's most unlikely recruits was Denis Rake. In 1947 the film star Douglas Fairbanks Jr was chatting with friends in the bar at White's Club and mentioned his problems in finding a butler. A few days later the telephone rang. 'I think I have just the man for you,' said the caller. There was just one condition. In no circumstances was Fairbanks to ask for references. But the man was top notch. Indeed, the War Office files would vouch for it.

Fairbanks was intrigued and Mr Denis Rake presented himself at his home soon after. 'He was short and stocky and was, I'd have guessed somewhere in his middle-forties. He was a jolly type of personality with an intelligent twinkle in his eyes . . . the shortened, rounded and jovial incarnation of Jeeves.' When they had guests, Rake waited on them with quiet efficiency, but at other times he would chat with the family. His passion was for the theatre, of which he evidently had first-hand knowledge. The family were also 'intrigued with his accentless fluency in French and German, both of which he volunteered to teach to our then small daughters'.

One day Fairbanks was sorting through his post and found a letter addressed to Major Denis Rake, MC. Major, he thought? Military Cross? He promptly asked Rake whether the letter was for him. 'Oh dear, I'd hoped you wouldn't know about all that nonsense,' replied Rake.

Slowly the story came out, but Rake's health was causing him problems and he had to leave. Nearly twenty years later Rake suddenly appeared again, and this time Fairbanks lost no time in persuading him to write his story. This duly appeared in 1968 as *Rake's Progress*, an apposite title. This delightful book can now be supplemented by Rake's recently released personal file, which was hidden away on a supplementary list at the end of the main index of SOE personal files. The reason appears simple. Immediately after the war he went to work as a passport officer (often a cover for intelligence work) and as a result his file was separated from the others.

Rake is also caught vividly in the famous 1969 film documentary by Marcel Ophuls on the Resistance, *Le Chagrin et la Pitié* (*The Sorrow and the Pity*). He appears as soft-spoken, charming man with a round face, grey hair and a button nose, as well as an engaging smile and affecting charm and directness. The film also picks out Rake's other great trait, his homosexuality. Rake explains: 'it's true that deep down inside I wanted to prove I was just as brave as my friends . . . And as a homosexual it was one of my great fears that I'd lack the courage for such things'.

Rake had two obvious qualifications for SOE, his French and his training in radio work. Maurice Buckmaster, the head of SOE's French section, was in desperate need of radio operators. Though the alarm signals repeatedly rang during Rake's training, and many thought he was quite unsuited to the hazards of an agent's life, Buckmaster took the risk.

Rake was born in Brussels in 1901. His father was the correspondent for *The Times*, his mother a singer attached to the Opéra Monnaie, well known as a soprano and famous for her leading roles as Louise, Butterfly and Lakmé. She had no time for her little boy, and he might have gone to a home had not a family friend suggested he should join Sarazini's Circus. Rake paints a wonderful picture of circus life for a little boy – he was soon prancing about the ring as a child tumbler and climbing to the top of the human pyramid. He travelled all over Europe by train and was well fed and looked after, though even as a four-year-old he had to wash his costume every day.

This enchanted life came abruptly to an end in the summer of 1914 when war broke out while he had returned for a holiday with his mother in Belgium. With the Germans in Brussels, the young Rake found himself playing the role of the go-between immortalised in L.P. Hartley's novel. For several weeks he carried messages for a Mrs Assernacher – American by birth but married to a German – to a man called Van der Ooft on the other side of the city. Then one day he was approached by a friendly German officer who had got on the same tram. He asked whether Rake had an envelope, which Rake, without thinking, handed over. It was a tragic situation. No one had primed him to be cautious and the pair were arrested. Rake was released as it was obvious he had no idea of what was in the notes. His father was also involved in resistance work, however – a member of the escape organisation run by Nurse Edith Cavell. Like her, he was shot by the Germans. It is an interesting point whether this early encounter with resistance work, providing the young Rake with excitement and possibly trauma too, was to lead him to seek to enter the clandestine life.

Rake was now taken to London by his mother, and soon she was travelling all over the country singing to soldiers. Here he was taught English by a Portuguese diplomat, a Mr Lem, and at the end of the war went to work for Lady Aberconway, a leading suffragette who had organised a hospital for officers in her Belgravia home. Rake waited at table

and ran errands. But Lady Aberconway took a keen interest
and sent him – providentially – to the Earl's Court College
of Cable and Wireless.

Quite by chance, while passing the Albert Hall, Rake saw
that his mother was singing there. The pair reunited, she
took him back to Belgium, to Dinant in the Ardennes,
where Rake embarked on the first of the passionate friend-
ships, often with older men, that were to run through his
life. 'I was now nearly eighteen, and though I say so I was
quite good-looking and physically attractive. He was the
first person who showed me any real affection . . .' His new
friend was a high-ranking British diplomat, and Rake went
to live with him. After some months the diplomat's wife
returned and the relationship became more difficult. Rake
found a new job with the Circus Royal as an assistant to a
magician called Paulmann, a hypnotist who even exercised
his powers on wild animals.

Rake continued to see his diplomat, who one day
announced that he was being transferred to Athens and that
his wife did not want to come with him. Thrilled at the
prospect, Rake auditioned for a job with a theatre company
going to Greece. In 1920 he arrived in Athens, where he was
invited to a reception by the wife of the British ambassador,
Lady Bentinck. Rake had developed a good baritone voice
and was invited to sing, accompanied on the piano by
another guest, who he afterwards discovered was a 'prince
of a European Royal family'.

Meanwhile relations with his diplomat were rapidly de-
teriorating. Rake concluded that his friend must have fallen
for someone else – which the diplomat denied – though only
rather half-heartedly, Rake thought. At the end of the
reception the prince offered to drive Rake back to his hotel.
In the car he took his hand and said he hoped they would
meet very soon. The next morning Rake found a note

asking him to meet the prince that afternoon. 'A deep and intimate friendship quickly developed between us,' said Rake. Suddenly, for the only time in his life, he found himself living in a luxurious apartment, in Cephisia Street, flush with money and attended to by servants.

The one shadow was the prince's violent outbursts, which left Rake wounded but as much in love as ever. Rake does not say who his prince was but the indications are that he was a member of the Greek royal family. The prince was faced by national unrest in his country, where real power was wielded by a tough military prime minister who had raised the prince up only to become the agent of his fall.

Rake wrote: 'we had always tried to be the very soul of discretion, but it was not enough . . . The Prince had too many political enemies who were eager to make capital out of anything that the Prince might do that was at all out of the ordinary. In some sections of the Press I was openly referred to as the spoiled English favourite of royalty'. Rake was advised to leave the country and was told to go to Venice, where he took rooms at Danieli's. Soon after this the prince joined him – finally driven from his country. It was not the happy reunion Rake wished for. The quarrels and violent attacks became more frequent, and one day he simply packed his bags and left. Back in London his mother gave him an introduction that led to a small part in a touring musical comedy, *Suzanne*. For the next fifteen years Rake was on the stage in the West End and the provinces, and in the spring of 1939 was working with Ivor Novello at Drury Lane.

He started his wartime service as an interpreter with the BEF in France, and was one of the survivors of the troopship *Lancastria*, sunk by the Germans in 1940 after the evacuation from St-Nazaire. Rescued by HMS *Berkeley*, he was brought back to England and spent a brief time in hospital. As soon as he came out he was assigned to the French minesweeper *Pollux* to act as interpreter between British officers and the Free French crew. Rake's luck ran out again – the day after the first blitz of Portsmouth in July, the minesweeper hit a mine, sank and once more 'I was dragged out of the water'. Assigned to a depressing job in a shore establishment, Rake drifted down to a pub in Portsmouth one day in August, where he overhead a group of RAF pilots talking, a little carelessly he thought, about a call for volunteers to parachute into occupied France. Rake was intrigued, obtained a forty-eight-hour leave pass and went to London to look up a friend, Burnett-Brown, who knew influential people. Burnett-Brown presciently advised Rake strongly against the idea, but when Rake continued to insist he drafted a letter to the War Office which Rake copied and posted. A few days later he received a letter from Major Lewis Gielgud, brother of the famous actor Sir John, who was one of SOE's main recruiting officers, asking him to come to an interview. They spoke in French, and to Rake it felt like a theatrical audition and he was convinced he hadn't got the part. But soon he found himself signing the Official Secrets Act at Orchard Court, the block of flats near Portman Square used by SOE's French section. In this book Rake is often self-deprecating about his war work, joking about his unsuitability as an agent and the anxieties of his instructors. In fact many of his SOE training reports are very favourable. His first report from Wanborough runs: 'Very humorous and has personality. Always bright and cheerful . . . Very fit for his age and expresses a liking for exercise.' A week later the report added: 'very generous man and most popular with both students and staff.'

He was forty when he was arrived at the SOE training school at Wanborough in 1941. The Morse he had learnt at the college in Earl's Court came back to him at once, and in three or four days he was doing twelve to fifteen words a minute. SOE at this stage was desperate for radio operators. Thanks to his stage dancing Rake was reasonably in trim, but he flatly refused to take part in PT sessions, let alone rupturing himself, as he put it, on the parallel bars. The Coldstream Guards officer in charge of the school, Major Roger de Wesslow – 'an absolutely charming man, only thirty-eight, slim and very good-looking' – was understanding. But soon Rake was in trouble again. It had been found that he was taking sleeping pills by night and Benzedrine by day. Though the pills were kept openly by his bed he was accused of being a covert drug addict. He burst out laughing, and explained that he had been taking the pills ever since the *Lancastria* to combat insomnia.

'Well, what would happen in the field if you couldn't get them?' he was asked.

Rake replied, 'I'd have to do without them.'

'Do you think you could?' came the rejoinder.

When Rake answered 'I don't honestly know' he was told he was not suitable. He stormed out, his thoughts turning to finding a part in a musical comedy. A few hours later, he said, an emissary arrived from SOE to ask him to reconsider. He went back to Wanborough, gave up the pills and took up drinking instead. Within days a report had arrived alerting headquarters to his dangerous drinking habits.

After a spell at Grendon Underwood Wireless School Rake was sent to do paramilitary training at Arisaig. Here, he wrote: 'I refused to have anything to do with explosives, or to take part in any assault course that entailed the use of explosives; and I also refused to handle firearms.' Rake nonetheless made a favourable impression. 'The type of man who makes friends very quickly with anyone, as his pleasant manner and good humour cannot fail to please,' runs the report of 9 October 1941.

Next he went to Ringway for parachute training. Here Rake complained bitterly about the jumping suit. 'I felt like a chicken must feel ... all trussed up for the oven ... I couldn't walk properly but had to amble along like an old man with water works trouble.' Nonetheless Rake made five successful jumps from the plane at 600 feet – though each time he insisted on being pushed. When it came to a night jump from a tethered balloon, panic struck. He could not jump without the cushioning effect of the slipstream. Despite repeated appeals from his pained instructor Rake flatly refused to move and had to be ignominiously winched down. Again the SOE report from Ringway gives a rather different impression. 'One cannot help admiring this man for his courage. Although he is getting on in years he has taken part in strenuous PT to the best of his ability. Is fairly hesitant before leaving the plane, but by no means hesitant to go up and do the jump. Fit. Has the respect of all at this school.'

At the radio school at Thame Park, Rake was in trouble. He showed 'a serious lack of security mindedness' while on a one-week scheme at a farm early in February 1942. 'He spoke quite openly what his work was – what he was going to do. He talked in trains and other public places in a natural voice about his work.'

Rake was reprimanded, but a few days later another SOE radio operator was caught in Lyons and Rake was on his way. He was flown by seaplane from Plymouth to Gibraltar, where he was given a handsome room in the Rock Hotel. Here Rake began to worry about the gold propelling pencil Buckmaster had given him which he had noticed had '9 carats' stamped on it. The French, he knew, did not hallmark or assay their gold. He was now taken by armed trawler towards the French coast, transferring first to a submarine and then to a felucca. When Cannes loomed into view Rake made a fearful fuss, refusing to be landed somewhere so conspicuous and demanding to be taking to Juan-les-Pins, which meant a delay of a full twenty-four hours. The next evening he was ready, dressed in a dark blue and white pinstripe suit with genuine French labels made by a French tailor in London.

Rake landed on 14 May with Jean-Marie Emmanuel Van Haellebroucq (Yves). He went to stay with SOE's key local contact – Dr Levy, later known as Liewer. Liewer, whose name changed later to Staunton, is the agent who appears alongside Violette Szabo in the film *Carve Her name with Pride* on a mission to Normandy.

Haellebroucq went separately to his aunt's house and made the fatal mistake of telling her about his mission. She was a strong Pétainiste. Haellebroucq was promptly arrested and pressed into revealing his contacts. Rake meanwhile made his way to Lyons and made contact with SOE's Virginia Hall, an American citizen who had the excellent cover of being the accredited Vichy correspondent of the *New York Post*. Directed by her, he went to the help of Edward Zeff, the radio operator for the Spruce circuit in Lyons, who was oveloaded with work. Zeff was Georges 53 (initially all SOE radio operators were known as Georges). Rake meanwhile says he found time to live his cover as a cabaret artist, singing in restaurants and nightspots such as La Taverne Royale and La Cicogne. 'I am quite sure that this work which was more or less routine for me . . . helped me to face my secret life much more calmly.' Soon after, Rake says, he had the uneasy feeling 'that the barman at La Cicogne had told the police that I was not the Belgian cabaret singer I pretended to be'. Next he found he was being followed, though with his SOE training he was soon able to lose his tail.

He reported this to Virginia Hall, who confirmed through her contacts that the police were on the lookout for him. She advised him to return to England. The ever impulsive Rake decided to go instead to Paris, where he had heard that the radio operator of the Xavier circuit had been arrested and a new one was desperately needed. Virginia Hall agreed to send his set and luggage ahead by another route, using her courier Germaine. Germaine suggested Rake should cross the border with the help of a passeur known as the 'charcutier de la Rue Barré'. Rake later told SOE that 'this individual . . . was out to make money and sold a percentage of the people whom he helped to the Germans'. This was not normally as alarming as it sounds as the Germans 'treated them fairly leniently as they were fined only 200 francs, and given a few days in prison – 14 days for the first offence, 21 for the second, 28 for the third and so on.' For Rake it was not to be so simple.

After waiting in a café for a guide they were taken in parties of four across the fields and told to walk up a hill, 'where they would be all right.' Rake was in one of the last groups and paused to help a young girl who had broken a shoelace. Seeing people being stopped ahead, Rake remembered that if people were caught they were sent back to whichever side of the line they had started. To be surer of getting to the Occupied Zone Rake asked the girl to say that he had crossed from northern France and that she had persuaded him to turn back. When he was duly arrested he was searched and 47,800 francs was found on him. He told a story 'which was more or less believed' that he had owned a small café in Nantes which he had sold, as an uncle and aunt had bought the Brasserie Klébert in Lyons and he was going to work for them as maitre d'hotel. Rake knew the brasserie was for sale and was able to give satisfactory answers to questions by one of his

German interrogators who had been in the profession.

Rake was now transferred to a prison at Chalons-sur-Saone where he was questioned all morning and afternoon by four German officers, a member of the Gestapo and a French interpreter 'who was against him right from the start'. When he repeated the story about the café in Nantes he referred to his uncle and aunt as 'mes parents' – which the Germans seized on at once. The Frenchman demanded precise details about the sale of the café and then declared that Rake's address on his identity card had been checked by wire and nobody had heard of him. Rake countered that it was a boarding house and had probably changed hands – the Germans were more inclined to believe the story than the Frenchman, he said. When questioned again the next day, Rake was badly knocked about. He endured it, he says, by counting, the technique he had been told to use during his training as 'with the mind empty you can put up with quite a good deal of pain.'

Rake now faced the still grimmer prospect of further questioning in the fortress at Dijon. He was given his clothes and his suitcase while his papers and his money were handed to the German guard accompanying him. Rake now exercised his charm, telling the guard a story that he was working in the Black Market and stood to lose two million francs by the hold-up. After two hours the guard agreed to accept the 47,000 francs, allowing Rake to slip off the train at a small halt just outside Dijon.

Rake, with a few hundred francs and his identity papers, now took a train to Paris. He was without a ticket but remarkably 'nobody asked him for one, and he was able to obtain something to eat on the train'.

Unable to stay in a hotel without identity papers, Rake decided to try his luck at the Boeuf sur le Toit, a club where he had sung before the war, billed as the Anglo-German tenor. This was open all night. All hope of anonymity was dashed when the barman greeted him immediately by his stage name, Mr Greer. Rake hinted at his predicament, explaining that he had come to the occupied zone hoping to find work but had been caught crossing the demarcation line. The barman told him to go and see Jacques Artel, an old friend of Rake's playing at the Comédie Française, who would provide him with papers. At that moment Rake turned to see a man he describes as 'about forty, slim, very good-looking, with glorious deep blue eyes which were as sensitive as an artist's'. Though the man was in civilian clothes and spoke fluent French, Rake sensed at once that he was German.

Rake smiled and the man said, 'I was thinking of going to see Jacques myself at the theatre this evening. By the way, my name is Hadler – Max Hadler.' Rake introduced himself as Rocher – his cover name – adding that his stage name was Denis Greer. The barman reassured Rake that his new friend was violently anti-Nazi and from an old German family. They found Artel in his dressing room – like a large apartment – at the Comédie Française, and soon after the three were back at the Boeuf, Rake enjoying delicious food and drinking champagne. When they stood up to go, Rake exclaimed theatrically, 'I haven't a room . . . If I go out now I'm bound to be caught. I'm unlucky that way.'

'There's a bed at my flat,' replied Max. In *Le Chagrin et la Pitié* Rake says, 'I stayed with him for four or five months until I found myself thinking I was letting him down in my double game.' In his book he adds: 'I am quite sure that, had it not been for the demands of the war, we should have remained together for many years, if not for ever. I could never make out whether he had the slightest suspicion of what I was really doing; if he did he never once by word or gesture let me know that he did.'

Rake now made contact with another SOE agent, Edward Wilkinson (Alexandre or Alex, for short). They decided to travel back to Lyons, making the journey, this time undisturbed, in the fuse box of an electric train ('quite roomy' said Rake). In Lyons Rake went immediately to see Virginia Hall. Leaving Rake in her flat, she travelled to Cannes to discuss Rake's future with Peter Churchill, the most senior SOE agent in France at the time. He also took the firm view that Rake should go back to England. Meanwhile SOE's Ben Cowburn had been in touch, requesting Rake's help with radio work for a short while. So Wilkinson and Rake set off once again to cross into the occupied zone via Limoges. This time they were accompanied by a third agent, Richard Heslop, who published his own vivid memoirs using his code name Xavier as the title.

Presumably as a precaution, Rake stayed in one hotel and the two others in another. Fatally they had been seen at Rake's hotel. What they did not know was that the proprietress of his hotel was in league with the Surveillance du Territoire. Early the next morning Rake was arrested as a black marketeer and his identity card, hastily drawn up by the American consul in Lyons, was declared false. Worse, when his money, all in crisp new notes, was counted, it was not pinned in bundles of ten as all notes issued by French banks habitually were.

As he left with the police, the *patronne* told them to look out for his two companions. Rake tried to shrug this off, saying the two men were just people he had met on the train, but she gave such a precise description of their clothes that soon Heslop and Wilkinson were arrested outside the café where they had arranged a rendezvous. They never accepted Rake's explanation of their arrest and remained convinced that he had blabbed to save his own skin. Heslop provides a very different account in his book: 'I was bloody furious . . . That man had been a nuisance from the very first time I saw him, always frightened, always twittering away like an anxious sparrow.'

Rake told SOE that they were all now questioned 'by a very pleasant Alsatian named Guth, aged about 34. Guth declared that Rake must be German because there were no pin marks on the 20,000 francs he was carrying. He then asked, 'are you a German agent? We are very hard on them.' Rake took a large gamble and replied that he was a British agent. Guth promptly asked him why he had not said so in the first place. He then fetched in Wilkinson and Heslop, 'took all three into a back room, and asked if they had anything they wanted to hide'. They had left a radio set in one cloakroom and a couple of revolvers in another, so it was arranged that they should have pick up their property and go to Guth's flat where they had an excellent Black Market lunch and were primed with suitable answers to questions they might be asked.

The prison guard, Rake told SOE, became still friendlier after the news of the Allied raid on Dieppe and meals were brought to them by an Inspector Imar and a M. Lesoie, who gave them an enormous chisel and pincers. There were eight others in the cells and Rake made loud groans while the others chipped away at a door leading to the street.

Rake was now taken to hospital where he heard the others had been caught just as they opened the door. In the hospital a doctor, who had been a prisoner in Germany, arranged for Rake to be provided with a student's white coat. The plan was that he would wait in the eye section, pretending to talk to patients if necessary, until he could slip to a car which would be waiting outside. Unfortunately a nurse spotted him and he was hastily rushed back to bed. He was not punished he said, adding (just a touch theatrically perhaps) that four guards were placed around his bed.

Rake was now sent to Castres – 'the worst prison in France'. Here he was reunited in a cell with Wilkinson and Heslop. Tensions were still high and Wilkinson continued to refuse to talk to Rake. Rake was still suffering from dysentery and when they were put in separate cells a doctor named Cartel – 'a very pleasant man . . . who had once been on a coaling ship which visited Cardiff' – used to talk to him and put slips of paper through the door with the latest BBC news.

Rake was frequently taken from his cell and interrogated, and one particularly vicious young officer one day brought his naked jack boot down on Rake's bare foot crushing every bone.

Just as their imprisonment reached its grimmest stage, Rake, Heslop and Wilkinson were told that their status had been revised and they were to be transferred to an ordinary prisoner-of-war camp at Chambran. On stopping *en route* at Lyon, Rake told SOE they were 'put in a van, taken to the Gendarmerie, where they were received like heroes and given a lunch of six or seven courses.'

At Chambran they were well received, given battledress tunics and Red Cross parcels. Soon after they arrived came the news of the Allied landings in North Africa, followed immediately by Hitler's decision to take over the southern unoccupied zone of France. The prison commandant, Tournier, realised that the three British agents would be seized by the Gestapo and offered to set them free on condition that they took with them two British soldiers who had killed a German in an earlier attempt to escape. 'We were fitted out with civilian clothes, chocolate and cigarettes – but no money – and with a railway warrant to Marseilles,' said Rake.

SOE records provide slightly different details – namely, that Tournier supplied the prisoners with food tickets and a bus to take them to St-Marcellin. The two English sergeants, Hall and Foster, spoke not a word of French. Wilkinson and Heslop, convinced that Rake was a liability and not to be trusted, promptly left Rake and set off together to Paris. (Heslop returned to the UK by Lysander on 23 June 1943 while Wilkinson was instructed by London to proceed to Nantes and start a new circuit. Here he was arrested and escaped, only to be recaptured and sent to Mauthausen, where he was executed in September 1944.)

Rake bravely undertook to try to find a way of taking the two sergeants across the border into Spain. He relates that as they were leaving Chambran a French officer had come up to him, thrust a scrap of paper into his hand and whispered, 'Go there. He will help you if he can.' On it were scrawled the name and address of a doctor in Marseilles. The subsequent story, which has become something of a legend, is confirmed from several sources. The three survived a train journey partly spent in a compartment with four German military police. All the time Rake was thinking, how could the Germans not be suspicious of three Frenchmen, 'notoriously the most talkative race in the world, sitting absolutely mute'.

In Marseilles they arrived at the doctor's house and when they rang the bell two girls looked out of an upstairs window. The doctor was away, they said. Rake replied that a friend of the doctor had told them to come to him if they needed help. After an exchange of whispers the two girls descended and let them in. One was about twenty-five, the other twenty. Rake explained that they were escaped prisoners, hoping to cross the frontier into Spain. The girls readily agreed that they could stay there until their father, a Dr Rodocanachi, returned. The next morning the elder

girl suggested Rake should seek out a Greek who sometimes helped her father. When Rake found him he suggested they should continue to Perpignan, the last major
town before the frontier, and contact the Dutch consul. He
also gave Rake several thousand francs to help them on
their journey.

In Perpignan the Dutch consul also gave them money and
directed them to stay in a brothel, the one place where they
would not need to fill out a *fiche*, or registration form. Here
Rake admired the rooms in different styles – Japanese,
English, French – but the next morning they had a shock.
Curtly, the Dutch consul, told them he could not help them,
refusing to provide any explanation or suggestions. Rake
was explaining the predicament to the two sergeants in a
brasserie, the Palmarum, when he noticed a gendarme in
a splendid uniform, lined with First World War ribbons on
his chest, taking a friendly interest in them. Rake caught his
eye and impetuously went over to his table and asked
whether he could help, explaining that they were escaped
Belgian prisoners. With a twinkle in his eye the gendarme
replied, 'Are you quite sure you're Belgians. Your two
friends have English written all over them.' His new companion then introduced himself as Commandant Feti, chief
of the Perpignan gendarmerie, and suggested they meet
outside the café in half an hour, after he had talked to his
wife. The two sergeants were horrified and a fierce
argument followed, but as they left the brasserie the
commandant appeared and gave Rake the address of an
apartment in the Avenue des Mimosas. Here they found
Madame Feti and a large family of six sons and five daughters. They stayed for a week, with Rake assigned a bed in
the gendarmerie headquarters to avoid displacing more
children than necessary. The commandant then announced
that he had found a guide to take them across the Pyrenees.

The charge was to be 8,000 francs for the three of them, not the usual 25,000 francs – paid for with money the sergeants had earned while running a canteen in their prisoner of war camp and had hidden in an aspirin tube. Madame Feti and her daughters made them haversacks and filled them with food.

For Rake, with his bad foot, the long climb grew increasingly desperate, and his feet became so swollen he took his shoes off and slung them round his neck, his feet numbed by the snow. Eventually they reached a small hotel, slept for thirty hours and were then taken on to Barcelona. Far from being free, he was sent on to the notorious detention camp at Miranda. Rake's stay here was made bearable by a new friendship with Alex Shokolovsky, son of a French mother and a Hungarian father. The Spanish authorities were puzzled that Rake, was allowed to languish so long in Miranda, unlike other British officers, whose release was usually secured through the embassy in Madrid. It transpired later that SOE believed he had been executed in Dijon and suspected that the Rake who had now appeared was a German spy, planted to report on Allied escape networks. Fortunately the Spanish now decided to send Rake to Jaraba, a Spanish hydro where four large hotels had been turned into a more relaxed place of detention for officers. Here they enjoyed luxuries such as sheets and marble baths and were free to walk round the village, the Spanish food was excellent and the Rioja flowed. As each officer departed, a farewell party was given. Rake kept the menus, including one given to the agent H.P. Le Chene, who had set up a circuit near Clermont-Ferrand with his wife as courier. This included such choice items as *poulet froid evasion, dinde farcie manana* and *vins sans calcul ni ordonnance*.

Arriving at Gibraltar, Rake was sent to the Rock Hotel, where he found several fellow inmates from Jaraba, including the SOE agent Harry Peulevé, who had the mis-fortune to parachute on top of a police station. Back in London, during his debriefing Rake was given a heavy grilling over Heslop's and Wilkinson's arrests. He insisted that it was the woman at the hotel who had provided descriptions of their clothes and SOE appears to have accepted this. Buckmaster certainly had a continuing soft spot for Rake.

While he was staying in one of the SOE flats in South Kensington, Rake received a telegram that read: 'Help am imprisoned Alex.' His friend from Miranda had arrived in England and, like all foreigners claiming to have escaped from occupied Europe, had been sent to the Royal Patriotic Asylum, a large Victorian hospital in Wandsworth, where they were questioned relentlessly to ensure they were not German plants.

Rake himself, suffering from exhaustion and virtual nervous breakdown, was sent to Drimmin Hospital near Glasgow, where his foot was treated and he was given a silver plate to support it. Buckmaster now gave him the job of con-ducting officer, accompanying agents during their training. Rake was soon in trouble after questioning the ability of a group of French-Canadians to survive in France, but during this time met the redoubtable Nancy Wake, an Australian who had gone to live in Paris, married a prosperous and energetic businessman named Henri Fiocca and become involved in organising the Pat O'Leary escape line. When O'Leary had been arrested she had escaped across the Pyrenees. Now she was been trained to be dropped to the new Freelance–Gaspard circuit in the Haute Loire. The head of the circuit was to be John Farmer, who Rake also met at Milton Hall while he was lecturing on 'Being an agent in the field'. Against all expectations Buckmaster, faced once again with an acute shortage of radio operators, asked Rake to join Farmer and Wake. They had parachuted ahead of Rake into the Massif Central. Farmer later reported: 'We arrived in the Field on the night of 29/30th April 1944. I fell perfectly on to the lights, but Helene on the other hand fell some 300 yards away from the Field. She was eventually found by a search party, revolver in hand, ready to shoot.' Farmer's initial contact was Maurice Southgate, the very efficient organiser of SOE's Stationer circuit, but following their first meeting Southgate and his new radio operator were arrested by the Gestapo. Farmer and Nancy Wake rapidly moved on, while Rake, who was supposed to join them immediately, was delayed until 15 May, when he was flown in by Lysander, this time with the cover name of Roland.

To his amazement and delight Rake found that the agent who had come to meet him was his friend from Miranda, Alex Shokolovsky. Alex, he says, had obtained a front-wheel-drive Citroën, the kind used by the Germans, and a uniform of the Milice (the hated Gestapo-like French security police) and German pass.

Rake now met up with Farmer and Nancy Wake. They had established an HQ at Chaudes-Aigues, and Rake began transmitting at once. Farmer's local Resistance contact, Gaspard, had told him he had four groups of nearly ten thousand men urgently in need of arms. Rake initially had serious trouble with his codes and was in a state of panic, but Farmer sat down with him and spent several hours unravelling and encoding. The result was six successive nights of *parachutages*, which generated still larger numbers of recruits as the news spread.

As D-Day approached Rake received an urgent call for help from Alex, whose 'pianist' or radio operator had been arrested. On the night of 6/7 June Alex was due to receive a *parachutage* near Châteauroux. After a blissful afternoon spent swimming in a lake they set off to the landing ground. As they passed the great ornamental gates of a chateau a burst of machine-gun fire hit the car. They sped on but Alex was hit and slumped forward unconscious. Blood was pouring from him. Rake tried in vain to stanch the flow with a scarf pressed inside his shirt. By the time they arrived at the nearest safe house he was dead. 'He had been almost cut in half,' said Rake. Five days later a large crowd gathered openly for his cremation in Montluçon. 'I don't think, even if I had the words, that I would want to put down on paper exactly how I felt about Alex's death. I had loved him as I had never loved anyone before, and though our life together had been short, it had been triumphant and far too wonderful for me to describe it.'

Rake had told SOE he did not like bangs so it is not surprising his book is light on descriptions of the fighting. A vivid account is provided by the American lieutenant Rene Dussaq (Anselme), who arrived by parachute on 22 May. His plane had circled for so long looking for the reception ground that it had alerted a nearby German garrison, with the result that 500 Germans surrounded a small wood in which a Maquis group of thirty-three was sheltering. The quick-witted Dussaq explains that he withdrew 'the 33 boys . . . by taking advantage of a small river bed in the centre of the wood. The Germans opened fire on each side of the wood with no other result than the killing of some of their own men'.

Having now made contact with the Freelance circuit, Dussaq was collected by Nancy Wake and taken to Chaudes-Aigues and introduced to Farmer and Rake (whose field name was Roland). Dussaq started to give weapons training to the Maquis. Hearing that the Germans were preparing to attack, he did all in his power to convince the Maquis groups that 'it was suicide to maintain such a large group of men in one single spot with the type of weapons they had'. This prompted the ultimate in wishful thinking – a request for tanks and cannon to strengthen their positions. Dussaq insisted that their weapons were intended for guerrilla warfare, not pitched battles.

When the Germans attacked Monmoucher with 4,000 men they were bravely held in check by 1,500 French Forces of the Interior (FFI) for a whole day. Dussaq now had the chance to show the FFI that the bazooka 'could easily stop any enemy armoured car, with the result that from then on for the following four months, all the heads of the FFI in Auvergnes knew me under the name of "Captain Bazooka".' In this engagement, continues Dussaq, the FFI 'successfully stopped the advance of the Germans led by Geisler, the head of the Gestapo, [and] started their withdrawal from Monmoucher during the night, after having inflicted upon the Germans a loss of 1,400 killed . . . We sustained the loss of some 40 men, 25 missing and 15 certainly dead'. Explaining the figures for German losses, he says, 'When attacked by the Germans we would usually fight delaying actions until our ammunition would give out or our boys would just run away; therefore, we could not very well go around to count the number of dead the enemy had left on the ground. Concerning that particular action at Monmoucher, radio Vichy announced that the Germans admitted having lost 800 men.' Three days later they ambushed two German trucks at the Pont de Garabit and the captain 'just before dying told us they had lost 1,400 men at Monmoucher'.

To Dussaq's intense concern, when the Maquis established a new command post at St-Martial they repeated the mistake of assembling a large group, inviting German attack. 'I asked Roland, the radio operator, to send a message to London informing them that exceedingly unsound military tactics inviting disaster were being applied.'

He continued: 'Ignoring the instructions given by London, Gaspard's staff had moved to the small town of Chaudes-Aignes . . . The Germans attacked from three sides simultaneously,' using artillery. Though Farmer and Rake had established a new command post in some woods thought to be safe, they now found themselves in the path of the German attack.

Knowing that Rake and a group of pilots had been left in the wood, he decided to go and look for them. 'The Germans at the time were performing one of the poorest demonstrations of mortar fire I have ever witnessed.' Unable to find Rake in the woods, he rejoined Farmer. Farmer then managed a successful withdrawal, taking refuge with Nancy Wake in a nearby wood and then a deep gorge.

Farmer describes it as 'a real first-class attack', which lasted from approximately 7 a.m. until well past nightfall. 'When our positions became untenable the order to retire in a "*sauve qui peut*" manner was given. It was at this period that Roland lost contact with the UK.'

Farmer had arranged for them to retire from the village of Fridefont to a wood near by. Rake and four Canadian air force pilots came with them. Farmer and Nancy Wake then set off on a uniquely British mission – to fetch some tea, which had been left in a house. On their way back they met a French captain, who asked them to take an urgent message to Gaspard's HQ some 12 kilometres away. Returning to Fridefont, they found the village deserted but met Dussaq and took refuge in a deep gorge. Farmer continues: 'Unfortunately Roland, with the remainder of the party, had not been able to get back to Fridefont, owing to enemy shelling and troops which had come between them and the village.'

Dussaq searched the woods for Rake without success. This time the German attack had successfully routed the resistance forces, aiding by aerial bombardment and strafing by German planes (Ju-88s). Withdrawing his men 16 kilometres, Dussaq decided, at dead of night, to 'go back again to the woods in an effort to find Roland. Two days later, I found him, and on foot I led him to Saint Santin. We covered some 170 kilometres'. For Rake, with the pain from his injured foot, this must have been a major feat of endurance.

The Maquis had now been dispersed over three departments, and Farmer decided to split the area, leaving Dussaq and Rake in the Cantal. A new set of codes and crystals was dropped for Rake. Dussaq, who was now Rake's leader, was a tough, impressive, dedicated soldier who saw his mission from the moment of his arrival in France to look for Germans and attack them. He describes how he formed

small parties of three men that would constantly go out hunting Germans along national roads wherever the terrain would lend itself to such operations. Obtaining false papers I went into Aurillac and secured direct information from the German Kommandatur, which enabled us to ambush successfully a German column that was trying to leave Aurillac to rejoin their forces in Saint Flour. I made arrangements with a milicien to kill La Haye, the head of the milice in Aurillac, and provided him with a silent gun. My adjutant arrested a woman from the milice who had sold to the Gestapo 18 young men from the Maquis.

He relates how in St-Santin he confronted a mayor who was hostile to the Resistance. 'I went to see the mayor, and demanded that he gather the population of the town at the high school . . . I spoke very bluntly . . . that if it were not for the French resistance and for those who were falling before the German bullies, France would not be considered

259

among the foreign nations as a fighting ally; that the Allies would win this fight with or without the resistance, and that it was advisable for all Frenchmen to put themselves at this early date on the side of the Allies in anticipation of victory.' In his mission report, Dussaq paid Rake his finest tribute: 'I must say that one man with whom I have been associated for quite some time, the radio operator, Roland, should receive recognition for his devotion to duty, for his courage and for all the many friends he has made in France in the name of England. He is a man who, although not a soldier, has all the qualities one would like to find in a soldier.'

Though Rake made light of his second mission, SOE did not. Rake was awarded the MC in June 1945, the Croix de Guerre avec Palme in 1946 and made a *chevalier* of the Légion d'honneur in 1948. Recommending Rake to SOE for an award, Farmer said:

As is well known to you, this officer has undergone considerable physical suffering in the past, and the trials which he underwent during his escape after the Fridefont attack are worthy of special mention. Although it was obvious to everyone that he was undergoing extreme pain from his feet, he never once complained, and always remained cheerful in face of very considerable physical trial. On each occasion that we were attacked, by his personal behaviour and apparent fearlessness he contributed to a large extent to the good morale of the poorly trained Maquis.

Rake died in Manchester in 1976, bequeathing his body to medical research and asking for donations to be made to the Campaign for Homosexual Equality.

ENVOI

The SOE archives continue to yield up astonishing stories of courage and audacity. Philippe de Vomécourt organised one of the most successful mass escapes of the war. He was one of three brothers who worked for the French section of SOE. He used the cover of organising railway goods traffic to Germany while he continued to live with his wife and seven children at the family Château de Bas Soleil near Limoges, receiving arms drops on his own estate. Inevitably he came under suspicion and was arrested.

His SOE personal file provides new details of his astonishing escape from Eysse prison near Toulouse. This took place on the evening of 3 January, 1944. Five prisoners managed to absent themselves from the roll-call using pretexts such as reporting sick or going to the dentist. One of the keepers had agreed to help them and engaged the other keepers in conversation. The 'absentees' then overpowered the keepers, bound them and took their uniforms. When the time came for the rest of the prisoners to be marched back from roll-call in groups of seven, each group was accompanied by a friendly keeper who took them through the gate. Here they all separated and ran off, making for an agreed meeting place. 'The sentries on the walls were completely taken by surprise and when they had started firing it was getting dark and they lost sight of the prisoners. Fifty-four men got away, without a single casualty,' Vomécourt told SOE.

The rendezvous was on a road just outside the village of Cançon, where one of the escaping prisoners knew a woman who had offered help. When thirty had gathered at the rendezvous Vomécourt set off with his contact. He himself was in civilian clothes and equipped with identity papers, but his companion still wore his heavy coarse prison trousers. They found the house of Madame B – next to the police station, where two policemen were inconsiderately standing chatting on the doorstep. When the policemen at last went back inside, Vomécourt knocked quietly at the front door, which Madame B opened, beckoning them to come inside. 'She was a tall, fair-haired woman in her early thirties. She came back into the room, now dressed and carrying two cups of coffee. Then we broke the bad news to her. We told her there were thirty of us and another twenty or so somewhere on the road. She was clearly shocked.'

After a few moments she replied that there was a farm near by where the farmer had agreed to take one or two men. They could go to him. Vomécourt asked for some coffee for his comrades. When it was ready she offered to put a little alcohol in it. He agreed but soon came to regret it, forgetting that in this part of France fifty-fifty was the norm.

The farmer was as thunderstruck by the number of prisoners to be hidden as she had been. After an awkward pause he volunteered an old shed just behind his farmhouse. Vomécourt then took the coffee to his men and told them to hasten after him. One man had taken too much coffee and had to be carried and dragged a large part of the way. Now Vomécourt had to go in search of the others. Once again there was one man who could scarcely walk, but by dawn Vomécourt had shepherded them all into the shed. The next day the police came to search the farm. Vomécourt left the door of the shed open and miraculously the soldiers glanced only briefly inside.

The following night, with the help of Madame B, the whole party was distributed in twos and threes in houses around Cançon. Vomécourt remained at the farm with two British officers. Naturally there were complications. Some of the younger men started to behave amorously towards wives and daughters in the houses where they were billeted, causing fury among the husbands. Overnight Vomécourt had to find houses for them 'where there were fewer women, or so many that they would be inhibited'. Another man, who had always worked on a farm, insisted on going out into the fields to help, even though he was still in his convict trousers. By then Vomécourt had moved in with Madame B to make his nightly rounds easier. One evening she said, 'There's a visitor for you, somebody who wants to speak to you.' It was the local chief of police.

He explained with a smile, 'Madame has been buying big quantities of bread and black market meat lately. I knew it couldn't all be for herself . . . I put two and two together and made – how many is it? – *fifty-three?*' Over the next few days the police provided identity cards for the whole group and Vomécourt managed to scrounge clothing too. Like the others Vomécourt left the village in a Black Maria, having the pleasure of seeing two of his old warders as they drove past the prison at Eysse.

Another commanding SOE character was Squadron Leader Count Manfred Czernin, who carried out two missions in Italy. A note on his personal file reads: 'he possesses considerable charm of character, but from reports sent in by his immediate commanding officer it would appear when not engaged on work of an operational nature he was completely uninterested in duties of an administrative type'.

When recruited for SOE Czernin had already served valiantly as a fighter pilot in the Battle of Britain, continuing with the RAF until invalided home from the Far East. By this time he had undertaken 1,000 hours of flying, forty of them operational.

The Czernins were one of the leading families of the Austro-Hungarian Empire. The squadron leader's father, Count Otto Czernin, had married the Hon. Lucile Beckett. Manfred was born in Berlin in January 1913 and became a naturalised British subject in 1922.

Czernin's report from Beaulieu training school was glowing.

He is very intelligent and practical. He is highly educated and has a wide experience of the world in handling men. He has plenty of imagination. He is keen, worked hard and has outstanding initiative. He is a strong character and [has] plenty of determination. Without in any way being domineering he naturally takes the lead. He is inclined to be self-centred but not selfishly so. He showed occasional traces of vanity and a slight tendency to be impatient with people less quick-witted than himself. He is sociable, good humoured and a good mixer and a good raconteur. He is a natural leader and appears to have considerable organising capacity. He would inspire great confidence in his subordinates.

Czernin was dropped by parachute 16 kilometres inside the Italian–Austrian frontier in June 1944 on a reconnaissance mission. 'He dropped without the least knowledge of what he was likely to find on the ground and the aircraft circled round until he had reconnoitred and signalled that it was safe to drop the wireless operator. Contact was immediately made with the partisans in the neighbourhood and some Austrians found among them who were prepared to act as guides over the Austrian frontier.'

Following the arrival of another radio operator they were heavily attacked by a strong force of Germans. Though they lost their kit and equipment, all managed to escape. By the time Czernin was picked up by Lysander at the end of October 1944 he had established two lines across the frontier in Austria by which several agents had already been infiltrated. For this work Czernin was awarded the MC in addition to his DSO and DFC.

On Mission Herrington Czernin was dropped a second time behind enemy lines on 21 March 1945 near Edolo in north Italy. This time he came as Senior British Officer to the Bergamesque area, with the task of coordinating scattered partisan units into a unified command. He was then to carry out the directions of the 15th Army Group during the final stages of the Allied advance. 'To reach his destination, he had to cross the 9,000 foot high Passo del Diavolo which at that time was completely snowed under.' On 2 April he made two attempts which failed owing to the snow which was over 2 metres deep. He demonstrated his intrepid nature the next morning, setting out at 4 a.m. 'determined to make one further effort and after 24 hours continued march, suffering severely from cold, frostbite and lack of food he succeeded in making the crossing'.

Czernin immediately set about organising the various partisan groups and 'by his personality and energy quickly built up a large and aggressive partisan command. These forces, under his direction, went immediately into action'. On 26 April he personally forced an unconditional surrender from the enemy garrison in Bom.

The same day, with a large Union Jack draped over his car and accompanied by the leader of the partisan forces, he drove into Bergamo to demand the unconditional surrender of the German forces there. The Germans opened fire and he was forced to withdraw rapidly. Undaunted, he immediately ordered the partisans to attack the city, and arranged for the underground elements in Bergamo to rise up simultaneously. Despite the overwhelming superiority of German firepower, 'by midday on the 27th, only a small area of Bergamo was still in enemy hands'. At 7 a.m. the next day Czernin received an unconditional surrender 'of all German troops in the Bergamesco.'

Amédée Maingard, known to his family as Dédé, is a remarkable example of an untried talent flourishing under SOE. Born on the island of Mauritius in 1918, he came to London in 1919 and qualified as an accountant in 1938, volunteering for service in the King's Royal Rifle Corps on his birthday on 21 October 1939. The next year he was promoted to lance corporal but was considered unsuitable for a commission. So he turned to SOE, where he rose to the rank of major and was awarded the DSO. Maingard, often known by his cover name of Samuel, had been dropped as a radio operator to Squadron Leader Southgate, the very capable head of the Stationer circuit based on Châteauroux and Tarbes. Over the course of a year Maingard sent 248 radio messages and also trained two local recruits who were accepted by London as fully fledged operators. On 1 May 1944, Southgate, exhausted by the sheer number of night drops he had to attend, failed to notice a black Citroën of the type regularly used by the Gestapo in the street outside his new radio operator's house in Montluçon and was arrested. His large territory was divided into three, with Pearl Witherington taking over the northern Indre. Maingard's new circuit in the south was given the name Shipwright, and in four months he received 125 parachute drops, bringing 3,236 containers and a further 1,009 packages – these being items that did not fit into containers. Additional drops were made to Jedburgh teams in the area.

The daily reports on Shipwright in the OSS archives in Washington give a detailed picture of the extraordinary volume of intense active resistance work carried out under Maingard. Some, of course, say that the Resistance were prone to vastly exaggerating their successes, but in Maingard's case the enormous volume is corroborated by summaries of telegrams. On 2 July 500 men were ready to receive stores in the next large-scale daylight drop. On 4 July Samuel reported that he controlled the Vienne department south of a line Pleumartin–Poitiers–Lusignan. The men under his control would be increased to 2,000 when arms arrived. A Maquis group in the Forêt de St-Sauvent had carried out three derailments, three ambushes of road convoys and taken eight German prisoners, making a total of fifty-two in the camp.

On 8 July two enemy divisions moving north from the south were held up, one at Figeac, another at Uzerche, owing to lack of petrol, which had been stolen by patriots. On 10 July Maingard's men cut the 110,000-volt cable that supplied the German submarine base at Rochefort.

Three days later, at the request of the Maquis, two German infantry battalions at Bonneuil-Matours were bombed from the air and the barracks completely destroyed without a single civilian casualty. The next day 'All the villages in the region celebrated [Bastille Day]. There were military parades and Allied flags were flown from the houses. Enemy spies were executed after being tried by a military tribunal.' On 21 July, after the Germans had burnt twenty houses in the village of Jousse, the Maquis counter-attacked, killing two Germans and wounding five without losses of their own. On 26 July Maingard was present at the funeral of seven airmen who were brought down on the night of 23 July near Brillac. There were 2,000 people in the church, which was decorated with Allied flags. The next day the German general Boclet was killed in an armoured car.

The American first lieutenant Thomas Blackwell, who dropped into France on 25 August, said Samuel 'was really the dominant personality of the section. He had the entire situation in his pocket and was very competent. No one made a move without his OK, including the big Maquis colonels'. Second Lieutenant Robert McCarthy added that Samuel 'was the mental backbone of the Maquis etat-major'.

When Jedburgh team Ian, led by the American major Gildee, dropped into France on 20 June they were taken to Maingard the very next morning. He gave them the task of organising, arming and training the Maquis in the south-west of the Vienne. 'We had to travel a great deal. We used a car, transformed into a reconnaissance vehicle armed with two FM [light machine guns], on the road running through German occupied towns and villages because we believed the success of our mission lay in the rapidity of action and that our security would be better safeguarded by force of arms.'

The zone around the towns of Charroux, Confolens, Chasseneuil and Champagne-Mouton 'was transformed into a fortified bastion. We made barricades of trees and masonry on the roads and the bridges were mined'. Two hospitals were formed and nurses and surgeons recruited. On 20 July '800 Germans, well equipped and armed . . . pierced our defences and established themselves at Champagne-Mouton', entrenching themselves in the camp, surrounded by barbed-wire entanglements and ditches. They took numerous hostages, threatening to shoot them and burn the town if the Maquis attacked. The Maquis countered by entrenching themselves in front of the town. This had the desired effect. The Germans declined to fight and disengaged. They now sent in a column of 1,000 men, including militia, well armed with mortars and heavy machine guns. Another column attacked at La Rochefoucauld. 'Our whole organisation was at stake,' said Gildee. He continued:

Harassed by us, they could not penetrate our positions and had to disengage themselves. The column descending on Chabanais could not cross the Vienne. The bridges were badly damaged and the maquis, although young and with no previous experience of the firing line, were well trained by their leaders and armed only with FM, stens, carbines, rifles and grenades, did not give way under the mortar and machine gun fire. The enemy had to retreat and go back to Champagne-Mouton after having burnt a whole district of Chabanais and shooting a few civilians. The losses were numerous on both sides. About two hundred Germans and eighty French.' Summing up, Gildee said: 'For three months we harassed German convoys on the roads, destroying material, killing their men, blowing up railways, derailing trains, holding up transport causing German columns to become targets for aerial bombardment . . . finally freeing the whole of the Charente, all its large towns and a large portion of the coast.'

On 7 August Maingard was flown back to England by Lysander for a week of consultations and briefings on the Resistance. A week later he was awarded the Croix de Guerre with palms by General Koenig, the newly appointed head of the French Forces of the Interior.

Parachuted back on 14 August this time in uniform, Maingard was just in time to take part in the liberation parade at Poitiers, where 3,000 of the Free French who marched through the town had been armed by him. SOE's evaluation of his role reads: 'He showed a grip of his job and a wise determination surprising in one so young and in many ways so temperamental. He behaved admirably and with immense bravery during the fighting and showed great tact in smoothing out problems between leaders . . . What a grand lad.'

Charles Milne Skepper has a special place in the annals of SOE as he is one of very few agents whose fate has never been finally resolved. Sent to Marseilles in June 1943 to run the Monk circuit, he carried out an impressive series of sabotage attacks aided by his plucky courier Eliane Plewman (Gaby). Sheer determination to make a contribution to the war brought Skepper into SOE, which in his case was doubly impressive as he had already suffered brutal imprisonment by the Japanese.

Born in Richmond, Surrey in 1905, Skepper had been brought up in Paris. His nephew Edmund who compiled the family history writes, 'Charlie was bilingual in English and French, but also learnt and spoke Spanish, Russian, Chinese and German. He was for a time very "left wing" and visited Russia twice in the late twenties. My father told me how he returned completely disenchanted by Communism, saying it was no more than Fascism in another guise'. (MI5 had noted that he was a member of the Friends of the Soviet Union at the time).

Skepper had first studied and then taught at the London School of Economics from 1926 to 1931 when he was awarded a Rockefeller Fellowship. Professor Robson of the LSE wrote after Skepper's death 'He was a most delightful companion, eager, witty, spiritual, catholic in his interests and friends. He had naturally easy and distinguished manners, excellent taste in art, literature and music . . . [holding] advanced views on social, economic and political questions (he was for long a keen Fabian)'.

Skepper was also very interested in modern art and purchased paintings by Da Silva, Max Ernst and Edouard Cortès, though most of his collection was stolen from the family house at Rueil-Malmaison near Paris during the war.

In the 1930s he had become very interested in Chinese art and history going to live in Beijing. When war broke out in 1939 Skepper volunteered for military service, and was sent to Shanghai as director of the Shanghai broadcasting station run by the British Ministry of Information. When Shanghai was taken by the Japanese he was arrested for helping four American marines to escape. Escaping himself, he joined Chinese guerrilla forces operating in the neighbouring countryside and according to Robson 'was captured, tortured and incarcerated in a Japanese prison. He was literally starved by the Japanese and became so ill that he could afterwards recall very little of what occurred in prison. He did speak, however, of the extreme kindness of his Chinese fellow prisoners in the cage.' Skepper's life was saved when he was included in an exchange of diplomats between the UK and Japan in December 1941.

Returning to England in August 1942 his family found him looking worn and ill, but unbroken in spirit and determined to volunteer for further service. Early in 1943 he wrote to Robson 'I am going into the army on Monday . . . In peacetime of course I would never have got in!'

What can be told of his war work comes principally from his SOE Personal File and from a memoir given to the author Elizabeth Nicholas by Madame Régis, who had a villa named La Cavalière in the hills above St Raphael, which the circuit's young radio operator used for his clandestine transmissions.

A photograph on SOE files shows Skepper with an earnest, intelligent face with slight creases around the eyes and mouth suggesting a quick, warm smile. 'Has done extremely well in training' runs a report of 27 March 1943. Skepper was granted the acting rank of Lieutenant on 16 June 1943. He parachuted into France with the cover name of Henri-Edouard Truchot and the alias Bernard. A Madame Truchot had been his French teacher when he was a boy at Malmaison before the First World War. Three days later he was joined by Arthur Steele (Laurent) his radio operator who was to send nearly four hundred messages for the circuit.

Steele also received glowing reports during his training. Sergeant Holland at STS 5 wrote on 30 October 1942: 'This student is the son of a British father and a French mother, speaks both languages extremely well and is young modest and retiring.' Sergeant Fox at Beaulieu commented: 'In spite of his youth, this student is exceptionally keen and conscientious. He is completely absorbed in his work and is most security minded. In manner he is shy and retiring, but obviously he has plenty of self confidence and is obviously very highly thought of by everyone in the school.' On 23 February 1943 Holland added 'From the security point of view, he is admirable, he remains inconspicuous in public, a non-smoker, and practically a non-drinker, and has not yet been spoiled by his good looks, which make him seductive to women.'

Skepper had been sent to Marseilles to take up contacts given to London by Sidney Jones, who had landed at Marseilles by boat in September 1942 and been flown back to England to report the following February. Skepper travelled extensively using a small box of his own jade ornaments as 'cover' that he was an antique dealer. One day having almost run out of French money, he appeared at the offices of the family firm, Wood-Milne at Rueil, near Paris to the disbelief, surprise and then extreme anxiety of the company Secretary, a Mr Davoz, who had no idea that he was in France. Edmund Skepper explains 'Davoz was very frightened that Charlie would be seen and recognised by someone in the office and that tongues could wag or some ill-intentioned collaborator would give them away to the

Germans.' Fortunately no one recognised him and Skepper was able to depart with a large sum of cash from the Company safe (duly repaid by SOE at the end of the war).

A recommendation for an OBE (reduced to MBE) reads: 'among the many acts of sabotage organised by Skepper was an attack on a synthetic oil plant at L'Estaque, where three oil tanks were destroyed and six damaged, and the blocking of the important Cassis tunnel . . . by the derailment of a train inside it. He also carried out a successful attack on a cement works at Fos sur Mer'. In the first two weeks of January 1944 the Monk circuit was active in damaging thirty-one locomotives and, amazingly, another thirty-two on one day: 15 March.

Buckmaster's personal commendation read: 'very industrious, very serious-minded, he did a superb job. He attacked problems in an effective and scientific manner. Brave and disciplined he gave a fine example to all his colleagues and by his initiative and audacity produced first class results'.

Skepper, it was known, had been arrested by the Gestapo in his flat in Marseilles on 23 March. After the liberation, one of Monk's Marseilles contacts, the architect Jean Hellet, visited Skepper's apartment at 8 rue Mérentié and spoke to the Italian hairdresser opposite, who told him that he heard shots coming from the flat on the day of the arrest. Hellet added: 'The next day Laurent and Gaby went to the flat and were arrested . . . in all some ten Frenchmen walked into the trap.'

Further details of the betrayal came from Julien Villevieille (Marc), who had been arrested in the flat with Skepper. On his return from Dachau he said the arrests had been carried out by a man called Bousquet, who had shared a mistress with Schwab, also known as Peg-Leg Henry. Schwab supplied the circuit with transport and had bought a *camionette* on Skepper's instructions. According to Mme Régis he also supplied the special foods Skepper needed as a result of his illness: 'meat, eggs, butter and sugar, things that could only be obtained on the black market'.

Villevieille was put in the same cell as Schwab at the Beaumettes prison at Marseilles, where Schwab admitted having carried out some very advantageous transactions at the circuit's expense. He was seen again by Villevieille at the beginning of 1945 at Dachau being sent off in a convoy, 'probably for extermination as he had a wooden leg, and such infirmities were usually treated in this way by the Germans'.

Bousquet repeatedly denied involvement but had been seen accompanying the Gestapo to the apartment. Evidence to this effect was produced at his trial and he was later executed.

While SOE agents sent to the SD headquarters in Paris were usually cunningly interrogated, not tortured, Skepper, Steele and Plewman suffered horrendously at the hands of the Marseilles Gestapo. Hellet reported in December 1944 after his visit to Marseilles that it appeared that Henri, Arthur and Eliane were still alive, having admitted that they were British subjects, but apparently nothing more. 'One of the methods of torture they suffered consisted of applying a very powerful electric current between their eyes over several days.' He added they had last been been observed in a convoy at Compiègne en route for Germany.

Villevieille, when he came back from Germany, said he had been confronted with Skepper and his comrades in prison but he 'really did not know them. Their faces had been so swollen and deformed by the application of the electric current, they were truly unrecognisable'. Later Mme Régis recounted that Jean Hellet had heard that Skepper was interned in Hamburg and that the camp had been heavily bombed. A note on an SOE index card for Skepper reads 'seen in Hamburg Oct 44'. Steele's fate was worse. He was said to have been hanged by his feet – one of some thirty executed on 9 September 1944 in this way, according to the courageous Wing Commander Yeo-Thomas, best known as the White Rabbit. Eliane Plewman was executed at Dachau on 13 September 1944 with three other SOE women agents, Yolande Beekman, Madeleine Damerment and Noor Inayat Khan.

Despite their appalling treatment, no further arrests followed those at the rue Mérentié. 'It is clear that none of them gave away any addresses of friends,' said Hellet.

In 1943 Arthur Nicholls was in line to become the next head of SOE in Cairo, but the thought of a desk job pained him, and on 10 July 1943 he wrote to Colin Gubbins volunteering for active service in the Balkans. His earnest hope was to join the British officers coordinating guerrilla movements and 'to be parachuted into either Greece or Yugoslavia'. Born in Hampstead in 1911, Nicholls had gone to work in the Stock Exchange. While at Pembroke College, Cambridge, he had served in the Officer Training Corps and was commissioned into the TA and then the reserve of the Coldstream Guards. In 1939 he was mobilised and sent to France with the Guards, where he was appointed an intelligence officer on account of his French and German. He had been evacuated from Dunkirk while acting as ADC to General Alexander. Photographs show a handsome man with a forthright, confident look and lively, friendly eyes, with a warmth rarely found in official record photographs.

His short PF is astonishing principally for the way it records his formidable powers of endurance during a bitter winter in the Albanian mountains. Albania, with a strong and vicious German presence, was the grimmest of the many tough fronts on which SOE officers and men had to fight, made worse by internecine rivalries between different resistance groups. Nicholls had parachuted into Albania on 10 October, 1943, just as German occupying forces began a major offensive aimed at destroying resistance. In freezing winter conditions his mission was driven back into the deep snow of the mountains.

After they had been on the run for three weeks they were ambushed on the bare mountainside. Several were wounded and had to be left to the mercy of their captors. Nicholls managed to lead the survivors away, splitting them into groups. He went on with just two Albanian guides to try to pass on details of the mission's fate. Staff Sergeant B.A. Chisholm wrote to No. 1 Special Force HQ early in the New Year, describing the extreme hardships they endured.

The previous week with its continuous marching, privations and exposure had worn out Lt Col Nicholls' stamina and he was a very sick man. His boots were in pieces and his feet were covered in cuts, all of which had turned septic. The Brigadier . . . treated him as best he could with iodine . . . and wished to send [him] to Tirana, where although a prisoner, he would at least get the treatment he was so desperately in need of, but Lt Col Nicholls would not hear of this, tried to treat the matter lightly and begged to be allowed to try and make the journey south.

The last the sergeant saw of Nicholls was as he and his companion Major Hare tried vainly to rally the remaining partisans to make a stand at the top of a hill. The two escaped together and walked all through the night, though Nicholls had to make frequent stops because of his frostbite. Realising he could not continue, he ordered Major Hare to try to proceed south and contact another mission, informing them of the capture of Brigadier E. F. Davies, the senior officer sent in to unite Albanians against the

Germans. He laid low with two partisan boys until contacted by members of the Slender mission.

Later Hare explained that he had been unable to make contact with SOE headquarters in Italy but Nicholls, by 'his perseverance and courage in carrying on, travelling to the north when he was unable to stand without fainting with pain ... succeeded in contacting Major Seymour and his wireless. But for this fantastic feat of willpower and endurance nothing would have been heard of Brigadier Davies's mission for another four or five months or perhaps ever, and the last recommendations of Brigadier Davies, affecting our whole policy towards Albania, and indeed the Balkans, would never have been transmitted'. For this Nicholls was awarded a posthumous George Cross.

On file is a series of harrowing messages from the field sent by Major Seymour to Gubbins. That of 5 February reads: 'personal message from Arthur to CD [Gubbins]. He hopes CD will contact Mrs Nicholls. CD to be informed of casualty but not Mrs Nicholls. Arthur most insistent that his wife should not be informed'. A second message that day reads: 'Man who brought doctor out of Tirana ... took Arthur in his car and is hiding him in his own house in Ihsan Toptani, a friend indeed. Arthur will be under doctor at least two months.' A third message that day noted: 'Regret necessity amputate all toes front half both Arthur's feet. Osman, best surgeon in Albania, attends. Operation owing frostbite and gangrene which set in while Partisans made usual promises and did damn all.' The next day came a further cable: 'Arthur's feet very bad ... How he kept going God knows. Has shown endurance and fortitude beyond all praise and a wonderful example of guts and will power ... Hope this will get him finest award possible.' Three days later came better news: 'Operation on Arthur more successful than hoped for.

Only three toes entirely amputated . . . Arthur stood operation of two hours and reported making good recovery.'

It was not to be. A handwritten letter of 14 February
from Suleyman Toptani [the Albanian doctor] tells
Colonel Seymour: 'he got over the operation extremely
well and the wounds made good progress but he became
every day weaker. Although the weakness of the last two
days was rather alarming, all of us believed he would get
over it too. The reason proved to be the over exertion of
the kidneys and the heart.' Nicholls died soon after
midday on 11 February.

The letter continues:

As he was till the last minute in full possession of his mind and
as I was already attached to him . . . his death appeared to me
almost unbelievable and impressed me like the loss of an old dear
friend. I very seldom meet men with so many outstanding qualities . . . true frankness, gentility, intelligence and generosity of
mind and heart. I stood under the fresh impression of all this, so
that I was touched in a very peculiar way indeed . . . [He]
appreciated fully the very particular situation of Albania in this
war . . . [He] saw the problems of our country with due justice.
You know Albania has got very few friends in the world and
needs everyone of them immensely.

Another SOE agent with extraordinary powers of
endurance was D.T. 'Bill' Hudson. Born in Kent to South
African parents, he had attended the School of Mines in
South Kensington. This led to prospecting in the Balkans
and a job in an antimony mine in Yugoslavia. Hudson was a
man of formidable physique and great strength. He was very
attractive to women and in 1936 married a prima ballerina,
Ada Proskurnikova, one of many White Russians who had
fled the Soviet Union. But she could not adapt to life in his
mountain home and they divorced. Hudson never remarried.

In the autumn of 1939 he was recruited into Section D (D for destruction, some said). He was posted to Zagreb, where one British agent was murdered and he himself had a narrow escape when pro-German Croat extremists planted a bomb beneath his office. Undaunted, he recruited a network to carry out sabotage against Axis shipping in Dalmatian ports and in February 1941 blew up an Italian cargo ship.

Now absorbed into SOE, he was dispatched from Malta by submarine to the coast of Montenegro on 7 September 1941 with a bagful of sovereigns and a mission to find out who was fighting the enemy and to coordinate resistance. Julian Amery saw him ashore with two wireless sets. One of these was a battery set too weak for regular contact with his base, the other more efficient but dependent on mains electricity – hardly appropriate for guerrilla work in the mountains.

Few in Britain understood the complexities of the politics in Yugoslavia after the German occupation of April 1941. Hudson spoke fluent Serbo-Croat and within a few weeks had reported the essence of the situation, though it was to take well over two years before his analysis was accepted, such were the factions among the British as well as the Yugoslavs. Hudson met the partisans, led by the then unknown Josip Broz Tito, and then on 25 October 1941 moved on from Tito's headquarters to those of Draza Mihailovic, leader of the royalist Serbs known as the Chetniks. Though both were ostensibly fighting the German invaders, they were already deeply hostile to each other. Mihailovic had been appointed by the Yugoslav government-in-exile. Tito was setting up a Soviet-style people's republic.

Hudson gave his impressions in a message of 13 November 1941: 'Communists at head of partisans are genuinely anti-Axis. Montenegro is Partisan-organised and

Mihailovitch has only just started there . . . Partisans would compromise but Mihailovitch believes he holds all the trumps . . . Both parties have withdrawn large forces from German front . . . Civil war will be a long affair and nothing substantial against Germans for months.' The next day he continued: 'Suggest you tell Mihailovitch full British help not forthcoming unless attempt made to incorporate all anti-Fascist elements under his command.' Hudson went on to report bluntly on the failure of the conference between Mihailovic and Tito on 20 November 1941. 'My attitude to Mihailovitch has been that he has all the qualifications except strength. At present Partisans stronger and he must first liquidate them with British arms before turning seriously to Germans.'

The Germans took the opportunity for a punitive attack on both, driving Tito into Montenegro and Mihailovic into the mountains. Mihailovic abandoned Hudson, incensed that he had told SOE to drop no more arms for internecine warfare Hudson spent a desperate winter, deprived of his wireless by Mihailovic, in an area where the Germans were burning villages and hanging 100 Serbs for every German killed. He was twice captured, once by bandits, once by quislings, but escaped and survived thanks to the hospitality of Serb peasants, who shared their meagre food with him.

By April 1942 Mihailovic was back in radio contact with SOE and receiving arms, and he allowed Hudson to rejoin the Chetniks. Mihailovic continued to refuse to resume active guerrilla work against the Germans, citing the horrific reprisals. The vigour of Tito's partisans convinced Hudson that they were militarily stronger but the British authorities did not believe him and he was variously accused of being naive and left-leaning. Late in 1942 Colonel W.S. Bailey, another mining engineer, was sent to check on Hudson but quickly confirmed his analysis. Even so, it was not until December 1943 that Churchill took the final decision to drop Mihailovic and support Tito. All who wished to do so were now given permission to make their own way to the partisans. Hudson and two other missions took advantage of this.

In May 1944 Hudson was flown to London. Churchill and Eden were impressed by his plans but Tito was not prepared to make concessions and was now determined to conquer Serbia. In the violent struggle that followed the Chetniks were destroyed.

The best tribute to Hudson comes from William Mackenzie in *The Secret History of SOE*: 'He had done as much as any man can do, and it was no credit to the organisation that he was not brought out at all costs for consultation earlier.'

The jungle war of Orde Wingate and the Chindits has long been celebrated, as have the strategic victories of Field Marshal Slim. SOE had its own hero in the Burmese jungle, Hugh Seagrim, whose courage, endurance and ultimate self-sacrifice come alive not only in the reports of Force 136, as SOE was known locally, but also in the detailed first-hand testimonies from Karens who fought with him and hid him from the Japanese.

Seagrim was the son of a parson. He and his three brothers all gave remarkable war service. His elder brother was awarded a posthumous VC and Seagrim himself was awarded a posthumous GC for his service with SOE in Burma.

Seagrim was a major in the 19th Hyderabad Regiment when he was left behind in Burma by British forces retreating before the Japanese in December 1941. The next month he arrived in the Papun area to raise and organise bands of levies or partisans. This was the jungle home of the Karens, a fierce, independent people, then numbering four million, who after the war continued to fight the Burmese junta for over half a century.

The British had been in Burma for nearly a century, but under the Burma Act of 1937 the country ceased to be governed from India and a national assembly was established. The Burmans still had no control over their economy or foreign affairs, and secret negotiations began with the Japanese to oust the British. The Karens, who were mostly Christians and lived in the Irrawaddy delta and in the hills between the Sittang and Salween rivers, had long been strongly pro-British, as colonial rule had ended persecution by the Burmans.

The Burma Independence Army (BIA) was formed in December 1941 and fought alongside the Japanese at the start of the campaign. The BIA, though untrained and undisciplined, were equipped with superior arms, and Seagrim realised it would be impossible to attack them in the open. When the BIA set up an administration and demanded the surrender of arms, Seagrim allowed a few obsolete muzzle-loading pieces to be given up. At the beginning of March 1942 he became bolder, ordering his men to make daylight attacks on the BIA, who were demanding food for their men.

He set up his HQ at Pyagawpu. According to a summary of his activities, 'By the end of February he had a small army of keen men who he trained in hill fighting and his organisation of spies and informers was well in hand.' He selected Saw Di Gay as his second in command. 'His chief need at this time was for more arms and ammunition.'

Seagrim's units began to harry BIA forces and to defend the villagers against the dacoits who were ravaging the area. In March 1942 the BIA occupied Papun and told Saw Di

Gay that unless all arms held by Seagrim's men were handed over all Karen villages would be destroyed and the men's families killed. Shortly after this, Seagrim's men counter-attacked and successfully drove the BIA out. Seagrim now decided that he must obtain fresh supplies of arms and ammunition and told his men he might have to go to India for them. He instructed them to continue guerrilla activities. While he was away the enmity between the Karens and the BIA grew steadily worse.

In August Seagrim returned to the Pyagawpu area having failed in his efforts to secure arms. He ordered many of the men to return to their villages. The summary continues: 'With the remainder he planned to lay the foundation of a strong army for the day when the British should eventually return. He organised section leaders and an information service and told his men to keep as quiet as possible until he called for them.'

A local leader, Saw Taroe, related that the BIA said they were 'authorised by the Japanese that they must wipe out this Karen nation by slaughtering every Karen. From that day, those Karen elders who were detained in Papun were beheaded and the Karen women were mal-treated and even some women were forced to be prostitute for their military'.

He continues:

On the 25th February 1943 (at 4am) I received an information . . . that the Japanese will be arriving at my village (Pyagawpu) today definitely, so that I could arrange to hide Capt Seagrim as soon as possible. Therefore I sent Seagrim to the jungle (about 7 miles) from the village with my elephants, at 7am on the same day. Then the Japanese arrived at my village at 8am, and together with the elders I met the Japanese (about 100) and they asked me if there were any British soldiers to which I replied 'No'. They told me that they had heard there were about 2,000 soldiers. I argued that if there were 2,000 it would be quite evident from the traces in the village.

About the first week of October 1943, Saw Taroe says, he received a letter from Seagrim inviting him to a meeting. 'He told me not to be disheartened as the British troops will be returning to Burma very soon,' including paratroopers. Two British officers did arrive, Captain Nimmo on 18 October and Captain McCrindle in November.

On Christmas Eve Seagrim, always intensely devout, came to Taroe's paddy field asking to be taken to the Christmas service. Taroe thought this too great a risk and held a second service at his house.

A vivid description of Seagrim's camp in the jungle at Hticlerplaw was provided a year later, noting that it was a small, barren ground, circular in shape, with a radius of 100 yards but 'a magnificent hiding place, being situated deep in the hills and at the junction of two small hill streams. Major Seagrim's personal hut is still standing on its legs but in very dilapidated condition'.

On 13 February 1944 a large number of Japanese arrived from four directions at Taroe's village, demanding Seagrim. 'We replied that Capt. Seagrim had returned to Karenni State. They told us that Capt. Seagrim was still here. They showed me a file (2 inches thick) containing Capt. Seagrim activities in my place. So we could not deny anything concerning him.' The Japanese were convinced that Seagrim was near Komupwado village. Taroe told them that Seagrim could not be there as he himself had been there the day before. They insisted he took them to the village. When Seagrim could not be found the Japanese burnt down the whole camp.

Another levy leader, Jem Mg Wah, was arrested on 3 February and severely beaten. He related that he 'was given up to 8th February to inform them where Seagrim etc were, and draw a map of their camps, strength and sentry positions'. After his release he told a comrade, Saw Mg Kyaw, all that had happened; Kyaw saw the wounds on his wrists and took him to Seagrim.

Seagrim asked him why the Japanese had sent him into the hills. He explained. 'I told him I was ready to live and die with him. I asked him for guns and ammunitions and planes to fight the Japanese, as they now knew all about us and their information was correct.' Seagrim explained that the British did not want the Karens to start full-scale fighting yet. 'There were Japanese as well as Burmans to deal with, also the Karens were few and if we fought we would all be killed. He said the time had not yet come and we would still have to put up with suffering . . . He told me to return and God would guard me. We could not do anything but pray.'

Jem set off and met one of his comrades on the road. 'He said that all my weapons had been taken away by Japanese because Tin Gyaw had been arrested, tortured and had given us away . . . When I reached home my friends told me that everyone had got into trouble owing to me.'

On the morning of 8 February he went to report to the Japanese. 'This time they did not question me much, they said . . . I was the ringleader. I had not told them about my weapons, but they had found more.'

On 12 February the Japanese told him he was to go with them. 'On the 16th morning [they] went to the camp but Seagrim had gone,' but the next morning they caught Saw Yay and forced him to show them where Seagrim was, 'namely on a hill just east of Yemulawklo. The Japanese totall[ing] 300 split into two parties, and they fired at Seagrim party. McCrindle was killed. Loot captured was one set, six stens, three tommy guns, two rifles some money and revolvers. Seagrim escaped'.

In the village where Nimmo and McCrindle had been the elder was forced to admit that 'he had had two British officers in the village but as he was a poor simple man he had not realised the seriousness of the thing. He gave Seagrim's position as being four miles east four days previously'. The Japanese force split into two and attacked the camp but found that Seagrim and his comrades had once again departed. One villager was now tortured for further information but bravely held out. 'A net was then thrown round the area and about 9pm a patrol saw smoke coming from a paddy hut and on investigation Saw Yay was captured. Although he said he was a buffalo man, a pistol was found in his kit and he was obliged to admit he had just come from Seagrim who was about three miles east of his old camp.'

By this time Nimmo had also been killed. It happened when another Karen, Saw Myers, had been arrested and subjected to prolonged torture in Rangoon. He said nothing, but during the night a treacherous comrade whispered in his ear that everyone had surrendered and there was no point in holding out any longer. He confessed, and from this Nimmo's camp was traced and attacked on 16 February 1944.

Pa Ha, who was with Seagrim hiding in the jungle, went to his brother's house to ask for food and help. Tragically he was seen by a Japanese collaborator.

The whole of Pa Ha's brother's family was then tortured until they disclosed what they had been doing and the brother begged Pa Ha to give himself up. This he did to save them from further torture. All, though Pa Ha was repeatedly tortured he refused to give Seagrim away – saying that he was on his own. The Japanese then issued an order stating that all would cooperate in searching for Seagrim and that should he escape every house in the Papun district would be burnt – all who had any contact with him would be imprisoned.

The next day, unwilling to see such appalling suffering continue, Seagrim walked out of the jungle and gave himself up to the Japanese. He was taken to Rangoon and put in prison. One eyewitness said: 'Seagrim was the only man who successfully smuggled a bible into his cell. His firm belief in God and never failing courage won the admiration of all the RAF and USAAF personnel . . . in the lock up.'

On 2 September 1944 Seagrim and all the Karens were brought to the final court martial. An account by one of the Karens with him states: 'We were ordered to line up, with Seagrim on our extreme right, before the Judges . . . Seagrim said "the lads are innocent of all the crimes you accused them. I am alone responsible for their actions. I never taught them to be anti-Japanese, but only taught them to be good Christians. I beg to suffer alone."'

Later the Japanese major general S. Shiokawa gave his own account of the trial. Major Seagrim, he said, attired himself 'as if he were a Burmese' and 'Upon receipt of the sentence of death punishment, Major Seagrim said to us that he deserved to be condemned to death for his activities as a secret agent and that he wished to have the said punishment executed immediately. He prayed his last prayer at the execution ground and died with composure which was really solemn attitude.'

One of the Karens saw a truck carrying Seagrim, who 'waved to them, wished them goodbye and told them not to despair because the British would come back. He preserved a brave front. A Jap officer then entered the truck, sword in hand, and it drove off. Their last view of Seagrim was of Seagrim standing up in the truck jesting with his captors'.

ACKNOWLEDGEMENTS

John Harding has generously given me the benefit of his brilliant detective work in teasing out the forgotten details of Eric Sykes's life – further vivid details have been supplied by Angus Fyffe and Henry Hall. Gill Bennett the Foreign Office historian kindly gave me access to the FO files on Operation Performance. Stan Cowburn has provided most valuable material on Ben Cowburn's exploits. Louis Dalais in Paris has given me constant help on the Mauritian agents in this book. Andre Heintz in Normandy has shared his painstaking researches on Operation Aquatint. Help on Charles Skepper has come from Edmund Skepper, George Scott and Mary Chamberlayne. My thanks also to former members and agents of SOE – Guido Zembsch-Schreve (who sadly died in 2003 at the age of 86), Douglas Dodds-Parker, Leslie Fernandez, Jack Grinham, Peter Lee, Dick Rubenstein and Ernest Van Maurik.

Howard Davies at the National Archives readily responded to queries on SOE personal files and his colleague Hugh Alexander provided valuable help in supplying photographs. Informal guidance has come from Ben Chamberlain and David List. At NARA in Washington DC, Lawrence H McDonald gave me many helpful leads in using the OSS archives. John Pitt at the Special Forces Club has supplied both photographs and contacts. The foundation of all work on SOE is the superb and unceasing scholarship of Professor M.R.D. Foot, as well the important work of

Professor David Stafford. John Sainsbury has given me the benefit of his remarkable researches into medals granted to SOE agents. My own researches into SOE were first prompted by General Sir Michael Wilkes. Air Chief Marshal Sir John Cheshire kindly put me in touch with Clive Richards at the MOD Historical Branch (Air).

Among friends Crispin Hasler has given me constant advice while further leads have come from my cousin Adrian Fort. Edith de Richemont and her husband John Hardcastle have helped explained the nuances of documents in French.

My greatest debt is to Duncan Stuart, the former SOE adviser who has provided both material and guidance at every stage of my researches, and particularly on Gus March-Phillips, Graham Hayes and Arthur Nicholls. My warm thanks are also due to his former assistant Valerie Collins.

My literary agent Belinda Harley set this book in motion. In Rupert Lancaster at Hodder I have had an editor as thoughtful and helpful as any author could wish. Hugo Wilkinson, his assistant, has skilfully piloted the book through to press. I am in debt to Ian Paten for his dextrous editing of my text. And finally thanks to my wife and sons for encouragement and forbearance at every stage.

Picture Acknowledgements
Marcus Binney: 3. Daily Express/Express Newspapers: 4. Louis Dalais: 10. André Heintz: 8. NARA, Washington: 16. The National Archives, Kew: 2 (HS9/115/2), 5 (HS9/1183/2), 6 (HS/3/92), 7 (HS9/680/5), 9 (HS9/1011/7), 11 (HS9/1648), 13 (HS9/1240/3), 14 (HS9/1370/1). Private Collections: 12, 15. Special Forces Club: 1.

GLOSSARY

Abwehr	German military secret police
Baker Street	SOE headquarters from October 1940
BRCA	Bureau Central de Renseignements et d'Action
blind drop	Agents parachuting into France without a reception committee to meet them
cachette	An agent's hiding place
circuit	SOE's F Section was organized in circuits named after trades and occupations – Footman, Fireman, Salesman, Scientist, Stationer. Sometimes the head of the circuit is referred to by the name of the circuit, e.g. Cammaerts is referred to as Jockey.
Combat	French Resistance group in unoccupied zone (zone libre) working with RF Section, not F Section
coup dur	Heavy round-up of suspects including house searches intended to flush out resisters and partisans. In Italy called *rastrallimenti*
D/F	Direction finding, a technique used by the Germans for tracking radios when messages are being broadcast
D/F Section	A unit in SOE operating escape lines

Deuxième Bureau	The Polish government-in-exile had an espionage and counter-intelligence service named after its French equivalent
Englandspiel	'The English Game' – playing back by the Germans of captured SOE radios, using an agent's codes, to deceive SOE that the agent was sending them
Eureka	A transponder on the ground, used by the Resistance, sending out a beam guiding a plane to the dropping ground for agents or material
FANY	First Aid Nursing Yeomanry
Feldengendarmerie	German Military Police
felucca	Small sailing ships, merchant vessels, used in the Mediterranean
'the firm'	Colloquial term for SOE
FFI	French Forces of the Interior
Francs-Tireurs (FTP)	In full, Francs-Tireurs et Partisans Français: the military wing of the communist National Liberation Front
Free French	Those working for the movement, Free France, founded in London by Charles de Gaulle, and fighting against the Axis in defiance of the armistice signed by the French government on 22 June 1940 after the fall of France.
F Section	The French section of SOE
Geheime Feldpolizei	The German army's own secret police
George	Initially all SOE radio operators were referred to as George and given numbers to distinguish them
informant	The agent
Jedburgh	Army officers in uniform, parachuted

	into France to organize and arm the Resistance
Maquis	French guerrilla bands operating 1940–5
messages personnels	Phrases broadcast by the BBC to alert reception committees that an agent would be dropped in their area
Milice	Vichy French paramilitary police force, formed in 1943, which collaborated in rounding up Jews for deportation and hunting down Resistance groups
moon period	One week either side of the full moon when there was sufficient light for night flying
Musketeers	A Polish secret network, formed in October 1939 by an engineer and inventor called Witkowski, to continue the fight against the Germans and the Soviets
No. 1 Special Force	The name by which SOE was known in Italy
one-time pad	Rows of random numbers printed on silk (chosen for its light weight); each line of numbers was used for coding one message only, then was cut off and destroyed
OSS	Office of Strategic Services; the US equivalent of SOE (from 1947 the CIA)
PF	An agent's personal SOE file
poem code	Following Intelligence practice that agents' codes were better kept in their heads than on paper, SOE initially used codes based on famous poems and quotations, but these proved

	highly vulnerable to expert German code breakers
Polish Home Army	Poland's secret army
Rebecca	The instrument on board a plane that was able to receive signals from a Eureka
QSO	A conversation in Morse code between two operators
reception committee	A group of Resistance members who would set lights to guide planes carrying agents to the landing or dropping ground, help them on their arrival and carry away any containers or packages dropped with them
réseau	Resistance circuit or network
RF Section	De Gaulle's parallel French department to F section
SD	Sicherheitsdienst, Himmler's security service
Section D	A special unit within SIS for carrying out dirty tricks against the enemy
SHAEF	Supreme Headquarters Allied Expeditionary Force
SIS	Secret Intelligence Service
SNCF	Société Nationale des Chemins de Fer Français – the French state railway authority
SOE	Special Operations Executive, formed in 1940
S-phone	A device that allowed pilots to talk directly to the agent on the ground
STO	Service du Travail Obligatoire (forced labour for French men in Germany)
time pencil	A form of explosive that could be

	carefully pre-set, allowing agents time to get away; it was activated when an agent pressed a ridge on the pencil, allowing the release of acid that ate at a predetermined rate through a wire attached to a detonator
Todt Organisation	The Organization Todt (OT) was named after Fritz Todt, Hitler's young engineer and chief architect, and mustered huge numbers of men for the Nazi building and production programme, using both forced labour and prisoners of war as well as some volunteers lured in by propaganda
23-land	SOE code for Spain
27-land	SOE code for France
Volksdeutsche	Communities of German minorities in occupied countries who were often suspected of acting for the Nazis
WAAF	Women's Auxiliary Air Force
Wehrmacht	A blanket term – literally 'defence force' – embracing all Germany's armed forces
Welbike	A portable and collapsible mini-bike
W/T	Wireless telegraphy

NOTES ON SOURCES

Though many losses have taken place, the SOE archive remains a remarkable and thrilling body of documentation, supplemented recently by the arrival of many of the agents' personal files (PFs). Where these are now accessible I have provided the PRO references in the HS9 series. Not all of these have been opened and in some cases I have seen copies supplied to members of agents' families. In every case key reference works have been the outstanding histories by M.R.D. Foot, notably *SOE in France* for the French operations, and also in several cases William Mackenzie's *Secret History of SOE*. An additional rich source is the series of taped interviews with agents in the Imperial War Museum Sound Archive. For France a very useful reference work is Colonel E.G. Boxshall's typescript *Chronology of SOE Operations with the Resistance in France* (1960); a copy of this is in the library of the Imperial War Museum.

1 BILL SYKES

My principal source for this chapter has been John Harding, who, like Sykes, is an instructor in unarmed combat and through painstaking research has traced many hitherto unknown details of Sykes's life and work. Sykes's PF is not yet in the PRO. I have also talked to a number of

Sykes's fellow instructors at the training schools, including Leslie Fernandez, Angus Fyffe and Jan Maurik. The quotes from William Pilkington and Rex Applegate have been provided by John Harding. The information about Fairbairn and Sykes's initial involvement with Section D and MI(R) came from the former SOE adviser, Duncan Stuart. Sykes's role in the development of specialist weapons is discussed in *SOE: the Scientific Secrets* by Fredric Boyce and Douglas Everett. Information on John Wilkinson-Latham and the Fairbairn-Sykes commando knife can be found on the Wilkinson Sword website, www.wilkinson-swords.co.uk and www.bkcg.co.uk/guide/fsstory.html. Articles on the Shanghai Municipal Police appeared in the *China Weekly Review* on 13 October 1928 (see p. 205) and 29 December 1928 (see pp. 188–9). The message 'Give Bill Sykes our best wishes – tell him we won't miss' is quoted in Donald Hamilton-Hill, *SOE Assignment*, p. 89. The information on W.A. Ord comes from the former SOE adviser. A key source for Fairbairn, and to a lesser extent for Sykes is William L. Cassidy's *Quick or Dead*, which also contains a bibliography of Fairbairn's writings and (on pp. 58–9) describes how Fairbairn became acquainted with Sykes.

2 GEORGES BÉGUÉ

Bégué's PF (HS9/115/2) contains a number of reports and details of his service with SOE. Further information comes from Clement Jumeau's PF (HS9/815/4). His *Times* obituary (2 February 1994) can be found on the Internet. He also appears in the memoirs of other agents, notably Langelaan's *Knights of the Floating Silk*. Boxshall's *Chronology* has a useful section on 'First Steps by SOE to Start Operations in France'.

3 GEORGE BINNEY

This chapter is based principally on a large new cache of Foreign Office files on Operation Performance to which I was alerted by the Foreign Office historian Gill Bennett. Other papers on Performance, Rubble and later ball-bearing operations using MTBs are in the PRO and were used extensively by Ralph Barker in his excellent and comprehensive book *The Blockade Busters*. Further material on the 'Kvarstad Ships and Men' and 'Norwegian Merchant Fleet 1939–1945' can be found on www.warsailors.com.

4 BEN COWBURN

Cowburn wrote one of the best early books on SOE, *No Cloak, No Dagger*, published in 1960. His very substantial PF (over 250 pages) is particularly rich in material on the Troyes operation and also on his first mission reporting on the state of the oil industry in France. In addition I have used the PFs on Mulsant (HS9/1074/4) and Barrett (HS9/94/7).

5 GUS MARCH-PHILLIPS

Operation Postmaster is well documented in PRO files HS3/86, HS3/87, HS3/88, HS3/89, HS3/91, HS3/92, HS3/96, HS7/22 and ADM/219/24. March-Phillips's PF is HS9/1183/2. Further vivid detail is provided in a sixty-minute radio programme, 'If Any Question Why We Died', prepared, researched and narrated by March-Phillips's daughter Henrietta and broadcast on 20 August 1971. This includes contributions from several of her father's colleagues, including Tony Hall, Leonard Guise and her mother. Further material is in Suzanne Lassen's *Anders Lassen* and *Geoffrey*, a life of Geoffrey Appleyard by his father.

6 GRAHAM HAYES

The former SOE adviser kindly provided me with copies of German reports on Operation Aquatint. Hayes's PF contains correspondence about the circumstances of his arrest, imprisonment and execution. In addition I have had extensive help and guidance from M. André Heintz, who lives in Normandy and has carried out very detailed research on the Resistance there. His own book is scheduled for publication in the autumn of 2004.

7 PERCY MAYER

Operation Ironclad and the liberation of Madagascar are extensively documented in PRO files, notably HS3/10, HS3/23, AIR 25/793. Percy Mayer's PF is HS9/1011/7. Further details on the three Mayer brothers and Percy's wife Berthe can be found in J. Maurice Patureau, *Agents secrets mauriciens en France 1940–45* (Société de l'histoire de l'île Maurice, Port Louis, 1995).

8 HARRY REE

Ree's extensive PF is HS9/1240/3. The Sound Archive of the Imperial War Museum contains tapes of two interviews with Ree, 8720 and 8688, recorded in 1985 and 1983 respectively (see Kate Johnson, *The Special Operations Executive*,

1998). There is a chapter by Harry Ree on 'Agents, Resisters and the Local Population' in Stephen Hawes and Ralph White's *Resistance in Europe 1939–45*.

9 GUIDO ZEMBSCH-SCHREVE

In addition to an interview with Guido in 2001, my principal sources are his PF and his book, *Pierre Lalande*. I have also used the SOE debriefing of Claude Planel, W/T operator of the Pierre Jacques circuit, carried out by Major Hunt on 3 March 1945, and the brief details in the PF of Abbé Henri Jeglot. Guido is also included in MRD Foot's *SOE in the Low Countries*.

10 DENIS RAKE

Rake's PF is HS9/1648. The other main source is Rake's autobiography, *Rake's Progress*, published by Leslie Frewin, with a perceptive foreward by Douglas Fairbanks Jr. Rake also figures in the memoirs of other agents, notably Ben Cowburn, Richard Heslop and Nancy Wake. The 1969 film documentary on the Resistance by Marcel Ophuls, *Le Chagrin et la Pitié (The Sorrow and the Pity)*, includes an interview with Rake early on in Part II – copies can be obtained via the Internet. Major Farmer's report on the Freelance circuit is in the PRO (HS6/570). Fuller reports on Freelance are among the OSS files at NARA (NND 843091). See also Boxshall.

ENVOI

Philippe de Vomécourt's PF is in the PRO (HS9/1539/5). See
also his book *Who Lived to See the Day*. Manfred Czernin's
PF is HS9/386/6. See also Norman Franks, *Double Mission*.
Amédée Maingard information is from his PF and the OSS
reports on Shipwright at NARA in Washington. For Charles
Skepper I have been able to draw on material provided by
his family, included his PF and *An Account of some of the
Skepper Family History* by Edmund Cecil Skepper (1998,
privately printed), which contains an obituary written by
Professor W. A. Robson of the London School of
Economics. Information on Colonel Nicholls comes from
his PF, HS9/1644. For Colonel Hudson see William
Mackenzie's *The Secret History of SOE*. Seagrim's PF is
HS9/1334/7.

BIBLIOGRAPHY

Appleyard, J.E., *Geoffrey* (London, Blandford Press, 1946)

Astley, Joan Bright, *The Inner Circle* (London, Hutchinson, 1971)

Barker, Ralph, *The Blockade Busters* (London, Chatto & Windus, 1976)

Beevor, J.G., *SOE: Recollections and Reflections* (London, Bodley Head, 1981)

Bleicher, Hugo, *Colonel Henri's Story* (London, William Kimber, 1954)

Boatner, Mark M. III, *The Biographical Dictionary of World War II* (Novato, CA, Presidio Press, 1999)

Boxshall, Colonel E. G., *Chronology of SOE Operations with the Resistance in France* (1960)

Braddon, Russell, *Nancy Wake* (London, Cassell, 1956)

Buckmaster, Maurice, *Specially Employed* (London, Batchworth Press, 1952)

Cassidy, William L., *Quick or Dead* (Boulder, CO, Paladin Press, 1978)

Clark, Freddie, *Agents by Moonlight: the Secret History of RAF Tempsford during World War II* (Stroud, Tempus Publishing, 1999)

Cowburn, Ben, *No Cloak, No Dagger* (London, Jarrolds, 1960)

Cunningham, Cyril, *Beaulieu: the Finishing School for Secret Agents* (London, Leo Cooper, 1998).

Dalton, Hugh, *The Fateful Years* (London, Frederick Muller, 1957)

Dear, Ian, *Sabotage and Subversion: the SOE and OSS at War* (London, Arms and Armour Press, 1996, paperback edn London, Cassell, 1999)

Dodds-Parker, Douglas, *Setting Europe Ablaze* (Windlesham, Springwood Books, 1983)

Foot, M.R.D., *SOE in France: an Account of the Work of the British Special Operations Executive in France 1940–1944* (London, HMSO, 1966, new edn London, Frank Cass, 2004)

Foot, M.R.D., *Resistance* (London, Eyre Methuen, 1976, paperback edn London, Paladin, 1978)

Foot, M.R.D., 'Was SOE any good?', *Journal of Contemporary History*, 167, January 1981

Foot, M.R.D., *SOE: an Outline History 1940–46* (4th edn London, Pimlico, 1999)

Foot, M.R.D., *SOE in the Low Countries* (London, St Ermin's Press, 2001)

Franks, Norman L. R., *Double Mission: RAF Fighter Ace and SOE Agent Manfred Czernin* (London, William Kimber, 1976)

Garlinski, Jozef, *Poland, SOE and the Allies* (London, George Allen and Unwin, 1969)

Hastings, Max, *Das Reich: the March of the 2nd SS Panzer Division through France, June 1944* (London, Michael Joseph, 1981, paperback edn London, Pan, 2000)

Hawes, Stephen and Ralph White, *Resistance in Europe 1939–45* (London, Penguin Books 1976)

Heslop, Richard, *Xavier* (London, Rupert Hart-Davis, 1970)

Howarth, Patrick, *Undercover: the Men and Women of the SOE* (London, Routledge & Kegan Paul, 1980, paperback edn London, Phoenix Press, 2000)

Hughes, Jimmy Quintin, *Who Dares Who Wins* (Liverpool, Charico Press, 1998)

Johnson, Kate (ed.), *The Special Operations Executive: Sound Archives Oral History Recordings* (London, Imperial War Museum, 1998)

Langelaan, George, *Knights of the Floating Silk* (London, Hutchinson, 1959)

Marks, Leo, *Silk and Cyanide: a Codemaker's Story* (London, HarperCollins, 1998)

Marshall, Bruce, *The White Rabbit 1952* (London, Evans Brothers, 1952)

Millar, George, *Maquis*, London, Heinemann, 1945)

Nicholas, Elizabeth, *Death Be Not Proud* (London, Cresset Press, 1958)

Paturau, J. Maurice, *Agents secrets mauriciens en France 1940–45* (Société de l'histoire de l'île Maurice, Port Louis, 1995)

Rake, Denis, *Rake's Progress* (London, Leslie Frewin, 1968)

Richards, Brooks, *Secret Flotillas* (London, HMSO, 1996, new edn in 2 vols London, Frank Cass, 2004)

Rigden, Denis (intro. by), *SOE Syllabus: Lessons in Ungentlemanly Warfare* (London, Public Record Office, 2001)

Stafford, David, *Britain and European Resistance 1940–1945* (2nd edn London, Macmillan, 1983)

Stafford, David, *Churchill and Secret Service* (London, John Murray, 1997, paperback edn London, Abacus, 2000)

Sweet-Escott, Bickham, *Baker Street Irregular* (London, Methuen, 1965)

Verity, Hugh, *We Landed by Moonlight* (Wilmslow, Air Data Publications, 1994)

Vomécourt, Philippe de, *Who Lived to See the Day: France in Arms* (London, Hutchinson, 1961)

Wake, Nancy, *The White Mouse* (Melbourne, Macmillan, 1985)

Wake, Nancy, *La Gestapo m'appelait la souris blanche: une Australienne au secours de la France* (Paris, Editions du Félin, 2001)

West, Nigel, *Secret War: the Story of SOE, Britain's Wartime Sabotage Organisation* (London, Hodder & Stoughton, 1992)

Wilkinson, Peter and Joan Bright Astley, *Gubbins and SOE* (London, Leo Cooper, 1996)

INDEX